Investigating Prehistoric Hunter-Gatherer Identities: Case Studies from Palaeolithic and Mesolithic Europe

Edited by

H. L. Cobb
F. Coward
L. Grimshaw
S. Price

BAR International Series 1411
2005

Published in 2016 by
BAR Publishing, Oxford

BAR International Series 1411

Investigating Prehistoric Hunter-Gatherer Identities: Case Studies from Palaeolithic and Mesolithic Europe

ISBN 978 1 84171 854 5

© The editors and contributors severally and the Publisher 2005

The authors' moral rights under the 1988 UK Copyright,
Designs and Patents Act are hereby expressly asserted.

All rights reserved. No part of this work may be copied, reproduced, stored,
sold, distributed, scanned, saved in any form of digital format or transmitted
in any form digitally, without the written permission of the Publisher.

BAR Publishing is the trading name of British Archaeological Reports (Oxford) Ltd.
British Archaeological Reports was first incorporated in 1974 to publish the BAR
Series, International and British. In 1992 Hadrian Books Ltd became part of the BAR
group. This volume was originally published by Archaeopress in conjunction with
British Archaeological Reports (Oxford) Ltd / Hadrian Books Ltd, the Series principal
publisher, in 2005. This present volume is published by BAR Publishing, 2016.

Printed in England

BAR titles are available from:

           BAR Publishing
           122 Banbury Rd, Oxford, OX2 7BP, UK
EMAIL   info@barpublishing.com
PHONE   +44 (0)1865 310431
FAX   +44 (0)1865 316916
           www.barpublishing.com

CONTENTS

List of Figures ii

List of Tables iv

List of Contributors v

Preface vi

Fiona Coward & Lucy Grimshaw
Hunter-Gatherers in Early Prehistory 1

Lucy Grimshaw
Upper Palaeolithic Social Colonisation and Lower Palaeolithic Biological Dispersal? A
Consideration of the Nature of Movements into Europe During the Pleistocene. 7

Fiona Coward
Transitions, Change and Prehistory: An Ecosystemic Approach to Change in the
Archaeological Record. 27

Felix Riede
Darwin Vs. Bourdieu – Celebrity Deathmatch or Postprocessual Myth? A
Prolegomenon for the Reconciliation of Agentive-Interpretative and Ecological-
Evolutionary Archaeology 45

Hannah Cobb & Steven Price
We're Not Waiting Any More - Or, Hunting for Meaning in the Mesolithic of North-
West Europe 65

Hannah Cobb
Midden, Meaning, Person, Place: Interpreting the Mesolithic of Western Scotland 69

Aimée Little
Reconstructing the Social Topography of an Irish Mesolithic Lakescape 79

Steven Price
Can't See the Trees for the Wood: The Social Life of Trees in the Mesolithic of
Southern Scandinavia 95

LIST OF FIGURES

Figure 2.1
The number of Lower Palaeolithic and Aurignacian sites in Europe 13

Figure 2.2
Distribution of the Lower Palaeolithic sites dating to each division of the Pleistocene 14

Figure 2.3
Distribution of the Aurignacian sites dated to each category in Kyrs BP 15

Figure 2.4
Number of sites in each environment type 17

Figure 2.5
Number of sites in each landscape type 18

Figure 3.1
Parts of the landscape and paths potentially associated with summer hunting of chamois, ibex and red deer from Amalda during OIS 5a/c 34

Figure 3.2
Parts of the landscape and paths potentially associated with winter hunting of chamois, ibex and red deer from Amalda during OIS 5a/c 35

Figure 3.3
Parts of the landscape and paths potentially associated with year-round hunting of bovids and horse from Amalda during OIS 5a/c 36

Figure 4.1
Odling-Smee et al.'s triple-inheritance model 49

Figure 4.2
The Bromme site of Trollesgave 51

Figure 4.3
A hypothetical phylogenetic rendering of Late Palaeolithic armatures 53

Figure 4.4
The linear settlement pattern of the Hamburgian and Ahrensburgian people 55

Figure 6.1
The much-reproduced, sanitised image of the shell midden of Caisteal nan Gillean I 71

Figure 6.2
Caisteal nan Gillean I in 1881, prior to excavation 72

Figure 6.3
Bevelled ended bone tools and stone tools 73

Figure 6.4
The view of Rhum from the Mesolithic site of Camas Daraich, Skye 74

Figure 7.1
Map of study area 80

Figure 7.2
Late Mesolithic material eroding out of a bank of the River Inny 81

Figure 7.3
Late Mesolithic finds from Clonkeen, a Late Mesolithic site on the River Inny 82

Figure 7.4
Map of Clonava Island showing pre- and post-drainage water levels 84

Figure 7.5
Worked chert from Corralanna embedded in peat sod 85

Figure 7.6
View of Derravaragh from Clonava Island 88

Figure 8.1
Differences in tree bark 97

Figure 8.2
An example of a cross-cutting characteristics model of some plant categories 98

Figure 8.3
Cross-cutting characteristics model for Mesolithic tree use 100

LIST OF TABLES

Table 2.1
Number of Lower Palaeolithic sites in each landscape type in each assemblage size class 16

Table 2.2
The number of Aurignacian sites with recorded instances of portable art and personal ornamentation in each date category compared against the occurrence of parietal art 20

Table 3.1
Animal species represented in Amalda level VII 32

Table 3.2
Ageing data for ungulate species from Amalda level VII 32

Table 4.1
Neo-Darwinian theory and archaeology 46

Table 4.2
A summary table of the cultural processes during the Late Pleistocene in Southern Scandinavia 56

LIST OF CONTRIBUTORS

Hannah Cobb: Hannah.Cobb@postgraduate.manchester.ac.uk
Archaeology, School of Arts, Histories and Cultures, Humanities Bridgeford Street, University of Manchester, Oxford Road, Manchester, M13 9PL. http://www.art.man.ac.uk/ARTHIST/student_profiles/cobb.html
> Hannah Cobb is currently undertaking her PhD in the School of Arts, Histories and Cultures at the University of Manchester. Her thesis addresses *The Mesolithic experience of the world and the Mesolithic to Neolithic transition in the Northern Irish Sea Basin.* She is also a project assistant with the Higher Education Academy, History, Classics and Archaeology Subject Centre.

Dr Fiona Coward: fcoward@ukonline.co.uk
AHRC Centre for the Evolutionary Analysis of Cultural Behaviour at the Institute of Archaeology, University College London, 31-34 Gordon Sq. London, WC1H 0PY. http://www.fcoward.co.uk
> Having completed her PhD addressing *Transitions, Change and Identity: the Middle and Upper Palaeolithic of Vasco-Cantabrian Spain* at the University of Southampton, Dr. Coward is now a Post Doctoral Researcher with the AHRC Centre for the Evolutionary Analysis of Cultural Behaviour at the Institute of Archaeology, University College London.

Dr Lucy Grimshaw: l.c.grimshaw@durham.ac.uk
University of Durham, Dept of Archaeology, South Road, Durham, DH1 3LE.
> Lucy Grimshaw recently finished her PhD on *Population Movements into Europe during the Pleistocene: a comparative approach* in the Department of Archaeology at the University of Durham. Her research interests include the Palaeolithic Archaeology of Europe, the Near East and North Africa, as well as human-environment interactions, human evolution and archaeological detection of population movements.

Aimée Little: itiaimee@yahoo.co.nz
Department of Archaeology, John Henry Newman Building, University College Dublin, Belfield, Dublin 4.
> Aimée Little is a PhD student at the Department of Archaeology, University College Dublin and a Humanities Institute of Ireland scholar. Her thesis *Reconstructing memory and meaning: Mesolithic identities and landscapes in the northern Midlands* is concerned with reconstructing the social and physical topography of a Late Mesolithic landscape by integrating a range of multi-disciplinary techniques.

Steven Price: stevencprice@gmail.com
Archaeology, School of Arts, Histories and Cultures, Humanities Bridgeford Street, University of Manchester, Oxford Road, Manchester, M13 9PL. http://www.art.man.ac.uk/ARTHIST/student_profiles/price.html
> Steven Price is currently completing his PhD entitled *The Mesolithic-Neolithic Transition in Southern Sweden: To what Extent does the Change in Material Culture Reflect a Change in Social Structure?*, in the School of Arts, Histories and Cultures at the University of Manchester.

Felix Riede: fr227@cam.ac.uk
McDonald Institute for Archaeological Research, University of Cambridge, Downing Street, Cambridge, CB2 3ER. www.mcdonald.cam.ac.uk/genetics/FRindex.htm
> Felix Riede is currently undertaking a PhD with the McDonald Institute for Archaeological Research, University of Cambridge. His thesis considers The Earliest Postglacial Re-Colonisation of Southern Scandinavia using archaeological, genetic and ecological data. His other interests include Evolutionary Archaeological, prehistoric colonisation processes, Niche Construction and Neanderthal archaeology and biology.

PREFACE

This volume stems from sessions at the 2004 Theoretical Archaeology Conference entitled "Hunter-Gatherers in Early Prehistory" organised by Fiona Coward and Lucy Grimshaw and "Hunting for Meaning: Interpretive Approaches to the Mesolithic" organised by Hannah Cobb and Steven Price. The sessions came about as a response to a continuing lack of appreciation of new developments in theoretical approaches to the archaeology of prehistoric hunter-gatherers both in the Pleistocene and Holocene. The significance and potential of these new developments is reflected in the proliferation of sessions tackling the subject at previous TAG conferences and by the exciting discussions that our sessions provoked, and we hope that the papers presented here will stimulate further debate on these issues.

We would like to thank all participants who both gave papers in these sessions and who contributed towards the lively debate. We would also like to acknowledge those who gave papers in the sessions but were unable to contribute towards the volume, namely Paul Davies, Chantal Conneller and Caradoc Peters.

Hannah Cobb, Steven Price, Lucy Grimshaw and Fiona Coward

HUNTER-GATHERERS IN EARLY PREHISTORY

Fiona Coward and Lucy Grimshaw

University of Southampton
University of Durham

Abstract
The success of the post-processual critique of processual models of prehistory has led to the development of models of human behaviour that prioritise people and their activities in a social milieu. However, although some aspects of these approaches have crept in to the late Mesolithic, the vast majority of illustrations of such paradigms in archaeology have been post-Neolithic. Why is there no social archaeology of the Palaeolithic and Mesolithic? Firstly, the nature of the data is argued to be insufficient both quantitatively and qualitatively to address the lifeways of people in the past. The questions considered appropriate for the study of the Palaeolithic have thus been largely restricted to those considering the economics of subsistence or raw material procurement and lithic manufacture. Secondly, the problem is one of identification; the attitudes of researchers towards post-Neolithic farmers and Mesolithic and Palaeolithic hunter-gatherer (and particularly pre-human hunter-gatherer) populations have meant that the two branches of research are considered fundamentally different.

The effect of this process of estrangement of hunter-gatherer archaeology from the rest of the discipline is the establishment of an a-personal Palaeolithic. The pre-eminence of the evolutionary paradigm, which equates change and evolution, identifies the process of evolution as purely a factor of time; change is conditional only on time passing, and is thus virtually unrelated to humans and their activities. The focus of research into Pleistocene archaeology has been at continent-wide geographical scales and geological timescales, which have removed the possibility of accessing personal experiences and actions. In addition, the conception of a culture as a system seeking homeostasis means that change requires external causality – usually, in the Palaeolithic, the environment.

This session would like to reintroduce the not-so-radical notion of 'people' to the Palaeolithic and Mesolithic, as creators of the archaeological record, and as inhabitants of the Pleistocene world. How can we access aspects of the prehistoric hunter-gatherer past that would have had meaning for its inhabitants/creators? How does the recognition of hunter-gatherer 'persons' in prehistory affect the generalizing, continent- and geological/climatic- scale models of the Palaeolithic and Mesolithic which are current in the discipline? We invite papers that use new perspectives to 'crack open' the 'black box' of hunter-gatherer 'persons' of the Palaeolithic and Mesolithic to access new perspectives on and understandings of the period.

The rationale behind this volume is that, although the success of the post-processual critique of processual models of prehistory has led to the development of models of human behaviour that prioritise people and their activities in a social milieu, the vast majority of illustrations of such paradigms in archaeology have to date been in post-Neolithic contexts.

Although theories of agency and 'social' explanations of change have been extended tentatively into the Mesolithic, with the exception of studies of Palaeolithic art (e.g. Conkey 1982; Leroi-Gourhan 1968), such paradigms have not been a significant part of Palaeolithic research until very recently (Wobst 2000, 43). Examples include Charles' work considering 'ethnic signatures' as enacted through butchery practices (2000) and Dobres' on the social relations of hunting and butchery (2000), both in the Magdalenian and thus rather late in the Pleistocene. Slightly further back in time we can identify Sinclair's work in the Solutrean (2000), and further back still Gamble's work dealing mainly with the Upper Palaeolithic but also extending back to the Middle and Lower Palaeolithic of Europe (1999, see also 1996), and that of Field (2002), whose work addresses the lithic record of the Lower and Middle Stone Age of Africa and Lower Palaeolithic Europe.

Why is there no social archaeology of prehistoric hunter-gatherers, particularly Palaeolithic populations? The papers in this section tackle two major issues perceived to be problems in the application of social theories to Palaeolithic archaeology. These include:

1. The nature of the Palaeolithic and Mesolithic archaeological record.
2. The opposition between 'evolutionary' and 'social' explanations of change in prehistory.

1. The 'Scraps of Data' Argument

The nature of the Palaeolithic record, and the archaeological record of hunter-gatherers more generally, is often argued to be insufficient both quantitatively and qualitatively to address the lifeways of people in the past. According to this 'scraps of data' argument (Gamble 1999, 5), Palaeolithic archaeologists need more, and 'better' data, before those questions considered important in the post-processual paradigm, such as issues of agency, can be addressed (Legge, *et. al.* 1998, 92; Wobst 2000, 43; Clark 2001, 139). As long ago as 1951 Childe wrote that

> The Archaeological record is found to be regrettably but not surprisingly deficient in indications of the social organisation or lack of it in lower Palaeolithic hordes. From the scraps available no generalizations are possible (1951, 85).

Twenty-two years later, Leach continued the theme, arguing that although archaeologists were aware of

> ... the paucity of their evidence and ... take legitimate pride in the ingenuity with which they apply scientific procedures so as to make the most of such evidence as they have ... all the ingenuity in the world will not replace the evidence that is lost and gone for ever, and you need to be on your guard against persuading yourselves that you have discovered more than is actually discoverable (1973, 769).

Such considerations have been argued to justify the fact that the questions considered appropriate for the study of the Palaeolithic have thus been largely restricted to those considering the economics of subsistence or raw material procurement and lithic manufacture (Gamble 1999, 1). However, as the papers in this session will demonstrate, "empirical insufficiency is only part of the problem" (Clark 2001, 139; Miracle 2002, 85). The Palaeolithic's failure to address the social aspects of the record is not a product of the record itself but of an unwillingness to look again at the data in new ways, using new theories and approaches.

In the first paper Grimshaw demonstrates that the data available from the Lower Palaeolithic are at least as strong as the early Upper Palaeolithic, and can be more appropriate for the application of social theories, due to the timescale of dating accuracy better matching that of developments in the Lower Palaeolithic, and thus that social approaches should not be restricted to the late Pleistocene on the grounds of insufficient data from earlier periods. Likewise, Riede utilises high-resolution data from individual knapping episodes to access interactions between members of a late Palaeolithic group, and to consider questions of the transmission of identity and technology in a Palaeolithic society. Palaeolithic sites when recovered *in situ* can offer better preservation of individual activities than those of later prehistory, since later prehistoric sites have often been subject to multiple occupations and construction phases which destroy the original spatial location of artefacts. Thus, high-resolution Palaeolithic sites offer a chance to address individual actions, that is not possible in the majority of later sites, and the failure to utilise this data until recently cannot be accommodated within the scraps of data argument.

2. The A-Personal Palaeolithic

The theoretical standoff between evolutionary and social theories, with the former favoured in the Palaeolithic and Mesolithic, and the latter in later prehistory, has led to a sterile opposition between the methods considered appropriate for the period, restricting Palaeolithic archaeology to the lower rungs of Hawkes' infamous ladder of inference (1954). However, despite the often fiery rhetoric, the papers in this section look beyond the opposition to initiate rapprochement between the two approaches, demonstrating that they do not have to be considered as inherently opposed but as complementary; a combination of the two has the potential, highlighted here, to give us a much fuller picture of the past than either can do alone.

The effect of this process of estrangement of hunter-gatherer archaeology from the rest of the discipline is the establishment of an a-personal Palaeolithic. The challenge of the post-processual approaches was that processual and evolutionary paradigms deny the 'agency' of essentially active, intelligent individuals at the heart of the decision-making process in prehistory in favour of a heavy emphasis on 'process' and 'systems' as the prime movers of human history.

In such a paradigm, stasis or equilibrium becomes the norm for 'cultures' and for species, and change is thus made external to the system, separated from human action and compressed into the 'lines' separating discrete 'cultures' in prehistory. Evolution thus becomes merely a property of long periods of time (Field 2002; see also Davidson 1991, 195).

However, criticisms of the evolutionary approaches as used in archaeology have come from inside as well as outside of processualism: O'Brien and Holland in particular have argued cogently that evolutionary theory in archaeology is all too often used as little more than a justification for 'just-so' stories (1992, 36-7) about the course of human history. Concepts of adaptation and evolution become "an ex-post-facto argument aiding 'explanation' of change among prehistoric groups" (*Ibid.*, 35). 'Change' in the archaeological record is tautologically 'explained' away as 'evolution' – but an evolution sadly reduced to mere typology, a point discussed in more detail in Coward's paper.

This equation of change and evolution, combined with the perceived paucity of the record, has produced a focus in Palaeolithic research at continent-wide geographical scales and geological timescales, which has removed the possibility of accessing personal experiences and actions: hence the individual in evolutionary theory has been characterised, with some justification, as merely a

> plastic, malleable dope incapable of altering the conditions of his or her existence and always subject to the vagaries of external non-social forces beyond mediation or any realistic form of active intervention (Shanks and Tilley 1987a, 56).

The result is that, as Sassaman writes, "[h]unter-gatherer prehistory has a disturbing anonymity about it" (2000, 148). As early as 1973, Leach criticised the strong behaviourist ethos, virtually linear theory of social development and use of direct ethnographic analogy characteristic of much of Binford's work as akin to that of Malinowski, conducted some twenty years previously, concluding that "Archaeology must be concerned with people rather than with things" (1973, 768). This trend has perhaps been exacerbated by the continued use of 'classic' ethnographic accounts, such as the proceedings of the *Man the Hunter* conference (Lee and DeVore 1968), as a source of behavioural analogy for prehistoric hunter-gatherers. Much of the ethnography used in the Palaeolithic has been based on observations of groups such as the !Kung (Lee 1979), who were assumed to be leading an essentially unchanged Pleistocene existence, uncontaminated by contacts with outsiders, and incapable of historical change. Subsequently it has become clear that such hunter-gatherer groups are not ahistorical (Layton, 2001), but are the product of centuries of contact and change (Schrire 1980; Wilmsen 1989), and thus hunter-gatherer individuals are actively constructing their societies. However, this revisionist critique of ethnographic approaches to hunter-gatherers does not seem to have filtered into its applications in the Palaeolithic.

Conclusion

The continuing stand-off between these two strands of thought is argued to relate to fundamentally different ideas about the kinds of questions that archaeologists should be asking of the archaeological record.

For the 'historical' post-processualists, the discipline's subject is 'human experience' (Shanks and Tilley 1987b, 123 and *passim*) – in contrast, 'scientific' processualism "necessarily sacrifices concern for the individual human" (Straus 1991, 67) to address the long-term processes of change patterning the archaeological record; 'evolutionary explanation' rather than 'cultural interpretation' (Miracle 2002, 65). While such paradigmatic gulfs remain, it seems unlikely that there will be any rapprochement of the two 'sides' – see for example Wobst's discussion of the arguments surrounding the use of the word 'behaviour' (2000).

Because of its particular interpretation by processualists, the word became a 'red flag' for an overly mechanistic treatment of past humans, but has since been re-appropriated by agency and action theorists, following Giddens (1984), and is now widely used to mean very different things by both sides of the debate. Riede discusses this theme further by demonstrating that these differences are based on mutual misunderstanding of the opposing theories, reinforced by the isolation of the two camps from one another through mutually exclusive citation histories.

However, it has also been suggested that the historical, post-processual and the evolutionary, processual paradigms could be reconciled by regarding them as complementary and relating to different scales, "since social evolution addresses short-term social dynamics and cultural evolution, particularly with its focus on selection (either natural or cultural), deals with the long-term persistence of cultural forms" (Preucel and Hodder 1996, 217; see also Bailey 1983).

None of the following papers argue *against* the use of evolutionary or processual theory, nor the complete abandonment of scientific principles and methods. But they do recognise that the reluctance of Palaeolithic researchers to countenance any form of 'social' theory or theory of agency is limiting the scope of Palaeolithic research. Like Wobst, researchers increasingly "find it difficult to make sense of the past or of the present without reference to the folk who had produced them" (2000, 41). The recent awakening of Palaeolithic interest in individuals and change within a social framework is an encouraging development (see e.g. Gamble and Porr, 2005). However, it remains nascent and there is no consensus on how post-processual theories of agency can be integrated into Palaeolithic research. The papers in this section do not wish to contribute to the ongoing and ultimately sterile binary opposition between processual and evolutionary approaches on the one hand, and post-processual and social or humanistic approaches on the other, but to proffer a way in which the Palaeolithic record can be re-populated while maintaining a certain amount of "humility in the face of our ignorance" (Jochim, 1998, 28). Hence, Grimshaw discusses methodological and practical similarities between the two approaches and Riede offers a theoretical means of reconciling the evolutionary and post-processual ideologies through 'niche construction', while Coward focuses on an 'ecosystemic approach' which again draws from both perspectives.

One of the themes apparent in this section is a challenge to the familiar processual conception of the environment as deterministic, providing the external causality for homeostatic cultural systems. The papers in this session, however, parallel their integration of social and evolutionary theory in their approaches to the environment, treating it in a more holistic sense as composed both of social *and* ecological elements. Selective pressures are thus seen as deriving both from interactions with aspects of the ecological environment *and* also with other hominids and humans and the social realm. As Ingold has noted, by ecology:

> I do not simply mean a perspective that would incorporate external environmental variables as part of the explanation for behaviour. An approach that is genuinely ecological, in my view, is one that would ground human intention and action within the context of an ongoing and mutually constitutive engagement between people and their environment (2000, 27).

Certainly we cannot simply assume that pre-'modern' hominids behaved or thought or experienced in identical ways to *Homo sapiens*, archaic or 'modern'; sociality and culture are not concepts that can be uncritically applied to the archaeological record of the Palaeolithic. Nevertheless, the integration of social and ecological environments allows us to access both social and evolutionary theory into a single framework and thus to use both sets of tools to address 'social' aspects of the lives of hunter-gatherers – both 'modern' and pre-'modern'- in early Prehistory. Although the following papers do not pretend to have 'solved' the problem, a number of thought-provoking approaches are presented here that, together with parallel developments elsewhere (Gamble and Porr 2005), identify a number of potential lines of attack that provide a firm foundation for future developments in this vein.

One such avenue is the social construction of the environment, which is a key feature of all the papers, with the development of knowledge of the landscape, environment and resources highlighted as a means of accessing such a social environment at scales from individual valleys and small regions in Riede's and Coward's papers, to the traditional continental scale in Grimshaw's chapter. The development of important locations in a landscape, for reasons other than simple resource availability, is therefore suggested to be a potentially valuable area of research for future studies of Palaeolithic social and ecological environments.

Acknowledgements.

Thanks to all participants and discussants in both 2004 TAG sessions: in addition, this session developed as a result of discussions that followed the "Social Archaeology and the Palaeolithic/Mesolithic" session at TAG 2002 in Manchester organised by Erica Gittens, who we would also like to thank for inspiring debate.

References Cited

Bailey, G. N. 1983. Concepts of Time in Quaternary Prehistory. *Annual Review of Anthropology* 12: pp. 165-92.

Charles, R. 2000. Searching for ethnic signatures in the Late Upper Palaeolithic of northwestern Europe. *Archaeological Review from Cambridge* 17(1): pp. 45-65.

Childe, V. G. 1951. *Social Evolution*. London: Watts.

Clark, G. A. 2001. Observations of the epistemology of human origins research. In R. Corbey and W. Roebroeks (eds), *Studying Human Origins: disciplinary history and epistemology*, pp. 139-46. Amsterdam: Amsterdam University Press.

Conkey, M. W. 1982. Boundedness in art and society. In M. W. Conkey and C. A. Hastorf (eds), *The Uses of Style in Archaeology*, pp. 115-28. Cambridge: Cambridge University Press.

Davidson, I. 1991. A Great Thick Cloud of Dust: naming and dating in the interpretation of behavior in the Late Paleolithic of Spain. In G. A. Clark (ed), *Perspectives on the Past: theoretical biases in Mediterranean hunter-gatherer research*, pp. 194-203. Philadelphia: Philadelphia University Press.

Dobres, M.-A. 2000. *Technology and Social Agency*. Oxford: Blackwell Publishers.

Field, A. 2002. *The Middle Pleistocene in Transition: lithic assemblages and changing social relations between OIS12 and 6 in Europe and Africa*. uncorrected draft PhD, University of Southampton.

Gamble, C. 1996. Making Tracks: Hominid networks and the evolution of the social landscape. In J. Steele and S. Shennan (eds), *The Archaeology of Human Ancestry: power, sex and tradition*, pp. 253-77. London: Routledge.

Gamble, C. 1999. *The Palaeolithic Societies of Europe*. Cambridge World Archaeology. Cambridge: Cambridge University Press.

Gamble, C. and Porr, M. (eds.). 2005. *The Hominid Individual in Context*. London: Routledge.

Giddens, A. 1984. *The Constitution of Society: outline of the theory of structuration*. Cambridge: Polity Press.

Hawkes, C. 1954. Archaeological Theory and Method: some suggestions from the Old World. *American Anthropologist (n.s.)* 56: pp. 155-68.

Ingold, T. 2000. The Optimal Forager and Economic Man. In T. Ingold (ed), *The Perception of the Environment: essays in livelihood, dwelling and skill*, pp. 27-39. London: Routledge.

Layton, 2001. "Hunter-gatherers, their neighbours and the nation state", in C. Panter-Brick, R. Layton and P. Rowley-Conwy (eds.), *Hunter-Gatherers: An interdisciplinary perspective*, pp. 292-321. Cambridge: Cambridge University Press.

Leach, E. 1973. Concluding Address. In C. Renfrew (ed), *The Explanation of Culture Change: models in prehistory*, pp. 761-71. London: Duckworth.

Lee, R. B. 1979. *The !Kung San: Men, women and work in a foraging society*. Cambridge: Cambridge University Press.

Lee, R. B. and DeVore, I. 1968. *Man the Hunter*. Chicago: Aldine.

Legge, T., Payne, S. and Rowley-Conwy, P. 1998. The study of food remains in Prehistoric Britain. In J. Bayley (ed), *Science in Archaeology, an agenda for the future*, pp. 89-94. London: English Heritage.

Leroi-Gourhan, A.1968. *The Art of Prehistoric Man in Western Europe*. London: Thames and Hudson.

Miracle, P. 2002. Mesolithic Meals from Mesolithic Middens. In P. Miracle and N. Milner (eds), *Consuming Passions and Patterns of Consumption*, pp. 65-88. McDonald Institute Monographs. Oxford: Oxbow Books.

O'Brien, M. and Holland, T. 1992. The role of adaptation in archaeological explanation. *American Antiquity* 57: pp. 36-59.

Preucel, R. W. and Hodder, I. 1996. *Contemporary Archaeology in Theory: a reader*. Oxford: Blackwell Publisher.

Renfrew, C. 1994. Towards a Cognitive Archaeology. In C. Renfrew and E. B. W. Zubrow (eds), *The Ancient Mind: elements of cognitive archaeology*, pp. 3-13. Cambridge: Cambridge University Press.

Sassaman, K. E. 2000. Agents of change in hunter-gatherer technology. In M. -A. Dobres and J. E. Robb (eds.) *Agency in Archaeology*, pp. 148-168. London: Routledge.

Schrire, C. 1980. An enquiry into the evolutionary status and apparent identity of San hunter-gatherers. *Human Ecology* 8: 9-32.

Shanks, M. and Tilley, C. 1987a. *Reconstructing Archaeology: theory and practice*. Cambridge: Cambridge University Press.

Shanks, M. and Tilley, C. 1987b. *Social Theory and Archaeology*. Oxford: Polity Press.

Sinclair, A. 2000. Constellations of Knowledge: human agency and material affordance in lithic technology. In M.-A. Dobres and J. Robb (eds), *Agency in Archaeology*, pp. 196-213. London: Routledge.

Straus, L. G. 1991.Paradigm Found? A research agenda for study of the Upper and Post-Paleolithic in Southwest Europe. In G.A.Clark (ed), *Perspectives on the Past: theoretical biases in Mediterranean hunter-gatherer research*, pp. 56-78. Philadelphia: University of Pennsylvania Press.

Wilmsen, 1989. *Land Filled with Flies: a political economy of the Kalahari*. Chicago: Chicago University Press.

Wobst, H. M. 2000. Agency in (spite of) material culture. In M.-A. Dobres and J. Robb (eds), *Agency in Archaeology*, pp. 40-50. London: Routledge.

UPPER PALAEOLITHIC SOCIAL COLONISATION AND LOWER PALAEOLITHIC BIOLOGICAL DISPERSAL? A CONSIDERATION OF THE NATURE OF MOVEMENTS INTO EUROPE DURING THE PLEISTOCENE.

Lucy Grimshaw

University of Durham

Abstract

Palaeolithic archaeology has begun to consider the social aspects of the archaeological record, but these new approaches have largely been restricted to the Upper Palaeolithic and Homo sapiens. This paper will discuss whether the exclusion of pre-sapiens hunter-gatherers from a social and personal archaeology can be justified, and examine the presumption that the archaeological record of the Lower and Middle Pleistocene shows weaker evidence of people than that of the Upper Palaeolithic. I will reconsider the processes that occurred during the population movements associated with the initial occupation of Europe by pre-sapiens hominids during the Lower Palaeolithic and the spread of the early Upper Palaeolithic, particularly aspects of environmental and landscape learning and behavioural changes that take place during movement into previously unknown territories. Patterning in the composition of archaeological assemblages in space and time across Europe during these events will be investigated for signs of innovations and developments that may relate to the development of social identity among the migrants, and thus allow previously existing continental scale research to be utilised in the consideration of the social life of the Palaeolithic

Introduction.

Palaeolithic archaeology is closer in theoretical and methodological approach to Quaternary sciences, geology and evolutionary science than the humanities, and traditionally draws its interpretive methods from these disciplines. However, the recovery of high-resolution sites such as Pincevent in Northern France (Leroi-Gourhan and Brézillon 1972) and Boxgrove in Southern England (Roberts and Parfitt 1999), which preserve traces of activities at a brief moment in time, has led to a gradual increase in interest in personal action (Gowlett 1997), for example through *chaîne opératoire* approaches to manufacturing and transport (Böeda *et al.* 1990), which have allowed discussion of the skills and decision-making of the individuals who created Palaeolithic artefacts.

This interest in behaviour is gradually filtering into broader studies that require inter-site comparison (Conard 1994) and regional or continental study areas, such as colonisation, which has previously been a classic example of the use of a-personal continental scale approaches to explain the patterning of the Palaeolithic archaeological record. New theoretical and methodological approaches have been developed, and Upper Palaeolithic movements have been reconsidered as reflecting the behaviours of individuals in social networks (Davies 1999; 2001; Housley *et al.* 1997). However, this emergence of interest in social behaviours as an explanation of the form of movements has not been applied to pre-Aurignacian periods, with the exception of Gamble's (1986, 1993, 1998, 1999) work, which identifies a lack of modern social networks, communication and environmental awareness as constraining the possibilities for range expansion in the Lower and Middle Palaeolithic. Earlier periods of population movement are largely explained by biogeographical principles (Rolland 1992; 1995; 1998; 2001), without consideration of the behaviours undertaken by the individuals involved that allowed occupation to spread into new areas. Moreover, the lack of precise dating before the range of radiocarbon dates has supported the view that behaviours on a personal scale cannot be seen in the Lower and Middle Palaeolithic.

This paper will consider whether this binary division of the Pleistocene into a social Upper Palaeolithic and biological Lower and Middle Palaeolithic is justified, by re-examining the nature of population movements into Europe during the earliest occupation of the continent and the spread of the Aurignacian. Potential sources of analogy and models of behaviours during movements will be presented, followed by a consideration of the applicability of social and biological explanations to the archaeological record of both periods of hominin range expansion.

Models of movement and sources of behavioural analogies.

Palaeolithic archaeology has traditionally drawn upon two sources of behavioural models in order to interpret the Pleistocene archaeological record: hunter-gatherer ethnography and evolutionary theory. The study of Palaeolithic dispersal and colonisation has been hindered by the lack of a comparative ethnographic record, as no recorded hunter-gatherer groups have been observed to expand their ranges. In addition, population movements have been largely dismissed as explanatory mechanisms in later archaeological periods (Chapman and Hamerow 1997), and hence there is no archaeological theory or methodology concerning human migration for the Palaeolithic to draw upon.

As a consequence of these absences Palaeolithic archaeology has utilised biogeographical models of the range expansions of non-human species to interpret Pleistocene hominin movements (Rolland 1992; 1995; 1998; 2001). However, this approach assumes that episodes of movement in the Palaeolithic follow a non-human pattern, and that contemporary human behaviour cannot be compared to Pleistocene behaviour. This has resulted in a purely biological approach to Palaeolithic dispersals, even when the movements of *Homo sapiens* are being considered. Furthermore, Palaeolithic archaeology has only made use of historical biogeography, which considers movements at geological timescales and infers their causes as related to continental or global scale processes such as climatic change and the evolution of faunal communities. The focus on historical biogeography has resulted in climatic change and gradual adaptation being the major explanations of Pleistocene hominin range expansions, without an understanding of how these factors relate to ecologically observed movements. This approach has discarded the possibility of discussing the factors affecting individual migrants, effectively removing the action of the individuals and groups involved from any explanation of the events. At a broad scale the historical biogeographical approach has provided a means of understanding the timing and extent of Pleistocene movements in relation to climate and ecological community change, but cannot provide any detail of the responses of hominins to these factors, resulting in only a partial explanation of the Pleistocene spread of hominins from Africa. Ecological biogeography addresses the behaviours of groups undergoing expansion and their interactions with the ecological community, thus allowing movement to be considered at scales appropriate to the actions of the groups involved. Therefore, this paper will draw on both ecological and historical biogeographical theories, in order to provide a more complete picture of the behaviours surrounding non-human movements than traditional archaeological approaches.

Human geography and sociology have provided an abundance of observations of contemporary human movements and built a large body of theory concerning the behaviours, motivations and consequences of human migrations, which could be utilised by archaeology. Although these observations have not been derived from hunter-gatherer ethnography, there are many aspects of these models that may assist in the understanding of prehistoric movements. Furthermore, the use of such models allows Palaeolithic hunter-gatherers to be considered as more than non-human species responding to climatic changes, raising the possibility that the behaviours of the groups undertaking movements were significant.

This paper will consider the question of whether the biogeographical models form a better source of analogy for the behaviours seen during the earliest occupation of Europe, while the geographical and sociological models better explain the spread of the Upper Palaeolithic and *Homo sapiens*, as assumed in the traditional binary division of the Palaeolithic into biological pre-modern and social modern phases. This will be achieved by presenting a summary of both sets of models and then results of the testing of these models against the archaeological record of the Pleistocene.

Social models of movement.

Human geography and sociology have identified several factors that are commonly observed during contemporary human migrations. The decision to relocate is considered to be based on knowledge of the destinations, and their expected benefits (Sjaastad 1962; Bravo-Ureta *et al.* 1996; de Haan 1999). Small-scale local migrations therefore result from individuals becoming aware of the advantages of relocating over a short distance through personal knowledge acquisition, and can result in major movements developing over a considerable period of time through a series of short distance transfers, termed step migration (Ravenstein 1885). However, during long distance and rapid movements knowledge is acquired during an exploratory stage of a migration (Tilly 1978). Initially few individuals move, and then communicate the advantages of the destination to friends and relatives at the origin, creating a migration chain. Over time more moves take place as more people become aware of the advantages of moving and subsequently enlist further individuals into the migration chain (Akerman 1978). Therefore, migrations do not usually cause a severing of social networks, as people move within an existing set of ties and relationships.

Explorers are often young adults with relatively few commitments at the area of origin that might outweigh the benefits of relocation, and are moving to establish a social position better than that obtainable at their place of birth (Oberai and Singh 1983). Once a movement has occurred that individual is likely to move again, as the inertia of ties to the natal community has already been overcome (Anthony 1997). Therefore explorers may move considerable distances in a series of short moves. Followers are less liable to take risks and will only move when the information from the explorers is strong enough to indicate that migration would be beneficial (Haberkorn 1981, de Jong and Fawcett 1981). Nevertheless, the migratory followers are less conservative than the individuals who remain in the natal region, and therefore migration can result in stagnation in the resident source communities because the most resourceful individuals have moved away from the area (Lin and Liaw 2000). The followers of explorers are also liable to be young and usually have not established their own families (Oberai and Singh 1983), and are receptive to behavioural innovations (Haberkorn 1981), although they may not initiate changes. These characteristics of migrants result in a vibrant, resourceful and changing community on the move, in contrast to a conservative, often aging and impoverished community at the source (Skeldon 1997). Therefore, innovation in behaviour other than movement can be a product of colonisation, rather than its cause as has previously been assumed, since explorers are practical and inventive individuals, capable of envisaging improvements to their existing circumstances, and their followers also tend to be receptive to novel ideas that may lead towards improved conditions. Changes can also be promoted by the migrants escaping the social expectations and norms of the parent group, which may limit innovation. Therefore, behavioural changes between the source and destination are likely to be seen in the archaeological record of a long distance movement.

Often a specific subset of the population at the origin will move, since these are the people connected to the explorers (Hugo 1981). Migrations are hence expected to involve a biased sample of the original demographic group, in terms of age, gender and social status, which is associated with behavioural changes amongst the migrants. The lack of a representative sample of the parent group may result in a decreased range of behaviours. A strong ethnic identity has been observed to emerge among migrant groups, as a result of their strong internal links and relative isolation (Castles and Miller 1993). Also as migrants tend to be closely related and to come from a distinct sub-group within the original population, the identity they express may be different to that which they were part of before migrating. These identity markers are often highly standardised and seen among all the migrants originating from the same group. However, in a local migration a more representative sample of the population is likely to move due to the shorter distances involved and the maintenance of previous social ties, hence the innovations and behavioural changes seen amongst migrants in a long distance chain are unlikely to take effect (Tilly 1978).

Social models also reveal spatial patterning of movements. Local migration will result in the slow spread of a population, with destinations throughout the region close to the origin, as local knowledge allows individuals to move directly to suitable locations (Tilly 1978). In contrast, a chain migration exploratory phase is likely to involve small highly mobile groups, relocating on several occasions, resulting in long distance movements. The initial lack of knowledge of the destination will cause movement to a wide variety of destinations, as the advantages and disadvantages of particular locations have not been established. This may be seen in the archaeological record as an ephemeral and unfocused occupation spread rapidly over large areas.

The establishment of a 'chain migration' pattern of explorers followed by friends and relatives, leads to a pattern of nodal destinations (Wilson 1994). Movement will be directed towards areas that are known to be beneficial to the migrants because of communications from the explorers. This should be seen in the archaeological record as a pattern of occupation centred on a few areas. These may be far from the origin, but will possess high levels of resources and should be known to the migrants. The post-exploration stage is predicted to involve larger volumes of migrants but the moves may be over shorter distances, since the individuals involved are likely to be less willing to move repeatedly (Tilly 1978). Thus the establishment phase is expected to spread more slowly than exploration. At a later stage secondary dispersal is expected to occur, in which populations at the destination move to secondary nodes, since knowledge of the destination area has increased. Thus, the movement will follow a network of nodes reflecting the information flow between migrants and the decisions made by individuals, and will increase in complexity over time.

In summary, the chain migration model predicts that knowledge of the destination is central to movement. The level of local familiarity may be detected in the archaeological record in a variety of ways. An initial lack of local knowledge could be manifested in the archaeological record by the absence of use of local resources, with materials transferred over long distances from known sources (Rockman 2003). Sites could also be clustered in landscapes that are easily navigable without detailed local knowledge of the terrain, such as river-valleys, coasts and the foothills of linear mountain chains, as these create corridors through the landscape, and allow the easy re-location of other individuals and groups and of resources, by providing clear landmarks (Kelly 2003). A strong pattern of environmental preference could also indicate a lack of local knowledge, particularly if the environment occupied is similar to that at the origin, and therefore provides familiar resource types and distributions. Furthermore, clustering of sites at destination nodes, with little evidence of use of the hinterland would reflect a lack of awareness of other potentially useful locations. Therefore, the chain migration model may be inferred from the archaeological record through the presence of these proxy indicators of a lack of local knowledge in the initial phases of the movement, followed by the development of more widespread occupation in a range of landscapes and habitats, with the utilisation of the full range of available local resources. In contrast, local migration will show little sign of a lack of local knowledge, and will be broadly dispersed across the region to the edge of the source population, but will be slow to spread. Local migration is also unlikely to be associated with significant behavioural changes or the development of novel forms of identity expression.

Biological models of movement.

Biogeography considers the range of a species to be constrained by the abiotic conditions that it is able to tolerate, and by biotic interactions with other species (Hoffman and Blows 1994), as well as by its evolutionary history (Watts 1971). Range expansions occur when either the physical constraints are lifted, for example by major climatic change resulting in an increase in the habitable area (Brown and Gibson 1983), or when the biotic constraints relax due to the extinction of competitors, community restructuring resulting in the broadening of the niche, or adaptation facilitating dietary or other behavioural changes (Schoner 1988). Thus, historical biogeography predicts that range shifts will coincide with major climatic changes, as the distribution of plants changes in response to the climate and faunal communities adjust to the floral resources. Range expansion is also predicted to occur during large-scale faunal turnover and dispersal episodes as communities restructure (Myers and Giller 1988), although these events are often explained as a result of climatic changes. Thus, Palaeolithic explanations of hominin range expansions have focused on the global climatic record of the Pleistocene, and faunal responses to these events. However, ecological biogeography studies the effects of biotic release from range constraints, and has shown that individual species can adapt and overcome physical constraints without the external assistance of climatic change (Williamson 1996). Moreover, species adjust individually to their resources and constraints, rather than in a fixed position in the ecological community; thus, movements need not occur during major faunal turnover and dispersal events.

Ecologically populations consist of many subgroups inhabiting separate patches, connected by the dispersal of individuals between patches (Hanski 1991). At the scale of individual experience, that of each habitat patch and the corridors between them, movement is highly complicated. Large areas of the range are uninhabited, and unsuitable for colonisation (Sax and Brown 2000). Only a few areas contain enough resources to support occupation for a substantial length of time, and by a population large enough to become self-sustaining (Hanski and Gilpin 1991); thus, a nodal pattern of occupation is also predicted by ecological models. During expansion the patches colonised may not be the closest to the natal patch, resulting in some individuals moving far beyond the core of the population (Swenson *et al.* 1998). Subsequently infilling of the unoccupied patches will take place between the core and the furthest travelled dispersers (Shigesada and Kawasaki 1997), as is the case in the social network chain migration model. Ecological processes of patch colonisation result in the historical biogeographical process of diffusion into new territory, as patches beyond the edge of the range are gradually occupied over many generations. Thus, long-term expansion at a large scale can appear to follow a wave front pattern, of movement at a constant speed in a consistent direction, but at an ecological scale the spread is actually composed of many moves into habitat patches at a variety of distances and directions from the population front.

Successful dispersal into new areas is potentially related to a number of factors. Ecological similarities between the source and destination, in terms of resource type and distribution, play a strong role in successful patch colonisation, as adaptation to new conditions is not required during the establishment phase, when failure is likely to occur (Samways *et al.* 1999). The distance between the source and the destination, and the level of inhospitability of the habitat between the patches is related to the chances of successfully arriving at a new patch, and therefore successful patch colonisation correlates with short dispersal distances (Pulliam *et al.* 1992). The nature of the community at the destination patch also affects the chances of successful colonisation, as low species diversity and a high level of endemism offer little resistance to invasions of new species, particularly if vacant ecological niches are present (Case 1991; Baltz and Moyle 1993; Simberloff and Von Holle 1999). Movement into a vacant niche could result in the development of new behaviours and ultimately physical adaptations to the new lifestyle (Suarez *et al.* 1999).

The size of the population arriving in the new patch is also critical, as a small population is dependent on further arrivals of individuals, and thus a large population can more rapidly become independent (Channell and Lomolino 2000). Hence, biological models predict that larger populations will be more successful patch colonisers, which may be detected in the archaeological record by relatively large and abundant sites from first appearance of a population in a region. However, beyond the established range resources may not be sufficient for reproduction, and expansion may rely on continued flows of individuals from the core (Hanski 1991), despite the presence of a large adult population, until adaptation to the new area is achieved. This can result in a distinct establishment phase that precedes rapid spread, during which population size increases and behavioural or physical modifications may occur (Shigesada and Kawasaki 1997). Therefore, the archaeological record may reflect an initially small population, through aspects such as rare and sparse assemblages, as a result of biological processes as well as exploration in a social model of movement. The population that is involved in the expansion will be derived from the groups on the edge of the core range, and may not be representative of the overall population, allowing founder effects and isolation to further enhance the level of differences between the dispersers and the core, and rapid physical and behavioural adaptations may be seen (Barrett and Richardson 1986).

The individuals occupying the edge of the range are likely to be in sub-optimal conditions, and may be forced into these patches by a lack of competitive ability (Hanski and Gilpin 1991). In this scenario, spread will occur slowly and is unlikely to be accompanied by behavioural innovation due to a lack of behavioural flexibility among the dispersers. Alternatively, the lack of competition at the edge of the range may be attractive to the most competitive individuals, who are able to choose which patches offer the best opportunities (Stenseth and Lidicker 1992; Pusey 1992; Lidicker and Stenseth 1992; Ellsworth and Belthoff 1999). Therefore, the populations at the edge of the range may consist of innovative and resourceful individuals, as is the case in the social models of movement, resulting in rapid adaptation and behavioural changes.

In summary, ecological models envisage a two-phase process of rapid movement, behavioural changes and nodal spatial patterning similar to the predictions of the chain migration model in sociology and human geography. However, biological models also accommodate slow movement with little behavioural innovation and a broadly dispersed population, as is the case in local and step migration models. Thus, the form of movement reflected in the archaeological model is distinguished by the speed of spread, rather than the biological or social nature of the processes occurring.

Methods.

The relevance of these models of movement to the archaeological record of the initial occupation of Europe and the spread of the Aurignacian was investigated by the collection of data regarding the nature of the archaeological and environmental records in Europe, the Near East and North Africa. The study area was designed to allow comparison between the behaviours seen in the European destination area and the potential source regions of the migrants, in terms of the environments and landscapes occupied and the nature of the assemblages produced. Data regarding the dating, longitude and latitude, immediate environmental conditions, landscape setting and archaeological assemblage size and range of tool forms were collected for all sites in both periods. The Lower Palaeolithic case study included all the sites recorded as dating to Marine Isotope Stage (MIS) 11 or earlier, with the aim that this would enable possible exploratory phases of European occupation to be evaluated against a period accepted as representing settled occupation.

The earliest occupation of Europe.

The sites were assigned to one of six phases of the Pleistocene defined as:
- "Later Middle Pleistocene" (LMP), defined as post-Cromerian or Biharian in fauna, and coinciding with late MIS 12 and the whole of MIS 11.
- "Mid Middle Pleistocene" (MMP), including sites with fauna from the second half of the Cromerian complex, corresponding to MIS 15-12.
- "Early Middle Pleistocene" (EMP), containing fauna from the first half of the Cromerian complex, equivalent to MIS 19-16.
- "Late Early Pleistocene" (LEP), defined as falling between the Jaramillo and Brunhes-Matayama palaeomagnetic boundary.
- "Mid Early Pleistocene" (MEP), containing sites within the Jaramillo palaeomagnetic event.
- "Early Early Pleistocene" (EEP), consisting of sites within the Pleistocene before the Jaramillo event.

The landscapes in which sites were situated were recorded as:
- riverine,
- lacustrine,
- coastal,
- plains,
- hilly,
- mountainous,
- high plateau.

Sites were attributed to a category by the predominant landscape type in their surroundings; thus, sites in a river valley but not adjacent to the channel were described as riverine because the valley was considered to be the most important landscape feature relating to the presence of hominins.

The environment of each site was recorded following standard ecological biome categories defined by

Whittaker (1975). These are based on the structure of the habitat, in terms of the density and height of the vegetation cover, which divides biomes into classes of forest, woodland, shrubland, grassland, semi-desert and desert. Each habitat physiognomy is then sub-divided by climatic type. These categories provide a standardised means of assessing the environment of a site, without predetermining the features of importance to the hominin occupation of a site.

Lower Palaeolithic tool forms were classified as:
- cores,
- debitage,
- choppers,
- handaxes,
- cleavers,
- flake-tools,
- prepared-cores,
- bone or antler tools,
- wooden tools.

These categories were designed to be broad enough for inter-site comparison and to cover the full range of variation seen in the Lower Palaeolithic.

The assemblage sizes were recorded as the number of artefacts recovered from each site, with the aim of differentiating sites showing substantial evidence of occupation from those reflecting limited presence of hominins. The assemblage size included unmodified flakes and debitage, as well as finished tools, as sites with small numbers of tools but large amounts of debitage may reflect a high level of occupation, because tool production on site could reflect established settlement rather than exploration and the use of curated tools transported from regions of pre-existing occupation.

The Upper Palaeolithic.

The Upper Palaeolithic case study was restricted to Aurignacian sites as this industry is widely regarded as reflecting the initial *Homo sapiens* presence in Europe. The early Upper Palaeolithic transitional industries, such as the Chatelperronian and Uluzzian were excluded from the study because they may reflect acculturation or interaction between Neanderthals and *Homo sapiens* (Mellars 1999, d'Errico *et al.* 1998, Zilhão and d'Errico 1999, Zilhão 2000), and therefore cannot be used as clear proxy evidence for the presence of modern humans. Moreover, the behaviours associated with the meeting of resident and immigrating groups go beyond the scope of this paper. Additionally, Upper Palaeolithic industries post-dating the Aurignacian have been suggested to reflect further episodes of movement from the east (Otte and Keeley 1990), and thus their inclusion could confuse the picture of a single episode of movement by potentially repeating the behaviours seen at the beginning of the Aurignacian and including aspects of acculturation and interaction between groups.

The Aurignacian data were generated using the Stage Three Project database of calibrated radiocarbon dates (van Andel and Davies 2003), as this provided a large volume of well-dated sites. For the analysis the sites were assigned to six date categories of:
- >40 Kyr BP,
- 40-36.5 Kyr BP,
- 36.5-33 Kyr BP,
- 33-29.5 Kyr BP,
- 29.5-26 Kyr BP,
- <26 Kyr BP.

These divisions of 3500 years were designed to allow sites to be placed in a minimum of categories, by considering the size of the standard deviations of radiocarbon dates during the early Upper Palaeolithic, following the recommendations of Pettitt (1999). A division earlier than 40 Kyr BP was not used as no Aurignacian sites could be placed earlier than 43.5 Kyr BP. Radiocarbon dates represent the distribution of possible dates of a sample; therefore, the actual date may fall anywhere within the distribution given by the standard deviation, and thus all dates within this range are equally likely and must be included in all analyses (Pettitt 1999; 2000; Pettitt *et al.* 2003). Therefore, each site was placed in every category covered within the range of its minimum and maximum definite dates at two standard deviations. In the situation of a site having been dated using several samples, the overall minimum and maximum of all the unquestioned dates were used to assign the site to the date categories.

The landscapes, environments and assemblage sizes of Aurignacian sites were recorded in the same manner as the Lower Palaeolithic case study. The Aurignacian assemblages are substantially more diverse than the Lower Palaeolithic tools, and this analysis focuses on:
- beads,
- marine shell,
- mobilary art,
- perforated teeth,
- parietal art.

Results

Temporal patterns.

The trend in the number of sites over time during the initial occupation of Europe (Figure 2.1 a) shows an early phase of extremely low numbers of sites, followed by two periods of substantial increase in the number of sites. There are difficulties directly equating site numbers in the archaeological record with population size, as issues of group size, archaeological visibility of sites, the level of dispersion or agglomeration of the population, and the level of mobility and duration of occupation all affect the numbers of sites recorded. The models of movement predict that groups will initially be small and widely dispersed, and may produce a limited range of tools. Therefore, the initial sites are liable to suffer from problems of poor archaeological visibility. Hence, a low level of sites due to poor archaeological detection of small assemblages with alack of easily recognisable complex tools, would fit the model of exploration preceding major population flows and established settlement. Moreover, exploratory groups are predicted to be highly residentially mobile, with short occupation duration, and thus these factors could also explain the rarity of sites in the early Pleistocene. Furthermore, a subsequent increase in duration of occupation due to reduced residential mobility or increased knowledge of local resources, or an increase of population size and levels of agglomeration at nodes, would result in greater archaeological visibility and an increase in site numbers, and both causes of increased volumes of archaeological sites fit the expectations of the models of movement.

Therefore, the patterning of site numbers over time suggests that an establishment phase occurred, in which exploration and possibly failure to establish took place, before successful widespread occupation. The periods of increasing numbers of sites could be explained by either the arrival of more groups from beyond the borders of Europe in a chain migration model following exploration and communication, or by indigenous population growth in an ecological adaptation model.

In contrast to the initial occupation of Europe, the Aurignacian data (Figure 2.1 b) concerning site numbers over time do not show an early phase of low levels of occupation. The numbers of sites are high from the earliest time of the appearance of the Aurignacian, implying that at a continental scale, no distinct establishment phase occurred. However, given the limitations of radiocarbon dates at this time depth, it is possible that a phase of low intensity occupation occurred, but has been obscured by older dates being compressed into the period around 40 Kyr BP. At present these two possibilities cannot be resolved, and many sites during the early Upper Palaeolithic have only minimal dates. Therefore, the Aurignacian data are equivocal regarding the presence or absence of a two-phase process of colonisation.

Spatial data.

Likewise, the spatial patterning of sites over time in the earliest occupation of Europe (Figure 2.2), reveals a distinct spatial trend, with early sites concentrated in the south, particularly the southwest, and later spread into northwestern and central Europe and finally the northeast. Therefore, in the Lower Palaeolithic spread was slow enough to reveal the possibility of detecting exploratory sites. Furthermore, the initial sites are small and widely spaced, whereas in the late Early and early Middle Pleistocene clusters of larger sites appear in the major

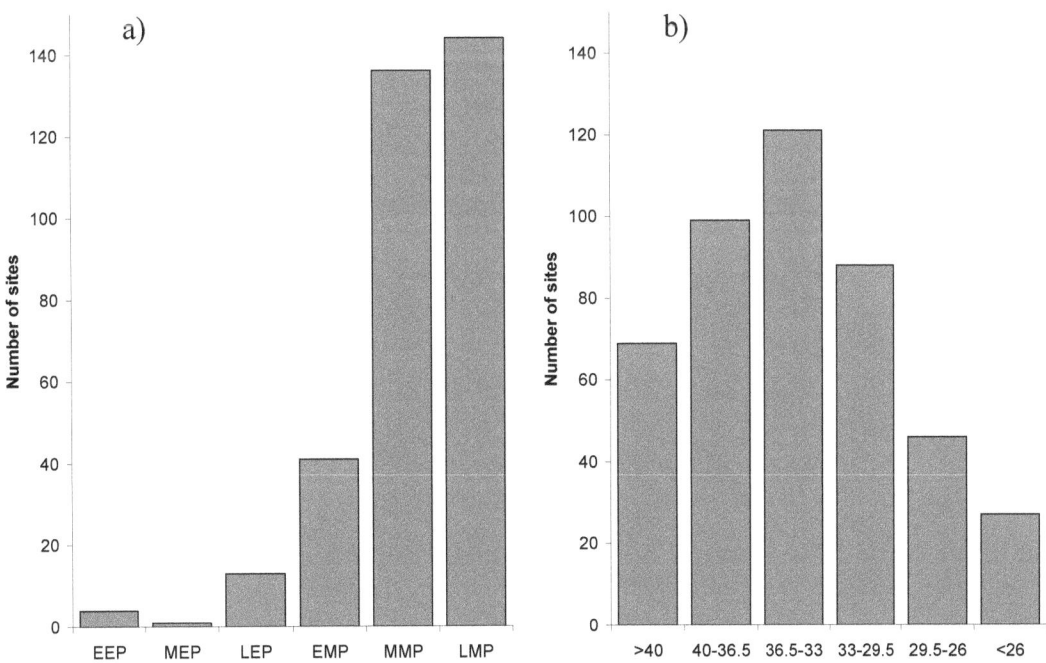

Figure 2.1 a) The number of Lower Palaeolithic sites in Europe during each of the divisions of the Pleistocene. b) The number of Aurignacian sites in Europe during each of the date categories in Kyrs BP.

river valleys of Europe. This spatial distribution tallies with the predictions of social networks operating as information conduits in a chain migration, to produce initially unfocused and low volume exploration, followed by major movements to destination nodes. Alternatively, this pattern could reflect resource distribution across Europe, as predicted in ecological models.

However, as the sites are dated to such broad divisions of the Pleistocene, it is unclear whether the sites in the clusters were genuinely contemporaneous or reflect repeated occupation of an area. Synchronous occupation of an area at several sites would show that a destination node was present, whereas repeated occupation could have taken place over several thousand years, and would not entail clustering of the population in a particular place. Nevertheless, repeated occupation implies that the location was known to be in an area with good resources, and was worth returning to, and therefore would fit the expectations of an increase in local knowledge in the later stages of a movement.

The Aurignacian spatial data (Figure 2.3) show a pattern of widespread occupation of Europe from the first appearance of the Upper Palaeolithic. The peripheral areas of the continent, such as the interior of the Iberian and Italian peninsulas and the British Isles were inhabited late, but the majority of mainland Europe appears to have been occupied rapidly in the earliest phases of the movement, leaving no traces of exploration in the spatial data. The presence of substantial numbers of sites throughout the core area of Aurignacian occupation from

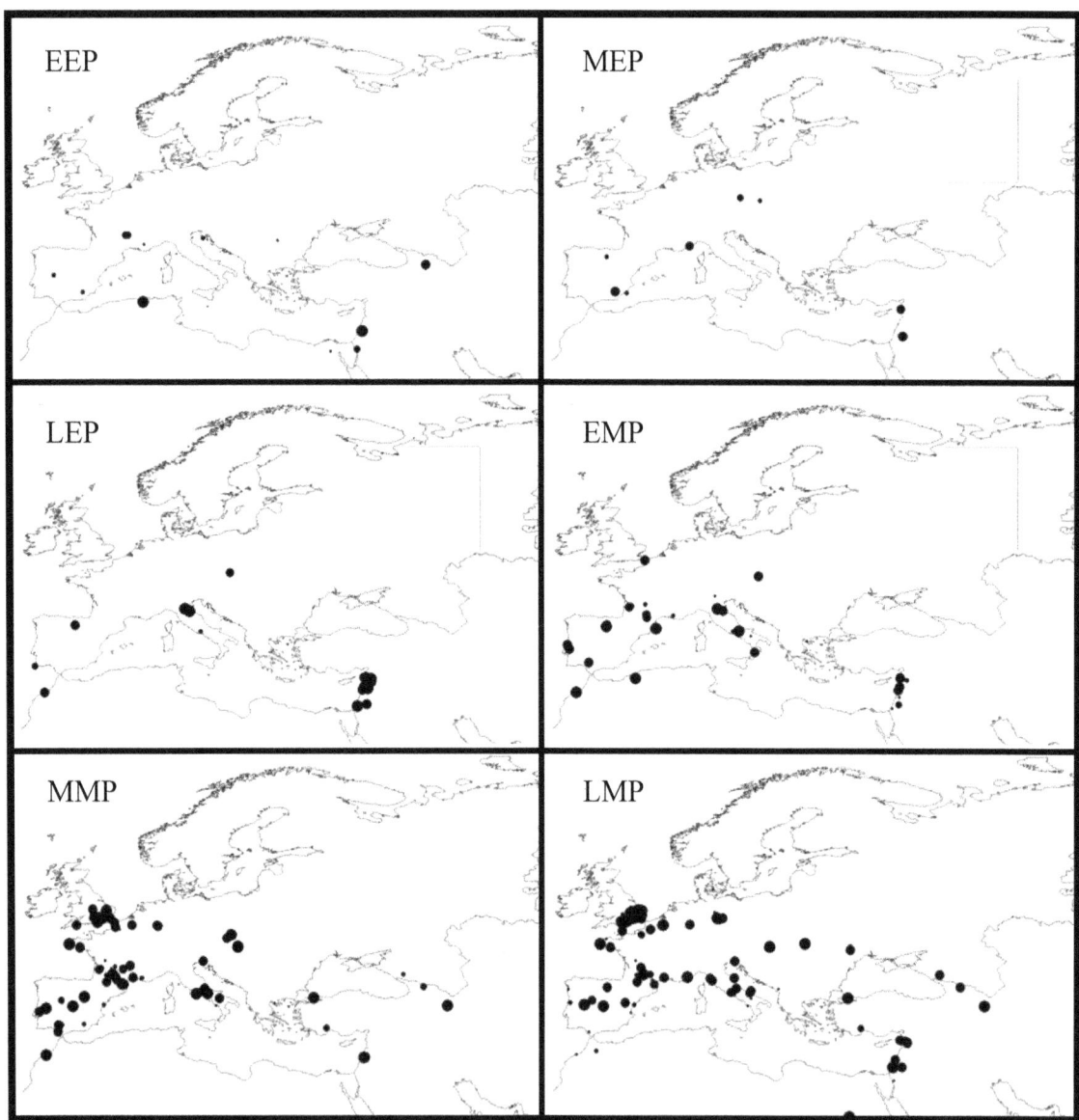

Figure 2.2 Distribution of the Lower Palaeolithic sites dating to each division of the Pleistocene, with points scaled to the size of the assemblage.

its earliest appearance could be explained in three ways:
- by an extremely rapid movement without a prolonged phase of exploration;
- by the radiocarbon dates compressing older sites into the period around 40 Kyr BP;
- or possibly by the earlier exploration not leaving distinctively Aurignacian assemblages due to the small group size and high levels of mobility associated with exploration, causing assemblages to be small and undiagnostic, thus preventing the recognition of exploratory sites.

However, the Aurignacian data do suggest that clustering of sites occurred and that major occupation nodes may have been present in areas such as southwestern France, northern Spain and southern Germany, as predicted in both social and ecological models, although these clusters may also reflect repeated occupation rather than contemporaneous sites.

Environments and landscapes occupied.

The types of environments and landscapes occupied were investigated in order to consider the question of the level of adaptation or behavioural change during the movements. However, these factors suffered from a substantial lack of data, with less than half of the sites in both study periods having a recorded local environment or landscape in the published record. Therefore, the results of these investigations are provisional.

In the initial occupation of Europe there is a distinct trend towards a greater diversity of environmental conditions inhabited over time, shown in Figure 2.4a, and the biomes occupied earliest, temperate woodlands and

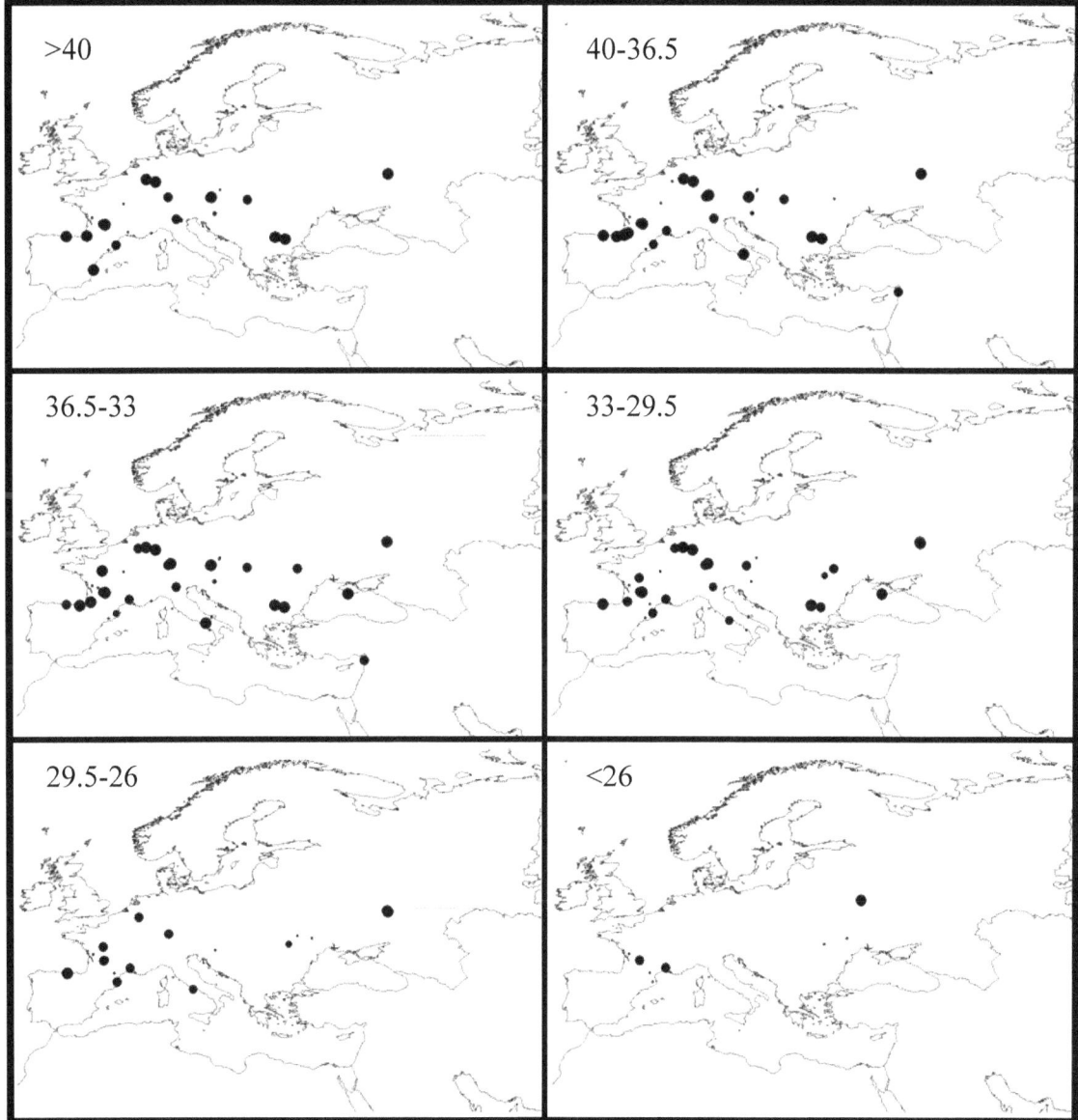

Figure 2.3 Distribution of the Aurignacian sites dated to each date category in Kyrs BP, with points scaled to the size of the assemblage.

shrublands, savannah and steppe, were those most similar to the conditions in the Near East and North Africa, the potential sources of the migrants. Ecological models suggest that similarity of habitat is a major factor in the success of a dispersal (Myers 1986), thus this pattern fits ecological expectations. Moreover, the sequence of habitats occupied over time follows a slow trend towards colder and more closed environments, with temperate forests, cool temperate bog and taiga occupied late, suggesting gradual adaptation to conditions in northern Europe. However, ethnographic studies have suggested that forested habitats present particular problems in terms of learning the location of resources, as landmarks are scarce, making these habitats extremely difficult to navigate without detailed local knowledge (Kelly 2003). Thus, the delay between the initial occupation of Europe and the appearance of sites in forested areas could be accounted for by landscape learning processes that occur in contemporary societies, and therefore are not necessarily indicative of biological adaptation.

Data concerning the types of landscapes occupied over time can provide further information about landscape learning processes. Throughout the early occupation of Europe the vast majority of sites were located in riverine landscapes (see Figure 2.5 a), which can provide corridors through unfamiliar regions, allowing easier navigation and location of resources (Kelly 2003). Coastal landscapes were also occupied in the early phases of the movement and can likewise form corridors in the absence of detailed local knowledge. The landscapes occupied later were those that demand a greater degree of local knowledge and experience, due to their lack of landmarks or navigable pathways, and consisted of plains and hills, high plateaux and mountains. These landscapes would have been extremely difficult to occupy without prior exploration, whereas the river valleys could have formed a network of corridors between areas of plentiful resources that appear as nodal destinations. Furthermore, the sites in the difficult landscapes contain small assemblages (Table 2.1) reinforcing the possibility that these were exploratory forays into new territory during the process of landscape learning, and preceding more substantial settlement. However, river valleys also provide a concentration of resources critical to hunter-gatherers, such as water and game animals, and therefore the heavily skewed distribution of sites towards riverine landscapes could reflect ecological preferences of the hominins, rather than landscape learning processes.

The landscapes occupied during the Aurignacian, (Figure 2.5 b) were also predominantly riverine. However, there was no sequence of occupation of landscapes, with coastal, hilly and mountainous regions inhabited throughout the existence of the Aurignacian. This lack of evidence for adaptation or landscape learning could be a factor of the lack of sensitivity of radiocarbon dates compared to the speed of the processes happening in the early Upper Palaeolithic. Alternatively, landscape learning took place very rapidly and mountainous or monotonous landscapes were not a significant problem for Aurignacian groups. Nevertheless, it appears that there is less evidence of landscape learning and knowledge development in the Upper Palaeolithic than in the Lower Palaeolithic.

Likewise, the Aurignacian environmental data, (Figure 2.4 b) show no chronological sequence of habitat occupation. Throughout the Aurignacian the majority of sites were located in steppic temperate grassland conditions, with some sites in temperate woodlands and shrublands and few in alpine grasslands. Therefore, the Aurignacian environmental data show no evidence of environmental adaptations following occupation of familiar habitats, as expected in biological scenarios, or of the learning of new biomes. However, as the Aurignacian was of a considerably shorter duration than the initial occupation of Europe, these processes may have occurred after the final Aurignacian sites, and in fact the following Gravettian techno-complex has evidence of expansion of occupation into colder and harsher environments, rather than retreat with the temperate woodlands, shrublands and grasslands as the climate cooled. Nevertheless, the comparison between the environmental data of the movements in the Lower and Upper Palaeolithic displays greater support for both ecological and social models of movement in the earlier data than the Aurignacian.

	\multicolumn{5}{c}{Assemblage size class}	
	0-10	11-50	51-100	101-1000	1001+	Total
Coastal	5	1	2	21	13	42
Riverine	34	37	24	82	44	221
Lacustrine	5	3	-	8	5	21
Hilly	5	4	-	13	2	24
Plains	-	1	-	1	-	2
High Plateau	5	-	-	1	-	6
Mountainous	2	10	-	1	-	13
Total	56	56	26	127	64	329

Table 2.1 Number of Lower Palaeolithic sites in each landscape type in each assemblage size class.

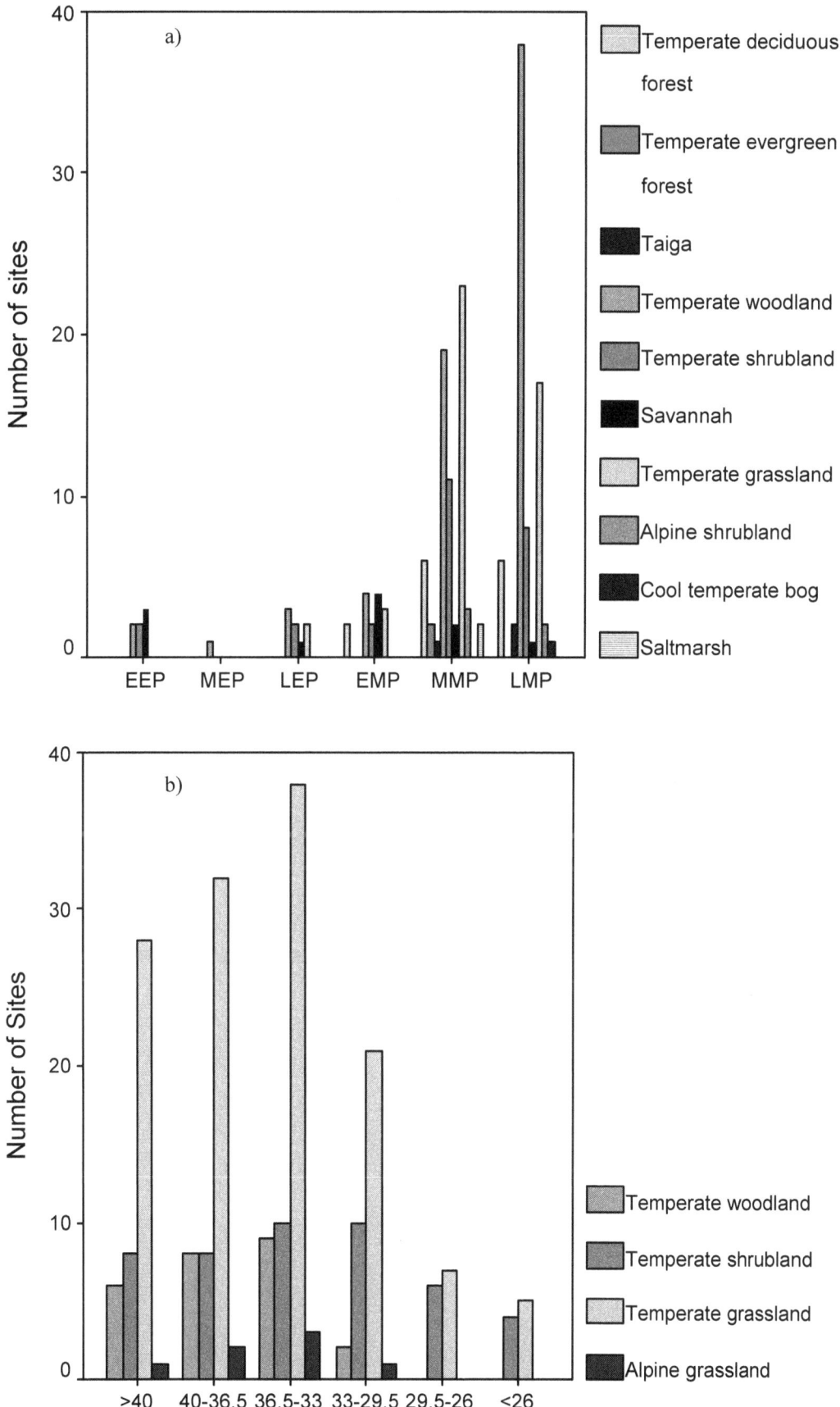

Figure 2.4 Number of sites in each environmental type. a) The Lower Palaeolithic in the divisions of the Pleistocene. b) The Aurignacian in the date categories (in Kyrs BP).

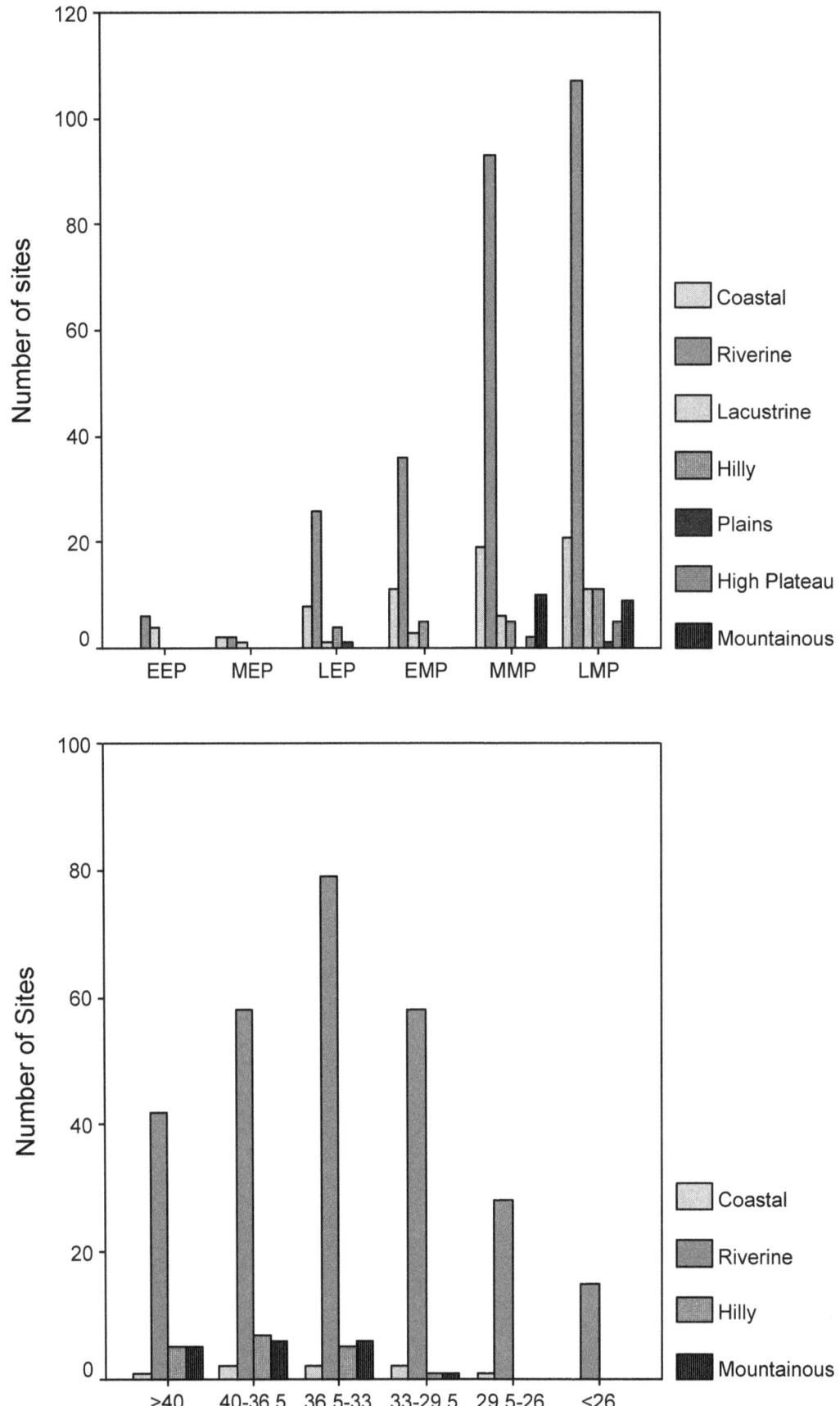

Figure 2.5. Number of sites in each landscape type. a) The Lower Palaeolithic sites in the divisions of the Pleistocene. b) The Aurignacian in the date categories (in Kyrs BP).

Behavioural context.

Both biological and social models predict that behavioural changes may take place during movements, either in the form of innovation or as a reduction in the range of behaviours undertaken. This was investigated through the consideration of the variety of tool forms produced during the movements and the types of technologies used in tool production.

The earliest occupation of Europe.

In the Lower Palaeolithic the overall level of behavioural variation is low and innovation is not seen; however, by looking at the distribution of tool types in Europe and its surrounding regions, a pattern of reduced behavioural diversity emerges over time. In Europe all regions have a non-handaxe phase of occupation preceding the appearance of greater numbers of sites, larger sites and sites with handaxes. This can be interpreted as an aspect of exploration, as small groups moving rapidly over large distances may have temporarily abandoned the use of handaxes and instead used a basic flake tool technology that required less time investment in manufacturing. Thus, the appearance of handaxes may represent the arrival of more substantial numbers of individuals, who were less mobile and more inclined to take the time to make more complex tools. Moreover, the arrival of larger groups could be associated with individuals who possessed a greater range of knapping skills and therefore could manufacture complex tools. Older individuals who have learnt the full repertoire of tool manufacturing techniques may be involved in the later stages of movement, in contrast to the explorers, who tend to be young adults and may have left their natal groups before learning to manufacture handaxes. Furthermore, handaxes have been suggested to have been linked to social interactions, such as mate selection (Kohn and Mithen 1999), and thus their absence from exploratory groups could be explained by the age and gender biases of these groups, which tend to be composed almost exclusively of young men, who would thus have little reason to manufacture handaxes in the absence of other demographic groups to signal to. It is possible that individuals within these exploratory groups competed amongst themselves using other means than the production of handaxes whilst in isolation from the broader demographic group. Moreover, Gamble (1998) argues that Lower Palaeolithic groups did not have the capacity to build relationships in absentia via symbolic material culture, and thus the members of the exploratory groups would not be expected to build a hierarchy relating to mate selection without a direct stimulus to do so. Alternatively, the slow spread of uncompetitive groups into the periphery of the range, predicted by ecological models, could explain the loss of complex behaviours.

A further possible explanation of the lack of handaxes due to high levels of curation of finished tools in areas away from known raw material sources and other fixed resources, such as watercourses (Potts 1994; Pope 2004), seems unlikely to apply since there is no evidence of any handaxes or of their production throughout the regions undergoing initial colonisation. The entire absence of handaxes or biface manufacturing debris over such large spatial and temporal scales implies that these tools were not a component of the tool kit in these regions, as otherwise some evidence of handaxes would be expected to be present, especially in gravel deposits that sample artefacts deposited throughout the catchment area, and thus are predicted to contain a representative sample of the lithics utilised in a region (Wenban-Smith 1998). Furthermore, there is no evidence in the Lower Palaeolithic of Europe of the transport of tools over the hundreds of kilometres necessary to explain the absence of handaxes at the edge of occupation by curation and transport from areas with evidence of their presence (Grimshaw 2004). Thus, curation may explain the lack of finished tools in a limited region, but not at a continental scale.

The Upper Palaeolithic.

In the case of the Aurignacian, the entire tool kit can be considered to be innovative in form as there are no clear precursors to Aurignacian technology in Europe. In the Near East transitional industries occur, but none contain the distinctive Aurignacian tools, such as carinated scrapers and split-based bone points, until considerably later than the appearance of these forms in Europe. Thus, it is possible that the Aurignacian emerged during the initial movement into Eastern Europe, and that the transitional phase has not been detected due to the very small population size likely to be involved as well as the poor resolution of radiocarbon dates during the Early Upper Palaeolithic. Groups in possession of the new Aurignacian forms could then have spread across the rest of Europe, leaving traces of a relatively uniform industry without clear precursors (Grimshaw 2004). This development of Aurignacian forms may have occurred as a response to the isolation of the migrating groups, and the release from the social constraints of their natal community. Social models of migration have emphasised the level of cohesion and development of new forms of ethnic expression among migrants, as a result of their encounters with resident groups of a different ethnicity and isolation from the community at home (Castles and Miller 1993). Thus, the emergence of the Aurignacian within Europe can be considered to fit these predictions. Nevertheless, as ecological models also predict behavioural changes this pattern is also compatible with a biological dispersal scenario.

A further aspect of identity expression during the movement of the Aurignacian is shown by the high levels of mobilary art, beads and perforated teeth in the sites dating to the first half of the Aurignacian. Personal ornaments such as beads can be used in expressions of social identity (Kuhn *et al.* 2001) and communicate group affiliation especially in situations where groups only encounter one another on an infrequent basis (Gamble 1980; 1982). In the later Aurignacian these artefacts become scarcer and parietal art appears for the first time, albeit at very low levels. These patterns may be linked to colonisation, as migrant groups are predicted to strongly express identity, and the forms seen in the early Aurignacian would allow this identity to be carried with the individual during movement. In contrast, parietal art implies the significance of a location, rather than an individual or group, since parietal art is static and cannot be transported, but may be viewed through repeated visits to the location. Although the art may be associated with the people that made it and their social identities and power negotiation, due to its importance as an act of creation (Gell 1998), artistic expression in a non-transportable format can also imply that the groups making and viewing the art could relocate these places, if reviewing and adding to existing art were also important. Therefore parietal art would be expected to occur once places had developed some significance to the Aurignacian groups, in parallel to the appearance of destination nodes and increasing local knowledge (Kelly 2003).

	Mobilary Art, Beads, Marine Shell and Perforated Teeth	Parietal Art
>40	38	-
40-36.5	56	-
36.5-33	56	1
33-29.5	35	1
29.5-26	11	-
<26	9	-

Table 2.2. The number of Aurignacian sites with recorded instances of portable art and personal ornamentation in each date category compared against the occurrence of parietal art.

Which models apply to the two events?

The data from the Lower Palaeolithic case study better fit an historical biogeographical model than the Aurignacian data do. The slow spread and lack of behavioural change during the Lower Palaeolithic events suggest that a process of historical biogeographical diffusion operated. However, many of the predictions of ecological biogeographical species invasions are also fulfilled by the Lower Palaeolithic data, providing insights into the processes allowing the diffusion to take place at an ecological scale, particularly the technological loss that occurred in the areas undergoing colonisation, which can be explained by the nature of the groups that explore beyond the population front. Nevertheless, the data also fits the local or step migration models in the rate of spread, and the chain migration model in the presence of a two-stage process of movement. Therefore, although the events of the Lower Palaeolithic are well explained by a combination of ecological and historical biogeographical approaches, sociological or human geographical processes cannot be dismissed in the explanation of these events.

In contrast, the movement of the Aurignacian, with its rapid spread and nodal destinations, fits the chain migration model, although the lack of an exploratory stage undermines the certainty that this process took place. Nevertheless, the lack of the exploratory phase can probably be explained by the poor dating resolution in relation to the speed of the processes under investigation. However, a rapid biological invasion with the formation of satellite populations in resource patches far beyond the primary population would also accommodate the patterns in the Aurignacian data. The slow spread of historical biogeographical and the step or local migration models do not match the findings of the Aurignacian data. It is currently impossible to differentiate between the two possible sets of processes that operated during the Aurignacian movement, as the archaeological proxies of both models predict the same findings. Therefore, the movement of the Aurignacian can equally plausibly be explained by biological or cultural processes.

Limitations of the models with regard to the Pleistocene.

A major problem with the application of the social models to the Palaeolithic is the expectation of knowledge of the destination, brought about by communication, and resulting in networks of nodes. In the absence of modern communications it is difficult to envisage how information transmission at a continental scale could have been maintained. However, return migrants are expected during migrations (Kearney 1986), and would be able to transmit information. Also, as the people involved in movement during the Palaeolithic would have been highly mobile, knowledge of areas beyond the original range is likely. Furthermore, communication need not have occurred between exploratory groups at the periphery of occupation and residential groups in the source regions at the edge of Europe; rather, local transfer of information and subsequent relaying of these communications to groups further from the periphery through the social networks involved in the migration chain could have taken place. Therefore, knowledge of remote areas could be communicated without modern long distance technology. However, the issue of communication is further complicated by suggestions that pre-*Homo sapiens* hominins or even early members of our own species lacked modern cognition and potentially possessed a restricted language ability (Foley 1995; Klein 1998; Wynn and Coolidge 2004), although other species do achieve communication without human language. Moreover, it would be unwise to dismiss the possibility that models based on contemporary human behaviour can be applied to other members of the genus *Homo*, as aspects of modern behaviours are likely to have a deep time depth, during which they developed and evolved.

A further problem concerning the application of social models to Palaeolithic movements is the extremely long duration of the episodes of spread into Europe compared to the contemporary migrations used to provide the analogy. It is possible that such long duration events do require explanation by factors that have not been, or cannot be, observed by studies of modern human behaviours. Nevertheless, the extremely slow spread of groups into Europe may have involved observed behaviours at the local microscale. Furthermore, the problem of poor chronological resolution could also be obscuring more rapid movements, failure to establish and subsequent recolonisation, which could have taken place at a more human timescale. However, further work considering how the predictions of contemporary social models could be manifested over substantial periods of time would be beneficial to their application to the Palaeolithic.

Problems in the application of ecological biographical models to the events of the Pleistocene centre on the difficulties of obtaining accurate dates of archaeological sites. Many of the ecologically observed range expansions have taken place extremely rapidly, and are therefore likely to appear to be instantaneous in the Pleistocene archaeological record. This problem particularly concerns the detection of the initial phase of movement, as a lack of a chronology at an appropriate scale to the processes that occurred would destroy the possibility of recovering a detailed sequence of events. Nevertheless, such rapid movement would imply that biological invasion rather than gradual adaptation in the context of climatic change occurred, and hence that ecological biogeography is a more appropriate model than historical biography for the particular case of spread being studied. A more complicated chronological limitation is the problem of rapid exploratory movement into a region, abandonment and reappearance at a timescale faster than can be detected in the Pleistocene, as these events may appear to describe a slow spread following historical biographical principles, or a social movement based on only local movement, when rapid biological invasion or social chain migration were actually involved. This situation results in a regional palimpsest of occupational histories, and would require much greater dating precision to resolve, through methods such as better regional correlation of biostratigraphical and geological sequences.

There is also a need for work to be undertaken on the application of these models to mobile hunter-gatherer groups, for whom residential movement was not an exceptional event, but an aspect of everyday life. Movements may have been even more common amongst Palaeolithic hunter-gatherer groups than recently observed migrants, as the inertia of ties to the current location may not be an inhibiting factor. Possibly larger groups of people may have been involved, as the young adults would not be the only mobile group in the population. However, young adults may still have been the most mobile and most likely to be pioneers during the exploratory stage.

Nevertheless, the combination of both social and biological models provides a spectrum of behaviours that possibly occurred during the movements of hominins in the Pleistocene, creating a stronger framework for the interpretation of the archaeology of dispersals and colonisations than the use of a simple historical biogeographical model. Moreover, in the absence of an ethnographic record of hunter-gatherer movements, these models provide the only available means of generating a picture of the behaviours surrounding movements based on observations rather than speculation.

Conclusions

In conclusion, this study has also shown that it is possible to address the scale of social behaviours in the Palaeolithic, despite the traditional continental scale approach, and opens avenues of research at the local level, which may provide stronger support for the use of these models in identifying behaviours. However, it is clearly very difficult to differentiate between social and biological predictions through traces of movements in the archaeological record. Both sets of models predict similar features, such as nodal networks of destinations and significant levels of behavioural change. Nevertheless, the fact that both the Lower and Upper Palaeolithic episodes of movement show traces of the predicted features demands that both types of models are considered in the treatment of all periods of the Palaeolithic. Moreover, the similarities in the models result in the social and ecological aspects of the Palaeolithic being inseparable in practice as well as theory. Furthermore, radiocarbon dating of the early Upper Palaeolithic provides a poorer record of the behaviours surrounding movement than the less precise dates available for the Lower Palaeolithic, as the timescale of the processes in operation in the Aurignacian is shorter than radiocarbon dates can access. Thus, a lack of radiocarbon dates does not support the dismissal of the social. Moreover, as the biological models predict similar features to the social models, the same dating constraints should operate in the application of both sets of predictions. Therefore, the division into an early purely biological phase and a later strongly social phase of Palaeolithic behaviour, constructed by Palaeolithic archaeology, is not justified.

Acknowledgements

I would like to thank Peter Rowley-Conwy and Mark White for their advice throughout this research project, and Paul Pettitt for his help with the use of radiocarbon dates. I would also like to thank Karl Pederson, Phil Howard, Neil Wharton and Ian Clark for their technical assistance with the use of GIS and SPSS. This research was made possible by the award of AHRB grant number 00/3061. The Stage Three Project was supported by Grant number F/757/A from the Leverhulme Trust, together with a grant from the McDonald Grants and Awards Fund, and was compiled by William Davies.

References Cited

Akerman, S. 1978. "Towards an Understanding of Emigrational Processes," in *Human Migration: Patterns and Policies*. Edited by W. H. McNeill and R. S. Adams, pp. 287-306. Bloomington: Indiana University Press.

Anthony, D. 1997. "Prehistoric Migration as Social Process," in *Migrations and Invasions in Archaeological Explanation*, 664 edition, *British Archaeological Reports International Series*. Edited by J. Chapman and H. Hamerow, pp. 21-32. Oxford: Oxbow Books.

Baltz, D. M., and Moyle, P. B. 1993. Invasion Resistance to Introduced Species by a Native Assemblage of California Stream Fishes. *Ecological Applications* **3**:246-255.

Barrett, S. C. H., and Richardson, B. J. 1986. "Genetic Attributes of Invading Species," in *Ecology of Biological Invasions*. Edited by R. H. Groves and J. J. Burdon, pp. 21-33. Cambridge: Cambridge University Press.

Böeda, E., Geneste, J.-M., and Meignen, L. 1990. Identification de chaînes opératoires lithiques du Paléolithique ancien et moyen. *Paléo* **2**:43-80.

Bravo-Ureta, B. E., Quiroga, R. E., and Brea, J. A. 1996. Migration Decisions, Agrarian Structure, and Gender: The Case of Ecuador. *Journal of Developing Areas* **30**:463-475.

Brown, J. H., and Gibson, A. C. 1983. *Biogeography*. St. Louis: C. V. Mosby Company Press.

Case, T. J. 1991. Invasion resistance, species build-up and community collapse in metapopulation models with interspecies competition. *Biological Journal of the Linnean Society* **42**:239-266.

Castles, S., and Miller, M. J. 1993. *The Age of Migration: International Population Movements in the Modern World*. London: MacMillan Press.

Channell, R., and Lomolino, M. V. 2000. Trajectories to extinction: spatial dynamics of the contraction of geographical ranges. *Journal of Biogeography* **27**:169-179.

Chapman, J., and Hamerow, H. 1997. "Introduction: On The Move Again- Migrations and Invasions in Archaeological Explanation," in *Migrations and Invasions in Archaeological Explanation*. Edited by J. Chapman and H. Hamerow, pp. 1-10. Oxford: British Archaeological Reports International Series 664.

Conard, N. J. 1994. On the Prospects for an Ethnography of Extinct Hominids. *Current Anthropology* **35**:281-282.

Davies, W. 1999. The Aurignacian as a reflection of modern human population dispersal in Europe. Unpublished Ph.D Thesis, University of Cambridge.

Davies, W. 2001. A Very Model of a Modern Human Industry: New Perspectives on the Origins and Spread of the Aurignacian in Europe. *Proceedings of the Prehistoric Society* **67**:195-217.

de Haan, A. 1999. Livelihoods and Poverty: The Role of Migration- A Critical Review of the Migration Literature. *Journal of Development Studies* **36**:1-47.

de Jong, G. F., and Fawcett, J. T. 1981. "Motivations for Migration: An Assessment and a Value-Expectancy Research Model," in *Migration Decision Making: Multidisciplinary Approaches to Microlevel Studies in Developed and Developing Countries*. Edited by G. F. de Jong and R. W. Gardner, pp. 13-58. New York: Pergamon Press.

d'Errico, F., Zilhão, J., Julien, M., Baffier, D., and Pelegrin, J. 1998. Neanderthal Acculturation in Western Europe?: A Critical Review of the Evidence and Its Interpretation. *Current Anthropology* **39**:S1-S44.

Ellsworth, E. A., and Belthoff, J. R. 1999. Effects of social status on the dispersal behaviour of juvenile western screech-owls. *Animal Behaviour* **57**:883-892.

Foley, R. 1995. "Language and thought in evolutionary perspective," in *Interpreting Archaeology: Finding meaning in the past*. Edited by I. Hodder, M. Shanks, A. Alexandri, V. Buchli, J. Carman, J. Last, and G. Lucas, pp. 76-80. London: Routledge.

Gamble, C. 1980. Information exchange in the Palaeolithic. *Nature* **283**:522-523.

Gamble, C. 1982. Interaction and alliance in Palaeolithic society. *Man* **17**:92-107.

Gamble, C. 1986. *The Palaeolithic Settlement of Europe*. Cambridge: Cambridge University Press.

Gamble, C. 1993. *Timewalkers: The Prehistory of Global Colonization*. Cambridge, Massachusetts: Harvard University Press.

Gamble, C. 1998. Palaeolithic society and the release from proximity: a network approach to intimate relations. *World Archaeology* **29**:426-449.

Gamble, C. 1999. *The Palaeolithic Societies of Europe*. Cambridge: Cambridge University Press.

Gell, A. 1998. *Art and agency : an anthropological theory*. New York: Clarendon Press.

Gowlett, J. A. J. 1997. High Definition Archaeology: Ideas and Evaluation. *World Archaeology* **29**:152-171.

Grimshaw, L. C. 2004. Population movements into Europe during the Pleistocene: a comparative approach. Unpublished PhD Thesis, University of Durham.

Haberkorn, G. 1981. "The Migration Decision Making Process: Some Social-Psychological Considerations," in *Migration Decision Making: Multidisciplinary Approaches to Microlevel Studies in Developed and Developing Countries*. Edited by G. F. de Jong and R. W. Gardner, pp. 252-278. New York: Pergamon Press.

Hanski, I. 1991. Single-species metapopulation dynamics: concepts, models and observations. *Biological Journal of the Linnean Society* **42**:17-38.

Hanski, I., and Gilpin, M. 1991. Metapopulation dynamics: brief history and conceptual domain. *Biological Journal of the Linnean Society* **42**:3-16.

Hoffman, A. A., and Blows, M. W. 1994. Species borders: ecological and evolutionary perspectives. *Trends in Ecology and Evolution* **9**:223-227.

Housley, R. A., Gamble, C. S., Street, M., and Pettitt, P. 1997. Radiocarbon evidence for the Lateglacial Human Recolonisation of Northern Europe. *Proceedings of the Prehistoric Society* **63**:25-54.

Hugo, G. J. 1981. "Village-Community Ties, Village Norms, and Ethnic and Social Networks: A Review of the Evidence from the Third World," in *Migration Decision Making: Multidisciplinay Aproaches to Microlevel Studies in Developed and Developing Countries*. Edited by G. F. de Jong and R. W. Gardner, pp. 186-224. New York: Pergamon Press.

Kearney, M. 1986. From the invisible hand to visible feet: Anthropological Studies of Migration and Development. *Annual Review of Anthropology* **15**:331-361.

Kelly, R. L. 2003. "Colonization of new land by hunter-gatherers: expectations and implications based on ethnographic data," in *Colonization of Unfamiliar Landscapes: The archaeology of adaptation*. Edited by M. Rockman and J. Steele, pp. 44-58. London: Routledge.

Klein, R. G. 1998. "Why anatomically modern people did not disperse from Africa 100,000 years ago," in *Neanderthals and Modern Humans in Western Asia*. Edited by T. Akazawa, T. Aoki, and O. Bar-Yosef, pp. 509-521. New York: Plenum Press.

Kohn, M., and Mithen, S. 1999. Handaxes: products of sexual selection? (Stone Age archaeology). *Antiquity* **73**:518-526.

Kuhn, S. L., Stiner, M. C., Reese, D. S., and Gulec, E. 2001. Ornaments of the earliest Upper Paleolithic: New insights from the Levant. *Proceedings of the National Academy of Sciences of the USA* **98**:7641-7646.

Leroi-Gourhan, A., and Brézillon, M. 1972. Fouilles de Pincevent. Essai d'analyse ethnographique d'un habitat Magdalénien (La Section 36). *Gallia Préhistoire Supplement* **VII**.

Lidicker, W. Z. J., and Stenseth, N. C. 1992. "To disperse or not to disperse: who does it and why?," in *Animal Dispersal: Small Mammals as a Model*. Edited by N. C. Stenseth and W. Z. J. Lidicker, pp. 21-36. London: Chapman and Hall.

Lin, J.-P., and Liaw, K.-L. 2000. Labor migrations in Taiwan: characterization and interpretation based on the data of the 1990 Census. *Environment and Planning A* **32**:1689-1709.

Mellars, P. 1999. The Neanderthal Problem Continued. *Current Anthropology* **40**:341-364.

Myers, A. A., and Giller, P. S. 1988. "Biological Processes in Biogeography: Introduction," in *Analytical Biogeography: An Integrated Approach to the Study of Animal and Plant Distributions*. Edited by A. A. Myers and P. S. Giller, pp. 149-163. London: Chapman and Hall.

Myers, K. 1986. "Introduced vertebrates in Australia, with emphasis on the mammals," in *Ecology of Biological Invasions*. Edited by R. H. Groves and J. J. Burdon, pp. 120-136. Cambridge: Cambridge University Press.

Oberai, A. S., and Singh, H. K. M. 1983. *Causes and Consequences of Internal Migration: A Study in the Indian Punjab*. Delhi: Oxford University Press.

Otte, M., and Keeley, L. H. 1990. The Impact of Regionalism on Palaeolithic Studies. *Current Anthropology* **31**:577-582.

Pettitt, P. B. 1999. Disappearing from the world: an archaeological perspective on Neanderthal extinction. *Oxford Journal of Archaeology* **18**:217-240.

Pettitt, P. B. 2000. Chronology of the Mid Upper Palaeolithic: the radiocarbon evidence. *Analecta Praehistorica Leidensia* **31**:21-30.

Pettitt, P. B., Davies, W., Gamble, C. S., and Richards, M. B. 2003. Palaeolithic radiocarbon chronology: quantifying our confidence beyond two half-lives. *Journal of Archaeological Science* **30**:1685-1693.

Pope, M. 2004. "Behavioural implications of biface discard: assemblage variability and land-use at the Middle Pleistocene site of Boxgrove," in *Lithics in Action: Papers from the conference Lithic Studies in the Year 2000*. Edited by E. A. Walker, F. Wenban-Smith, and F. Healy, pp. 38-47. Oxford: Oxbow Books.

Potts, R. 1994. Variables versus models of early hominid land use. *Journal of Human Evolution* 27:7-24.

Pulliam, H. R., Dunning, J. B., and Liu, J. 1992. Population Dynamics in Complex Landscapes: A Case Study. *Ecological Applications* 2:165-177.

Pusey, A. E. 1992. "The primate perspective on dispersal," in *Animal Dispersal: Small Mammals as a Model*. Edited by N. C. Stenseth and W. Z. J. Lidicker, pp. 243-259. London: Chapman and Hall.

Ravenstein, E. G. 1885. The laws of migration. *Journal of the Statistical Society* 48:167-227.

Roberts, M. B., and Parfitt, S. A. 1999. *Boxgrove: A Middle Pleistocene hominid site at Eartham Quarry, Boxgrove, West Sussex*. London: English Heritage.

Rockman, M. 2003. "Knowledge and learning in the archaeology of colonization," in *Colonization of Unfamiliar Landscapes: The archaeology of adaptation*. Edited by M. Rockman and J. Steele, pp. 3-24. London: Routledge.

Rolland, N. 1992. The Palaeolithic Colonization of Europe: An Archaeological and Biogeographic Perspective. *Trabajos de Prehistoria* 49:69-111.

Rolland, N. 1995. "Biogeographie et prehistoire: le cas du peuplement paleolithique inferieur de l'Europe," in *Nature et Culture*. Edited by M. Otte, pp. 11-61. Liege: University of Liege.

Rolland, N. 1998. "The Lower Palaeolithic settlement of Eurasia, with special reference to Europe," in *Early human behaviour in the global context: the rise and diversity of the Lower Palaeolithic record*. Edited by M. D. Petraglia and R. Korisettar, pp. 187-220. London: Routledge.

Rolland, N. 2001. "The initial peopling of Eurasia and the early occupation of Europe in its Afro-Asian context: major issues and current perspectives," in *A Very Remote Period Indeed: Papers on the Palaeolithic presented to Derek Roe*. Edited by S. Milliken and J. Cook, pp. 78-94. Oxford: Oxbow Books.

Samways, M. J., Osborn, R., Hastings, H., and Hattingh, V. 1999. Global climate change and accuracy of prediction of species' geographical ranges: establishment success of introduced ladybirds (Coccinellidae, Chilocorus spp.) worldwide. *Journal of Biogeography* 26:795-812.

Sax, D. F., and Brown, J. H. 2000. The paradox of invasion. *Global Ecology and Biogeography* 9:363-371.

Schoner, T. W. 1988. "Ecological Interactions," in *Analytical Biogeography: An Integrated Approach to the Study of Animal and Plant Distributions*. Edited by A. A. Myers and P. S. Giller, pp. 255-297. London: Chapman and Hall.

Shigesada, N., and Kawasaki, K. 1997. *Biological Invasions: Theory and Practice*. Oxford: Oxford University Press.

Simberloff, D., and Von Holle, B. 1999. Positive interactions of nonindigenous species: invasional meltdown? *Biological Invasions* 1:21-32.

Sjaastad, L. A. 1962. The costs and returns of human migration. *Journal of Political Economy* 70:80-93.

Skeldon, R. 1997. *Migration and Development: A Global Perspective*. Harlow: Longman.

Stenseth, N. C., and Lidicker, W. Z. J. 1992. "Presaturation and saturation dispersal 15 years later: some theoretical considerations," in *Animal Dispersal: Small Mammals as a Model*. Edited by N. C. Stenseth and W. Z. J. Lidicker, pp. 201-223. London: Chapman and Hall.

Suarez, A. V., Tsutsui, N. D., Holway, D. A., and Case, T. J. 1999. Behavioral and genetic differentiation between native and introduced populations of the Argentine ant. *Biological Invasions* 1:43-53.

Swenson, J. E., Sandegren, F., and Soderberg, A. 1998. Geographic expansion of an increasing brown bear population: evidence for presaturation dispersal. *Journal of Animal Ecology* 67:819-826.

Tilly, C. 1978. "Migration in Modern European History," in *Human Migration: Patterns and Policies*. Edited by W. McNeill and R. Adams, pp. 48-74. Bloomington: Indiana University Press.

van Andel, T. H., and Davies, W. Editors. 2003. *Neanderthals and modern humans in the European landscape during the last glaciation: archaeological results of the Stage 3 Project. McDonald Institute Monographs*. Cambridge: McDonald Institute for Archaeological Research.

Watts, D. 1971. *Principles of Biogeography: An Introduction to the Functional Mechanisms of Ecosystems*. New York: McGraw-Hill Book Company.

Wenban-Smith, F. F. 1998. "Clactonian and Acheulean industries in Britain: their chronology and significance reconsidered," in *Stone Age Archaeology: Essays in Honour of John Wymer*. Edited by N. Ashton, F. Healy, and P. Pettitt, pp. 90-97. Oxford: Oxbow Books.

Whittaker, R. H. 1975. *Communities and Ecosystems*. New York: MacMillan Press.

Williamson, M. 1996. *Biological Invasions*. London: Chapman and Hall.

Wilson, T. D. 1994. What Determines Where Transnational Labor Migrants Go? Modifications in Migration Theories. *Human Organization* 53:269-278.

Wynn, T., and Coolidge, F. L. 2004. The expert Neanderthal mind. *Journal of Human Evolution* 46:467-487.

Zilhão, J., and d'Errico, F. 1999. The Chronology and Taphonomy of the Earliest Aurignacian and Its Implications for the Understanding of Neanderthal Extinction. *Journal of World Prehistory* **13**:1-68.

Zilhão, J. 2000. "The Ebro Frontier: A Model for the Late Extinction of Iberian Neanderthals," in *Neanderthals on the Edge: Papers from a conference marking the 150th anniversary of the Forbes' Quarry discovery, Gibraltar*. Edited by C. B. Stringer, R. N. E. Barton, and J. C. Finlayson, pp. 111-121. Oxford: Oxbow Books.

TRANSITIONS, CHANGE AND PREHISTORY: AN ECOSYSTEMIC APPROACH TO CHANGE IN THE ARCHAEOLOGICAL RECORD.

Fiona Coward

University of Southampton

Abstract

Current thinking in the Palaeolithic divides the archaeological record into a succession of discrete 'cultures' defined in terms of lithic industries, thus creating 'points' of 'transition' such as the infamous 'Middle-Upper Palaeolithic transition', where differences in the archaeological record have been explained away as being the result of 'evolution', applied in a simplistic post hoc, accommodative way.

Such a 'top-down' perspective assumes qualitative differences between Neanderthals and 'modern' humans, particularly in terms of their mental abilities regarding abstract thought. Such assumptions are dangerous in the limitations that they place on the interpretation of the record - hominids, sites, industries, etc., can only ever be 'modern' or 'non-modern', with both categories pre-defined and pre-'explained'. A 'bottom-up' approach can be developed from the conceptualisation of both hominid and human populations as inevitably immersed within a four-dimensional world as a fundamental fact of their existence. Crucially, these ecosystems are not individual and discrete but are inescapably shared with other 'persons', whether these are hominid, human or animal, with whom interactions occurred on a daily basis. Thus the archaeological record - and particularly the faunal record - can be seen as demonstrating the signatures of certain kinds of interaction, providing clues to the 'place' and 'time' at which they occurred and therefore to the kinds of movement and interaction that constituted the identities and personhoods of the people who deposited material there.

This paper presents a methodology for addressing the four-dimensional structure described by the potential paths of movement and activity that were centred on some of the Palaeolithic sites from Vasco-Cantabrian Spain, along with something of the quality of the interactions that occurred between the people who lived there and other persons and types of person in that ecosystem. The results demonstrate the way in which fragments of the narratives of the lives of persons in prehistory can be re-presented, and highlight the potential of this methodology for reconsidering the lives of past populations and the similarities and differences of Neanderthals and 'modern' humans.

Introduction

This paper critiques sterile typological approaches to the study of change in prehistory, arguing that the identification of discrete, typologically defined 'cultures' in the archaeological record hampers consideration of patterns of process and change. This is particularly true of the Palaeolithic, where such chronological and technological divisions are reified and 'explained' *a priori* by misused 'evolutionary' theory, rather than as analytical categories requiring continual re-evaluation. Using as a case study the faunal record from the Mousterian levels of the Spanish site of Amalda, I demonstrate how an ecosystemic approach can allow us, even in the Palaeolithic, to move away from such sterile classificatory systems. Although in this paper I focus on only one level of Amalda, I aim to outline the ecosystemic approach and its potential for yielding a fuller and more dynamic understanding of the past by considering change in terms of personhood and identity, established, negotiated and maintained through a web of daily movement, interaction and activity within a four-dimensional ecosystem.

Palaeolithic 'cultures' and change

Change in the archaeological record of the Palaeolithic is still mainly 'explained' either by traditional culture-history approaches, in terms of sequential social or ethnic groups or 'cultures', or by evolutionary and Processual theories which focus on the continuing adaptation of hominids to changing environments. The consideration of change in these overly narrow terms divides the Palaeolithic into a succession of discrete 'cultures' defined in terms of the typology of lithic industries.

Such change is tautologically 'explained' away as simply the result of 'evolution' - but evolution reduced to typology and a succession of discrete logocentric, essentialist typological units. Adaptational and evolutionary rhetoric is applied in a simplistic *post hoc* accommodative way that becomes little more than a justification for 'just-so' stories about the course of human history (O'Brien and Holland 1992, 36-7). The past becomes a series of self-explanatory adaptive and evolutionary 'transitions' between static 'cultural' states, and there is nothing more to say about the past than to assign parts of the record to the relevant box; the concepts of adaptation and evolution become "an ex-post-facto argument aiding 'explanation' of change among prehistoric groups" (*Ibid.* 35).

In this way great chunks of prehistory are reduced into discrete blocks of time and space, distracting archaeologists from questions about variation, discontinuities and process. Interpretation becomes a question of "how we – much less *they* – get from one pattern or 'system' to another" (Conkey 1987, 69 emphasis in original). Such chronological and technological divisions become reified rather than being seen as analytical categories requiring continual re-evaluation, 'fossilized expectations' instead of "gross abstractions and temporary expedients" (Wobst 1983, 224; see also Robebroeks and Corbey 2001, 67; Schumann 1997, 254, 261).

It is now largely recognised that a direct equation between archaeological 'cultures' and "identity-conscious social units analogous to the tribes, peoples and nations of history" (Clark 2001a, 43), is overly naïve. Nevertheless, change in lithic typologies, as in other aspects of the archaeological record, *is* apparent, and material culture *does* demonstrate patterning in space and time. As Straus argues, whatever their 'meaning' *per se*, "some of the larger formal typological groupings of the Upper Palaeolithic do seem to have consistency and practical analytical utility ... [and] ... serve as useful shorthands for talking about broad patterns" (Straus 1991, 77; see also Schumann 1997, 254; Field 2002). The interpretation of the factors underlying this patterning, however, remains sadly under-theorised. As Straus concludes,

> Assemblage typologies are indeed sterile, when they are the 'be-all and end-all' of archaeological research (usually of a normative, phylogenetic nature). But *as tools*, they are useful, descriptive instruments – just as are artefact typologies. What is important is the questions asked, the reasons for classification (1991, 77-8).

Such classifications and periodisations are merely tools for us to use; the danger lies not in their definition or use, but in Palaeolithic archaeologists' epistemological naivety (Clark 1997) – as Clark cautions, we should resist their "tendency to become 'fossilized'" (Clark 2001b, 141).

This paradigm provides a normative typological framework in which the past is reduced to a succession of little 'boxes' of near-static variation which become reified in our understandings of the past: as Conkey has pointed out, "we do not refer to Magdalenians, but to 'the Magdalenian'" (1987, 69).

Meanwhile, change in the past becomes a series of distinct 'transitions' between succeeding, static 'cultures', 'events' requiring special explanation. Change is compressed into the lines separating cultural units, representing a clear boundary or origin point between archaeological stages - as exemplified by the infamous Middle-Upper Palaeolithic transition, where the problem is exacerbated because of the conflation of biological and apparently cultural change in a 'transition' which is central to our own identity as a species.

Interest in the question of the origins of modern humans dates back centuries, and although the terms of the debate have certainly changed, the questions – and some of the answers – have not fundamentally altered (Alexandri 1995, 57), and long-term continuities are apparent in the kinds of narratives that are told about human origins, whether these are religious origin myths, classical philosophy, folktales or scientific accounts of human origin (Conkey and Williams 1991, 104; see also Landau 1992; Alexandri 1995; Moore 1995; van Reybrouck 2001, 77-8 and *passim*). Hominid research, like all archaeology, is unavoidably a discourse about our own human identity situated in the present, and the debates surrounding the 'Middle-Upper Palaeolithic transition' draw strongly from debates about the definition of 'humans' from the animal 'other' (Pellegrin 1986; Chazan 1995, 235; Serjeantson 2000, 179; van Reybrouck 2001).

The issue is of more than just semantic concern: archaeological and palaeoanthropological interpretations of hominid prehistory have been strongly affected by social and cultural factors (Graves 1991; Chazan 1995; Roebroeks 1995; Marks 1997; Drell 2000; Cartmill 2001; Roebroeks and Corbey 2001; Proctor 2003), and the perception and treatment of the archaeological record can be hugely affected by the side of the 'boundary' from which it derives. As Roebroeks and Corbey comment about a workshop on the Palaeolithic occupation of Europe:

> In dealing with the Lower and Middle Palaeolithic, a highly critical attitude prevailed in which, for instance, hearths and dwelling structures were concepts to be applied only after a careful scrutiny of the archaeological data. Similarly, there was also a double standard with regard to the association of faunal remains and stone artefacts: at earlier sites, the actual degree and type of interaction between humans and animals had to be convincingly demonstrated time and time again, whereas in the context of modern humans, such critical examinations seemed less important and interpretations of stones and bone flowed more freely in terms of hunters and their prey (Roebroeks and Corbey 2001, 68).

The dominance of this model of prehistory and change in Palaeolithic research has produced a straightforward 'top-down' model which, applied to the Middle/Upper Palaeolithic 'transition', assumes qualitative differences between Neanderthals and so-called 'modern' humans: the *a priori* assumption, simply stated, is that modern humans and their associated Upper Palaeolithic assemblages are more 'advanced' than Neanderthals and the Middle Palaeolithic record (see e.g. Simek 2001, 199 for discussion), a prophecy which has all too easily become self-fulfilling for many Palaeolithic researchers (see e.g. Clark 2001b, especially 141; Roebroeks and Corbey 2001, 69 and *passim* for examples). In summary, "the 'Moderns' are capable until proven incapable, whereas the 'Ancients' can be summarized as incapable, until proven capable" (Roebroeks and Corbey 2001, 72). In such 'top-down' models it can often seem that the Middle Palaeolithic and Neanderthals are used only to emphasise the sophistication of modern humans (Clark 2001b).

But these models are often little more than collections of preconceived biases and assumptions, and as such are dangerous in the severe limitations they place on any interpretation of the record – hominids, sites, industries, etc., can only ever be 'modern' or 'non-modern', with both categories pre-defined and pre-'explained' by misused 'evolutionary' theory. Such a 'just-so' approach to the Middle and Upper Palaeolithic of Europe is teleological in the extreme, erroneously assuming directionality in the record and allowing archaeologists to assume rather than demonstrate the abilities and behaviours of the populations represented in the archaeological record, their conclusions justified by a lazy, post-hoc accommodative use of evolutionary rhetoric.

However, the neat coincidence between biological and cultural change at the time of the 'Human Revolution' has now been thoroughly discredited, with the identification of the Châtelperronian – essentially an 'Upper Palaeolithic' technology – as produced by Neanderthals (see e.g. d'Errico *et al.* 1998 for discussion), and McBrearty and Brooks' thorough demonstration that the evidence in fact suggests that so-called 'modern' behaviours "do not appear suddenly together, but rather are found at points separated by sometimes great geographical and temporal distances. It seems inappropriate to label changes accumulating over a period of 200,000 years either a revolution or a punctuated event" (McBrearty and Brooks, 2000, 259; figure 13).

Rather than assuming such differences, 'bottom-up' approaches need to be developed to reconsider the bases for change in the archaeological record at this time, "observing and documenting what Palaeolithic hominids actually did and how their behaviour changed over time, not just whether or not they could do what modern humans did" (Roebroeks and Corbey 2001, 75). Nor would such an approach be limited to the Palaeolithic; it could rewardingly be applied to the coincidence of forms of change in various 'transitions' throughout prehistory (e.g. the Neolithic 'revolution' – see papers in Price 2000).

However, there is currently no well-developed explanatory framework justifying our expectation that different forms of change (whether 'cultural' or 'biological') should coalesce at various points in prehistory. Certainly, as discussed above, there has been a move away – at least, in later prehistory - from the idea that all archaeological periods have any straightforward 'cultural' or 'ethnic' associations in the sense that they were created by consciously self-identifying groups:

> the space-time distributions of prehistorian-defined analytical units (e.g. the Aurignacian), exceed by orders of magnitude the space-time distributions of any real or imaginable social entity that might have produced them ... whatever the Aurignacian is, it is manifestly not a 'culture' (Clark, 2001a: 43-4).

Evolutionary and social archaeologies and the four-dimensional ecosystem

In fact, as Clark and many others have pointed out, 'cultural' stability is in fact more difficult to account for than change (e.g. Allen 1989). Despite this, the dangerous attraction of post-hoc, tautological 'evolutionary' explanation has exerted considerable influence over interpretations of change in prehistory and particularly, as discussed in the introduction to this section, in the Palaeolithic. Criticisms of evolutionary theory have crystallised around the charge that it consigns the individual to an essentially passive role, driven by processes beyond his or her control, with social actors irrelevant and "mere components of the system" (Shanks and Tilley 1987, 139).

But the fault lies with the application in archaeology of evolutionary theory, rather than with evolutionary theory itself, and in fact neo-evolutionary theory conceptualises "adaptation as an active process of becoming, rather than a static state of being" (Mithen 1989, 486).

Evolutionary theory is in fact a genuine theory of agency: individuals, as the units of selection, are the driving force of adaptation, selection and speciation (e.g. *Ibid.*, 488 and *passim*; Quinney 2000, 12). As Graves-Brown argues, far from being deterministic and imposed upon hapless hominids and humans, "[e]volution is by its very nature entirely contextual and contingent; organisms do not and cannot plan for the future but must act in the present context to ensure their survival" (1993, 76). Speciation is regarded as epiphenomenal, effect rather than cause, and hominids and humans are seen as essentially active and creative in their behaviour, learning and making decisions in adapting to their dynamic environments (Allen 1989, 277; Mithen 1989, 487).

And it is this link between people and their environments that provides us with the foundations for establishing a 'bottom-up' perspective, because populations cannot be separated out from their environment. While as Lewontin states, "there is no organism without an environment", it is equally true that there is "no environment without an organism" (1982, 160).

The concept of 'the environment' has been badly maligned by post-processual and social theory, as deterministic or as imposing a set of rules and constraints on those who live in it. But in ecological theory the relationship between the individual and its environment is by no means one-way; instead we can visualise the much-maligned 'environment' in a more holistic fashion, as an 'ecosystem' (Tansley 1935; see also Preucel and Hodder 1996, 23-35) – "a continuum of physical features, other species and conspecifics" (Foley 1984, 5). Although the concept of the ecosystem was first studied in a systemic paradigm, in terms of energy flow, nutrient cycling and information feedback (Preucel and Hodder 1996, 35), and its use in archaeology has thus been criticised (see e.g. Ingold 1992, 41), I argue that the concept can be used to emphasise the embeddedness of humans and hominids within their environments.

Here the emphasis is on 'synecology', communities of plants and animals interacting in four-dimensional space and exercising considerable influence on one another, rather than individual species acting in isolation (van Valen 1973; Jochim 1998). Individuals and groups can thus be considered as *part of* an ecosystem in its fullest sense, adapting through the formation and adjustment of 'niches', the sum total of the adaptation of an organism and how it 'fits' into its particular environment. Thus the concepts of the 'ecosystem' and of the 'niche' should be considered essentially creative and reflexive, rather than something imposed upon its members; ecological theory thus takes a far more complex view of human/environment interaction than the simplistic 'environmental determinism' set up as a straw person by some of the more polemical relativist critics (e.g. Hodder 1985; Shanks and Tilley 1987a).

The view of a continuum of interacting biotic and abiotic aspects of the 'ecosystem' allows for a very different conceptualisation of hominid and human behaviour. In ecological terms, an organism constructs its niche by perceiving and acting on the affordances of the abiotic, biotic and conspecific environment (Gibson 1979, 129; see also Ingold 1989, 504), and in this way we can avoid a simplistic human/environment, subject/object dichotomy. Rather than prioritising either the physical or social environments, we need to accept that we cannot separate the two as part of an encompassing ecosystem.

Persons and the four-dimensional ecosystem

Such an ecosystem is also not simply an abstract, characterless 'container' for human activity (Tilley 1994, 9; Relph 2000 [1985]; see also Gamble 2001), a two-dimensional backdrop for objectively measuring human movement and activity that can be considered primarily in Euclidean, geometric terms. New approaches to geographic space in archaeology such as phenomenology (Heidegger 1962 [1927]; Bourdieu's practice theory (Bourdieu 1977), Gibsonian direct perception (Gibson 1979; Merleau-Ponty 1962), time geography (Carlstein 1982), naïve geography (Mark and Egenhofer 1996; Mark *et al.* 1997) etc., have opened up a variety of new perspectives from which to consider this evolutionary interaction between humans and hominids and the worlds in which they live. Although, clearly, each of these theoretical approaches is very distinct, what they do have in common is an emphasis on the immersion of the individual within a four-dimensional world as a fundamental fact of their existence, and an emphasis on embodied experience as inseparable from understanding and action. In this way, lives become a form of skilled performance, rather than a system of abstractly designed strategies; as Ingold has pointed out, many other societies do not separate humans out from their environments. Rather, a person is seen as "a being immersed from the start, like other creatures, in an active, practical and perceptual engagement with constituents of the dwelt-in world" (1996, 120-1).

While Processualism tended to 'envisage the environment as a vast container filled with objects, living and non-living, mobile and stationary, like a room or stage-set cluttered with furniture and decorations' (Ingold 1992, 41), an ecosystemic approach considers particular, specific landscapes and the activities occurring within them as part of an experiential whole. As Gosden argues,

> The space of human action is not a geometrical entity to be represented easily on a piece of paper, but rather room-for-manoeuvre, a space in which skills can be deployed. Our skills are created to fit the spaces in which they are used and the spaces of human life are the result of past skilled action (1994, 344).

This last comment also highlights another significant aspect of ecosystems: they are *four-dimensional*. If experience occurs at *locales*, it also occurs at *tempos* (Barrett 1991, 8) that arise out of *practice* (Bourdieu 1977) and are composed of activities and behaviours regardless of the calendar or clock that may be imposed on them (Parkes and Thrift 1980, 37 cited Bailey 1983;

Ingold 1993a; 1993b; 2000b; Gosden 1994; Mackie 2001).

The organism-person, then, is immersed from the start in its ecosystem: the basis of the 'dwelling perspective' championed by Ingold (2000, 153). "Organism plus environment" denotes "not a compound of two things, but one indivisible totality" (Ingold 2000, 19), and the ecosystem is thus comprised of and experienced by the individual's activities and interactions, both structuring and being structured by them.

And the concept of the ecosystem has another very important corollary: it is not individual and discrete but inescapably shared with other beings with whom we interact on a daily basis - not just humans but other animal species, with whom we also enter into interactions, as hunters, as prey, as husbanders. While in western thought there is a fundamental split between 'human' and 'non-human', with 'person' a subcategory of human, other societies start from an overarching category of person within which human person, animal person and even wind person, for example, are valid subcategories (Ingold 1996, 130; Hallowell, e.g. 1960). And as Ingold has pointed out, such a re-conceptualisation of human-animal relations obviously has significant ramifications when considering hunter-gatherer subsistence practices (*Ibid.*). Far from being an encounter between culture and nature, the wild and the tame (e.g. Cartmill 1993), or a form of technical manipulation of the natural world, hunting is seen as a kind of ongoing dialogue between persons, integral to the total process of social life: hunting becomes personal (Ingold 1996, 128-9; 2000 *passim*)

Our practical day-to-day experience, then, is composed of constellations of habitual interaction with co-denizens of our ecosystem, including other humans and hominids, but also other kinds of entities. These other persons also describe their own matrices of movement in space and time, and these are inevitably familiar to their co-denizens, who in turn constantly alter and shift their own movements in an ongoing co-evolutionary negotiation of behaviour and identity. Thus the pathways of movement in space and time created by humans and hominids inevitably interlink and intersect with those created by these other entities, and each of these intersections provides an arena for various kinds of potential interaction.

In addition, our ecosystemic interactions also extend past the obviously 'animate' species to plant species and to geological and physical features of the particular ecosystem in which we live, as well as material objects created by ourselves or by the people we live with. Such an idea is hinted at by the southern Asian concept of the dividual, described by Strathern as "a person constituted of relationships" (Strathern 1988, 68), an emergent identity arising from the sum total of the relationships that he or she engages in (see also Marriott 1976; Thomas 2002, 34).

In this paradigm, people are not seen as concrete, separate entities *per se*, but as discrete but not bounded persons, composed of relations and connections. Identity, in this view, arises out of the everyday practices and interactions which comprise the ecosystem (see e.g. Gamble 2001, 206).

But these dividuals (e.g. Strathern 1988, 68) and their distributed personhoods (e.g. Gosden and Marshall 1999, 173) do not exist in a vacuum: these ongoing relationships, encounters and interactions occur *in the world*, at specific times and in specific places.

And these places also have histories or biographies acquired by the virtue of the interactions that have occurred there before. Such places do not exist in isolation but are connected by paths and tracks of movement that link places and activities and interactions into a narrative, enacting movement between persons as well as between places, such that for Australian Aboriginals, for example,

> the life of a person is the sum of his tracks, the total inscription of his movements, something that can be traced out along the ground ... who one is becomes a kind of record of where one has come from and where one has been (Wagner 1986, 21).

Palaeolithic identities

An ecosystemic perspective goes some way towards re-informing our understandings of change in prehistory. Rather than visualising aspects of the archaeological record ('subsistence'; 'lithic technology'; 'symbolic behaviour') as separate and discrete, all become implicated in the everyday movement and activity that constitutes life in a real, four-dimensional world.

The solution to these problems with Palaeolithic archaeology, therefore, is not to throw the baby out with the bathwater and reject the evolutionary framework outright, contra Shanks and Tilley (1987, 175). In fact, the evolutionary framework, with its emphasis on ecosystemic (rather than 'environmental') context, can actually help us approach the Palaeolithic in ways which admit the active individual.

Rather than being seen as a series of arbitrarily divided 'cultures', the archaeological record can be viewed as having been formed through the construction and continual negotiation of identity through movement, activity and interaction within the four-dimensional ecosystem. The material objects of the record – in the Palaeolithic, largely stones and bones – are metaphors for patterns of interaction between persons of different kinds, and also act to materialise and immemorate occasions of interaction with other denizens of the world, mnemonic of real, physical encounters with real, physical animals at particular times and places in the world.

From an analytical perspective, then, the faunal record contains within it the signatures of the interactions of which it is comprised, providing clues to the 'places' and the 'times' at which they occurred as well as to something of the quality of those interactions. The detail of the reconstruction of the environment is beyond the scope of this paper (see http://www.fcoward.co.uk) but in brief, the likely location of animal species and thus the potential arenas for hominid interactions with them is deduced from the consideration of ecosystemic and topographical factors such as steepness of gradient and changing sea and snowlines which affect the ease of access of various animal species to different parts of the landscape (see Sturdy and Webley 1988; Sturdy et al. 1997). The landscape offers, for example, ibex and horses very different kinds of affordances in terms of elevation and slope. Topography also has a significant effect on vegetation, which again has ramifications for where animals prefer to feed. By considering seasonal variation, we can also consider the ways that animal behaviours change over time, in terms of aggregation and dispersal, migrations and movements, and reproductive cycles and variations in condition and behaviour over the course of the year. From these forms of data we can begin to consider real places, connected by paths and tracks of embodied experience through a real landscape with its own distinct character that impacts on perception and movement and affords particular kinds of interaction with other persons – human, hominid and 'other'.

In this way we can work backward from the fauna to start to access something of the process of the structuring of movement, activity and interaction via the reconstruction of some of the potential pathways that form a composite, holistic matrix of movement out across the landscape, centred on the site from which the material traces of it were recovered. Each of these pathways, besides representing potential set of movements between persons and places through the ecosystem, had a distinct flavour or texture that drew from the *quality* of the interactions and activities from which it arose. And crucially, as the following section demonstrates, because the goal is not to access the direct, subjective experience of persons in the past but rather the kinds of ways in which their experiences structured and were structured by personhood and identity, such an approach can be applied to pre-sapiens populations as well as 'modern' human groups.

Middle Palaeolithic identities at Amalda, Vasco-Cantabrian Spain

Level VII of the site of Amalda in the Urola valley of the Spanish Basque country in northern Spain is dated to the Middle Palaeolithic of OIS5a or c, both warm phases of the end of the last glaciation around 80,000-100,000 years ago. The lithic industry has been identified as Mousterian, associated with pre-sapiens Neanderthals (Altuna et al. 1990).

Although level VII of Amalda is virtually polinically sterile itself (Dupré 1990), a reconstruction of the environment of substages a and c of OIS 5 suggests that the steeper areas of the valley were probably largely open, with alpine meadow and bare rock the dominant ecotype in the immediate vicinity of the cave but open pine and birch parkland with some deciduous trees on the higher, more gentle slopes above the valley and possibly oak, hazel and alder in the wider, more sheltered areas of the valley itself, lining the stream (see also Eastham 1990) and the Urola river (Figure 3.1: all figures referred to in this section, as well as maps and more detailed versions of those presented here, are available at http://www.fcoward.co.uk)

Chamois and ibex

Clearly, the most significant animal species with which hunters interacted at the time – in terms of individual animals represented – was chamois. At least 16 are represented in the faunal assemblage from the level (Table 3.1). This is an emphasis that persists throughout the levels at this cave site, from the Mousterian through to the Upper Solutrean. Pathways leading to and from hunting grounds associated with this species, then, were clearly well-known and formed a major part of the complex of pathways of movement and activity centred on the cave. At least three of the 16 individuals represented at the cave were infant animals (Table 3.2) killed during summer (May – June).

During these summer months, the mixed herds of adult females and young associated with these areas of the landscape, although generally small, were probably more easily located in their c. 75 hectare ranges than the scattered, lone adult males. Chamois could have been taken individually by single hunters by stalking or coursing, a time-consuming, solitary activity: stalking has been likened to three-dimensional chess (Cooke, 2004). However, chamois are notably wary animals said to post 'sentinels' to warn of danger (Freeman 1973, 10). The most efficient method (prior to the invention of the rifle) was probably to drive animals towards concealed hunters or natural traps (*Ibid.*) – such a technique would obviously involve a number of hunters working closely together.

During the winter months following the rut, chamois probably descended to lower altitudes in search of more sheltered, wooded areas in which to forage, being displaced from higher, barer slopes by the descent of ibex driven down from snow and ice bound summits (Figure

	Amalda Level VII			
	NISP	NISP%	MNI	MNI%
Red deer/Cervus elaphus	150	15.5	5	10.2
Roe deer/Capreolus capreolus	3	0.3	3	6.1
Chamois/Rupicapra rupicapra	536	55.4	16	32.7
Ibex/Capra pyrenaica	61	6.3	5	10.2
Bovids/Bovini	58	6	3	6.1
Horse/Equus caballus	48	5	4	8.2
Ungulates	**856**	**(88.5)**	**36**	**(73.5)**
Cave bear/Ursus spelaeus	58	6	5	10.2
Brown bearUrsus arctos	0	0	0	0
Hyaena/Crocuta crocuta	3	0.3	2	4.1
Wolf/Canis lupus	17	1.8	3	6.1
Cuon/Cuon alpinus	1	0.1	1	2
Fox/Vulpes vulpes	29	3	2	4.1
Leopard/Panthera pardus	3	0.3	1	2
Carnivores	**111**	**(11.5)**	**13**	**(26.5)**
Total identified	**967**	**(11.6)**	**49**	
Total unidentified	**7340**	**(88.4)**		
Total	**8307**			

Table 3.1. Animal species represented in Amalda Level VII (after Altuna 1990, table 8.8.).

	Cervus elaphus	Capreolus capreolus	Bovini	Rupicapra rupicapra	Capra pyrenaica	Equus sp.
Infant	1	1	1	3	1	2
Juvenile	1	1	1	2	2	1
Adult	3	1	1	11	2	1
Total	**5**	**3**	**3**	**16**	**5**	**4**

Table 3.2. Ageing data for ungulate species from Amalda level VII (after Altuna 1990, table 8.8., see Table 3.1 above for common names of species).

3.2). From these hunting grounds, virtually whole carcasses of chamois (as indicated by the pattern of anatomical representation; Figures 3.1, 3.2 and 3.3)[i], weighing somewhere in the region of 20 – 50kg apiece (Boyle 1990, 92); males 30 – 60kg, females 25 - 45kg (MacDonald and Barrett 1993)[ii] were carried downstream to Amalda by paths which followed the Alzolaras stream downriver northwest from the head of the valley

Clearly at least some ibex were also targeted in summer and thus around the highest peaks of the area (of the minimum of five represented, one was an infant killed during its first summer [June]; Table 3.2.; Figures 3.1, 3.2 and 3.3). Patterns of movement associated with their hunting (Figures 3.1, 3.2 and 3.3) are clearly rather similar to those of chamois; the two species share rather similar yearly cycles of behaviour (e.g. West 1997, fig. 4.2.) and were probably thus hunted in similar ways. Ibex kills, however, were more thoroughly butchered than those of chamois and the meatier elements of the hindlimb as well as some of the more marrow-rich extremities, were carried back to Amalda – many phalanges show evidence of impact and fracture marks typical of those produced by marrow extraction (Altuna 1990).

Bovids and horse

However, while chamois may be the dominant species in terms of number of individuals transported to the cave, the relatively small size of the species means that the rarer but larger bovids and horse whose remains were recovered from the site were probably more significant in terms of the overall meat that kills represented[iii]. The bovid material identified from this level may in fact have only derived from three individual animals. One of these was an infant killed during its first summer (Table 3.2.; May-June), one a juvenile and one an adult; the small mixed groups in which these bovids lived were largely restricted to the coastal plain (Figure 3.3), easily reached within a day by hunters from Amalda, although, still within a day's walk, there are also other potential hunting grounds further south, especially around the relatively flat inland valley of the confluence of the Urola and Ibaiuda rivers to the southwest of the cave. The open-ground

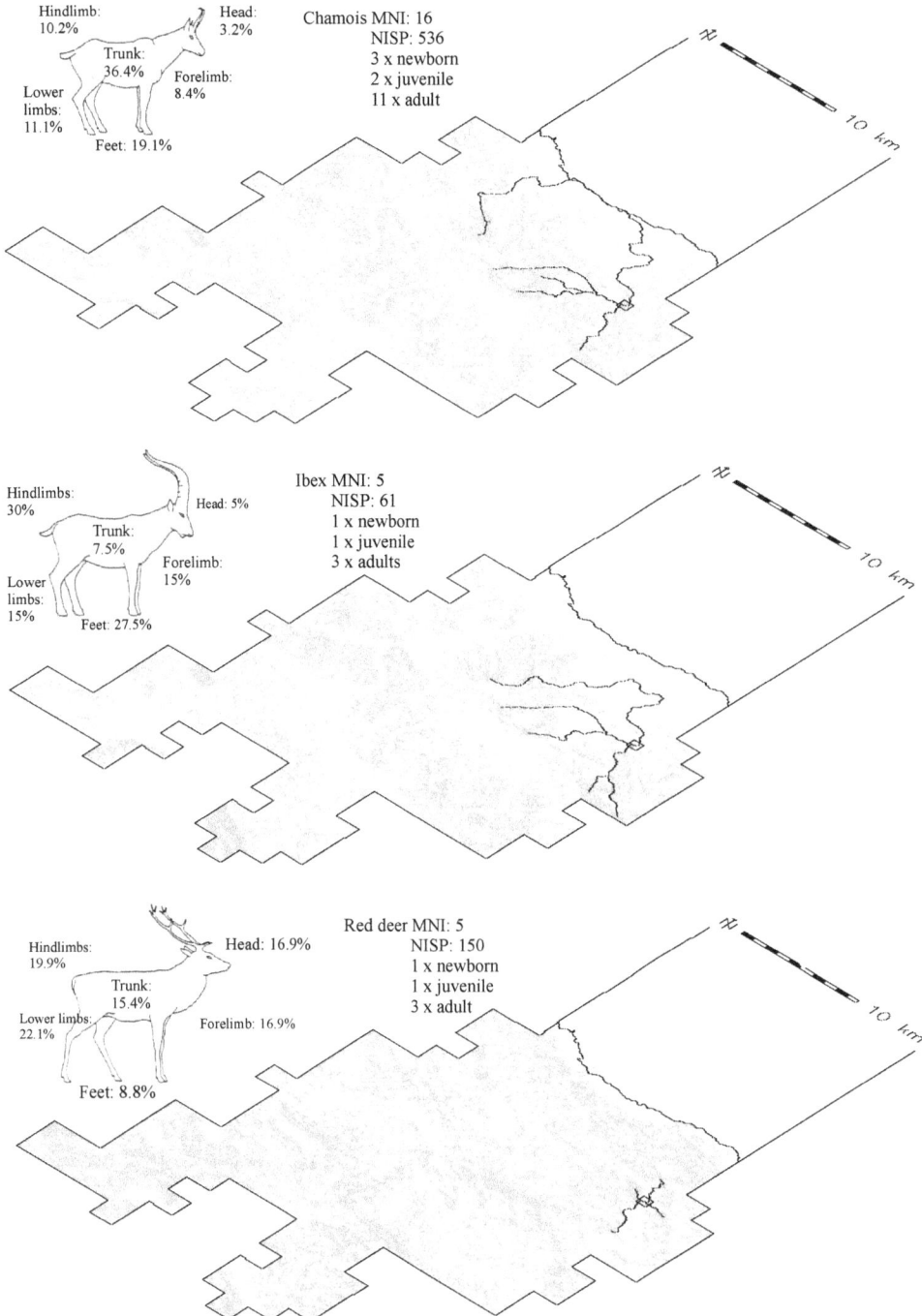

Figure 3.1. Parts of the landscape (shaded grey) and paths potentially associated with summer hunting of chamois (top), ibex (middle) and red deer (bottom) from Amalda during OIS 5a/c

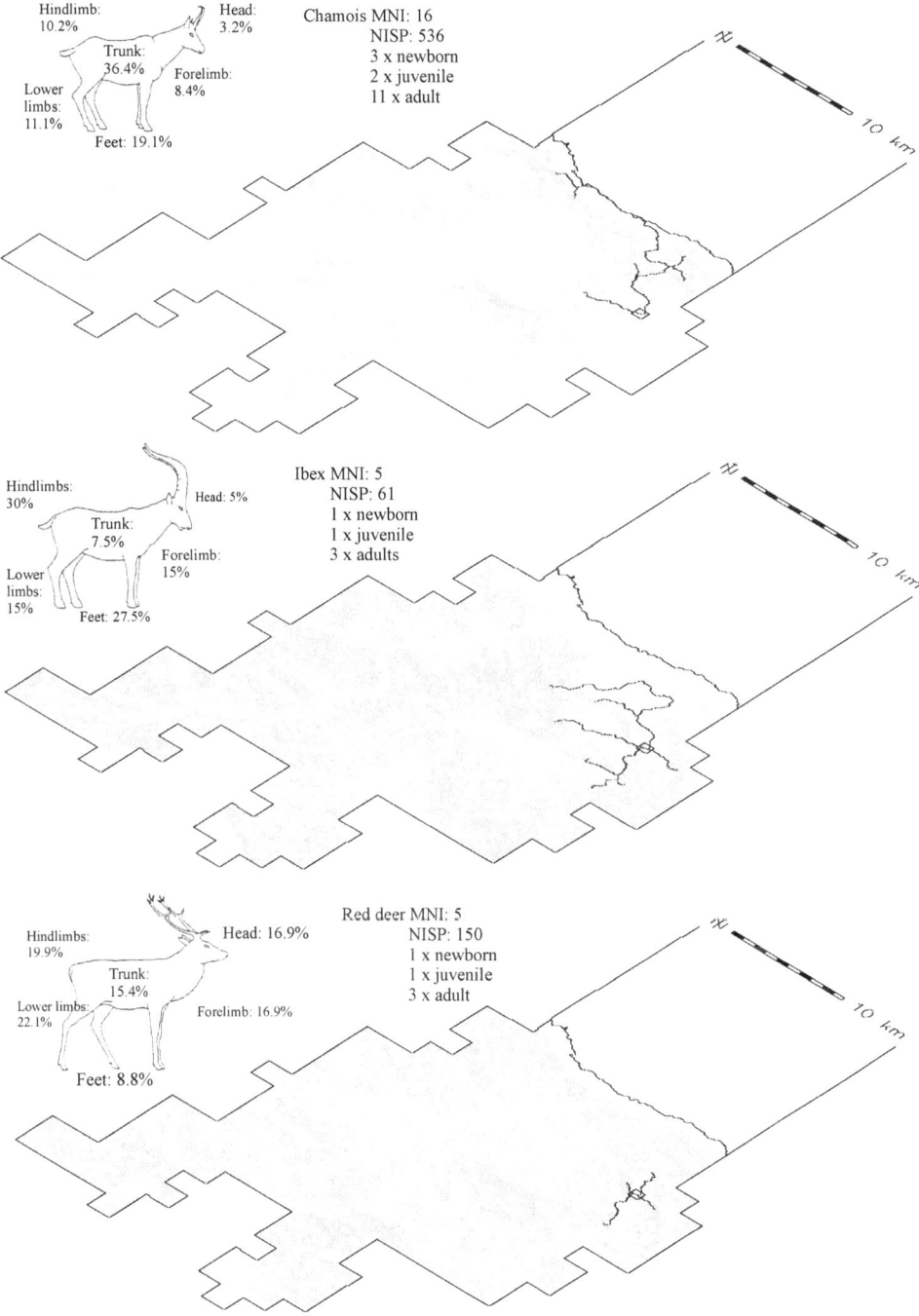

Figure 3.2. Parts of the landscape (shaded grey) and paths potentially associated with winter hunting of chamois (top), ibex (middle) and red deer (bottom) from Amalda during OIS 5a/c

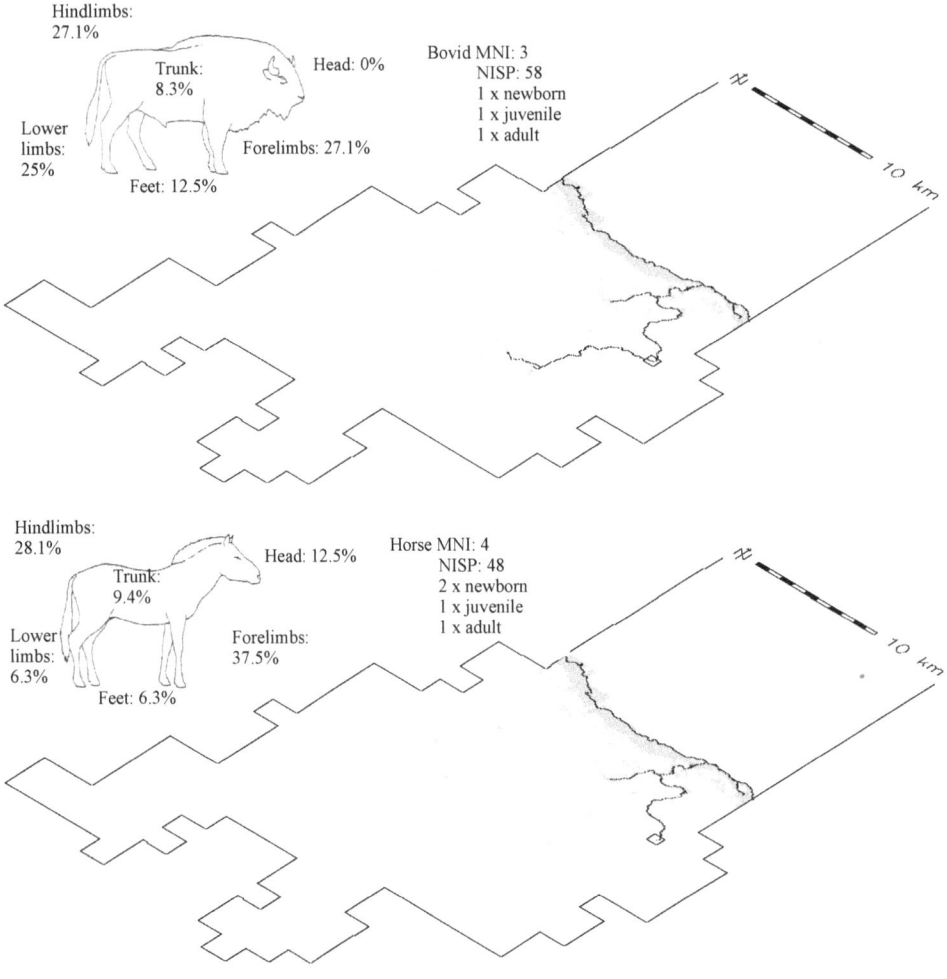

Figure 3.3. Parts of the landscape (shaded grey) and paths potentially associated with year-round hunting of bovids (top) and horse (bottom) from Amalda during OIS 5a/c

parts of the landscape preferred by bovids probably did not change significantly between the summer and winter months – although the shorter days are likely to have placed the more southerly potential hunting grounds beyond a day's return walk from Amalda.

Individual, systematic hunting by coursing or stalking is a possible strategy for bovids. But communal or co-operative hunting is also a good strategy, usually aiming to surround animals in the open and drive them into an ambush. Bovid herds are easily frightened and once stampeded have little control over the mass movement of the herd; they may be stampeded at speeds of up to 32mph over short distances (Boyle 1990, 86) over cliff faces, or in winter driven into deep snow drifts (although a moderate covering of snow presents bovids with few difficulties). Where there is a fairly large hunting party and a relatively small herd, the herd can be surrounded and driven in circles until exhausted and relatively easily dispatched (Freeman 1973; Boyle 1990), probably by hand-delivered thrusting spear (Churchill 1993)[iv]. These kills were clearly extensively butchered in the field and only selected anatomical parts (both meatier elements such as the femur and other elements more suggestive of marrow exploitation (Binford 1978)[v] returned to the cave: a relatively high NISP/MNI possibly relates to a greater degree of fragmentation of the bones, although Altuna makes no explicit comment about taphonomic findings regarding marrow extraction in this level. There is considerable overlap between the bovid and horse hunting grounds illustrated in Figure 3.3, although with horses also concentrated on the coastal plain as well as along the flatter parts of the northern reaches of the Alzolaras and Urola valleys rather than in the flat meadows of the Urola/Urestilla confluence preferred by bovids. At least four individual animals are represented, two of which were infants killed in their first summer (mid April – mid June; Figure 3.3; Table 3.2).

Horses probably grazed in small family 'harem' units of 5-6 mares, foals and yearlings and a stallion, which show considerable loyalty to their ranges year after year – thus these are likely to be well-known to hunters in the area. As with bovids, the size of the herd, speed of the animals and tendency to stampede makes co-operative driving a good bet, although of course systematic hunting techniques such as coursing and stalking may also be practised – particularly in suitable terrain with plenty of cover (Freeman 1973; Boyle 1990) – modern Hadza, however, are known to kill zebra on foot (O'Connell *et al.* 1990; 1992; cited West 1997, 48).

West suggests that harem groups are more likely to have been targeted by hunters because of their relatively more predictable behaviour, shorter movements and smaller home ranges (*Ibid.*). Bachelor groups are significantly less predictable in their behaviour, only occasionally returning to territories year on year. Without young they are also better able to outrun predators and are likely to flee danger rather than fight – if cornered, they are generally stronger and more vicious than most individuals in harem groups.

The trails created and followed by horses are often well-defined through frequent use. With young at their heels, harem groups do not move far during the day and while the foals are young groups will re-use sleeping areas which are easily recognisable from the accumulations of dung. They will also return every day, or every other day, to predictable water sources, and both harem and bachelor groups can be ambushed at waterholes where they regularly drink – historically, Siberian groups are known to have captured wild horses by digging pits close to their waterholes (*Ibid.*).

West envisions a possible hunting strategy thus:

> In ambush fashion, hunters could locate horse trails and wait for the dominant mare to approach followed by other members. The lead mare and her foal would be the first two animals wounded. Alarmed by screams at the front of the herd, the stallion would rush to the defense and would be dispatched. Milling

mares and foals could be wounded at this point (West 1997, 48).

Red deer

At least five individual red deer are also represented in Amalda Level VII; red deer are a notably catholic species and fairly ubiquitous in the ecosystems of the Deba and Urola valleys in both summer and winter (Figures 3.1 and 3.2). Large-scale migrations were probably not a feature of red deer ecology in northern Spain at this time (Bailey 1983; Boyle 1990), and in winter they are likely to have congregated in sheltered valleys with relatively dense tree cover and thus little snow. Stags and hinds usually prefer separate winter ranges although they may overlap, and particular areas of winter habitats may become associated with groups of particular sex year after year.

The areas frequented by deer throughout the year were probably quite apparent to hunters; their feeding practices leave rather striking and characteristic feeding signs, including broken and 'torn off' shoots and twigs and damage to trees that may result in very recognisable patterns of tree growth, particularly where young trees are targeted repeatedly (Bang and Dahlstrom 1974, 88). Larger trees along the edges of favoured wooded areas may also be cut off at a certain height, and signs of 'barking' resulting from cervid feeding activity (which differ significantly according to the season they are inflicted; *Ibid.*) are often obvious. Strips of antler velvet or signs of tree 'fraying' produced by stags rubbing growing antlers against trees may also provide clues to the locations of animals and their sex and age. During the rut, of course, animals are easily found; the males' fights create a considerable amount of noise, and mud 'wallows' used at this time of the year are common and smell strongly (*Ibid.*). Such signs would have been distinctive to experienced hunters, and if they were operating year after year in the area, they may well have rut, of course, animals are easily found; the males' fights create a considerable amount of noise, and mud 'wallows' used at this time of the year are common and smell strongly (*Ibid.*). Such signs would have been distinctive to experienced hunters, and if they were operating year after year in the area, they may well have been able to locate preferred targets in terms of age and sex to very particular areas.

This is of course significant because stags and hinds have rather different temporal cycles of behaviour and

condition, with body-weights fluctuating as much as 20-30% over the course of the year (Boyle 1990). Males are best hunted for meat in late summer and early autumn before the rut – at this time, they may have a layer of subcutaneous fat of up to 2cm thick, and as much as 30kg of subcutaneous and internal fat can be obtained from a single adult male. Nearly a third of a stag's bodyweight is

lost over the course of the rut from the end of August to October; however, if antler is the prime goal of hunting, males may be targeted between early November and late February (antlers are cast in March/April). In contrast, females retain good quality meat reserves throughout the winter until the birth of young in May or June. However, without knowing whether the antler fragments from this level were shed or otherwise, and with no indication of the sex of the animals killed, it is difficult to evaluate the extent to which such targeting was the case among hunters operating out of Amalda during OIS 5.

This potential for the precision-targeting of individual animals is particularly relevant given the probable hunting techniques used to pursue red deer. Like other small-group or solitary woodland species (e.g. roe deer, three of which are also represented in level VII), red deer are best hunted systematically by stalking or coursing. Deer stalking is of course still practised today; it is of necessity an activity undertaken by individuals or at the most small groups. Deer are mainly active in the mornings and evening although they may feed all day (Boyle 1990; MacDonald and Barrett 1993, 201), often leaving forage for saltlicks around sunset, and modern-day deer stalking generally involves early morning 'harbouring' or reconnaissance to locate suitable prey.

> Having located the prey, the hunter must approach stealthily downwind prior to dispatching his target. Stalking is a time-consuming activity during which concealment may be necessary. Thus the positioning of the hunter is of importance if the expedition is to be a success (Boyle 1990, 100).

Deer-hunting was thus probably a close-quarters, one-on-one process, involving the close identification and selection of the individually targeted animals. Following the kills represented in Amalda level VII, meat-bearing elements were carried back to the cave, with considerable numbers of mandibulae combined with few skull fragments suggesting that the rich, fatty tongue was also targeted, as were metapodials, particularly metatarsals.

Carnivore species

In addition to the ungulate species, a number of carnivore species are represented in Amalda level VII - particularly cave bear (see Straus 1992, 54 and Altuna 1990, 162-166 for discussion of the role of Amalda as a cave bear denning site), and it is clear that Mousterian hunters operating out of Amalda shared the landscape and overlapped in their hunting practices with a number of large carnivore species, including (in addition to cave bear) wolf, hyaena and leopard (Table 3.1).

With the exception of the cave bear and the two foxes, most carnivore species were represented by low NISP's[vi] and high frequencies of teeth/skull fragments and extremities (phalanges, carpals, tarsals etc.). Few of these species are likely to have presented much of a direct threat to hominids or humans unless provoked (e.g. Binford 1978; 1981), or even to have been in direct competition with them (e.g. Kurtén 1968; Altuna, *et al.* 1990, 156, see also Freeman 1973, 4), and most are unlikely to choose as a den a cave subject to any significant disruption or activity (Stiner 1994, 331). Nevertheless, the findings of carnivore toothmarks on much of the faunal material suggest a certain amount of carnivore activity – probably, the accumulations of bones provided a good scavenging resource for unfussy carnivore species, and in any case hominid and human inhabitants of Amalda would certainly have been aware of its use by other species: caves undoubtedly represented a potential node of interaction in the intertwining patterns of movement of carnivore and hominid species, and such interaction would have occurred within and been structured by a wider sphere of understanding of relations between the species – many traditional societies regard carnivore species with particular respect (see e.g. Binford, n.d., 8 for a discussion of how bears are viewed among the Nunamiut and in many boreal traditional societies generally).

Living in the OIS 5 a/c ecosystem of the Deba and Urola valleys

From the materials recovered from Amalda level VII, then, we can begin to identify some of the interactions of the hominid creators of the archaeological record with co-denizens of their ecosystem, and from this begin to reconstruct the habitual paths of movement and activity within those ecosystems. In addition to this, the faunal record adds to these something of the quality of the interactions represented in the level; the seasons in which kills were made, some educated guesses about the experience of locating and tracking other animal species – tracks and signs such as wallows, caught hair, grazed or browsed vegetation and so on - and about likely strategies of pursuit and killing as well as the butchery and transportation decisions made in each situation.

The aim is not to provide whole 'stories' attempting to present the subjective experiences of the persons who created the deposits of Amalda level VII – the focus is not so much the 'meaning' of the archaeological record as the ways in which meaning is constructed and structured through practical, habitual activity within a real world. In this way, I argue, we can begin to access the four-dimensional matrices of movement, activity and interaction that constituted the daily lives of hominid and human populations without having to first assume a pre-existing, overarching cognitive structure to their lives; comparison between 'archaic' and 'modern' populations is not then simply a matter of *post hoc* explanation by 'just-so' stories that misuse evolutionary concepts.

Instead, by reconsidering the sites and their material finds in terms of the clues they provide to movement and interaction in the ecosystem of which the cave and its inhabitants were a part, we can start to see fragments of the narratives created by the hominid and/or human persons who created the archaeological record: individual animals killed at particular 'intersections' in their paths of movements, at particular 'points' in space and time – at particular times of the year, and in particular places in the landscape.

Each of these aspects of activity adds another thread to the overall understanding of the faunal record and the archaeological record more generally – a full representation of hominid ecosystemic behaviour involves the consideration of the sum total of these interactions and activities as well as the paths and tracks created by patterns of movement associated with other activities such as those related to lithic raw material sources. No one such aspect can be separated out: every activity, every interaction, is enmeshed within a web of further such interactions and patterns of movement. Thus subsistence practices both structure and are structured by considerations such as the technical expertise and weaponry of hunters, involving them in ongoing interactions regarding access to lithic raw materials and manufacturing skills, as well as a working understanding of wider technological 'delivery systems' (Churchill, 1993), including hunting techniques and behaviours: undoubtedly prehistoric hunters would have been aware of particularly 'good' nodes in the matrix of interaction and movement that comprised their lifeways – places and times that afforded advantageous intersections between themselves and particular animal species. Tied in to this awareness, of course, were other factors such as the technical expertise and weaponry of hunters, and their perceptions of the affordances of the landscape; how to use topography, vegetation, wind direction and weather, for example, to its best advantage in stalking, ambushing, driving, disadvantaging.

In addition, every particular intersection has its own quality, some aspects of which are further preserved in the archaeological record. For example, a successful kill also necessarily involves further kinds of interaction during the process of butchery and transport – between hominids and animal species (who should butcher the carcass, *how* it should be done with respect for the spirit of the dead animal, etc.) and between hominids (how portions of the meat are divided, who gets the hide, antler, bone, teeth, how the carcass is transported, etc.), which again draw from a pre-conscious understanding of such factors as the time of year or season, the need for food, questions about the status and social links of the hunter and his or her family, friends, co-hunters, the 'right' and habitual ways of doing things in particular circumstances, and the potential danger presented by other carnivore species in the landscape, perhaps in competition for the meat or for caves or shelter.

Such decisions arise out of of understandings derived from previous such interactions and also, for hunters with a deep comprehension of the behaviour and movements of other animal species vis-à-vis their own, from a complex of pre-conscious understandings of the ecosystem of which they are a part (see e.g. Brody 1981, 37) that is part and parcel of the *habitus* of living in their world. All of these factors feed more or less consciously into the decision-making process at every stage, and every such intersection, every such event is necessarily unique, creating its own 'node' in the four-dimensional architecture of movement and interaction within an ecosystem. Every task and activity therefore ties further into a dense web of understandings derived from habitual interactions, and it is these wider understandings that constitute 'group' identities, into which individual persons are always and inescapably linked.

In entitling this section 'living' in the OIS 5a/c ecosystem, I aim to bypass a sterile opposition between approaches prioritising 'dwelling', experiential and phenomenological readings of activity in the landscape, and those emphasising 'adaptational' and 'evolutionary' readings: humans necessarily both 'dwell' and 'adapt', and as argued above, a separation of the two would be artificial. Rather, the one inevitably entails the other. 'Adaptations' are not necessarily discrete genotypic characters (although of course they may be). Rather, here, they are seen as arising out of the practices of dwelling. As Ingold argues,

> It is not by assigning the position where I currently stand to spatial coordinates that an answer to the 'where' question is arrived at, but rather by situating that position within the matrix of movement constitutive of a region (2000, 237).

Conclusion: An ecosystemic perspective on prehistoric change

From an ecosystemic perspective, then, sites can be considered not so much as discrete, bounded assemblages but as 'places', nodes inevitably and inextricably linked in to their encompassing four-dimensional ecosystem through a matrix of embodied movement that both arises out of and acts to comprise the movements and activities of individual people, their links and their groups between places and times.

This four-dimensional ecosystem is a shared one, occupied not just by individuals and groups of hominids but also by individuals and groups of other animal and plant species as well as other-than-animate aspects of the landscape such as geological or topographical features, each of which may be known and understood as having its own distinct character within peoples' overall comprehension of the ecosystem.

These other 'entities' also describe their own matrices of movement in space and time, and these are inevitably familiar to their co-denizens, who in turn constantly alter and shift their own movements over various timescales in an ongoing co-evolutionary negotiation of behaviour and identity. Thus the pathways of movement in space and time created by humans and hominids inevitably interlink and intersect with those created by these other entities, and each of these intersections provides an arena for various kinds of potential interaction.

Archaeology, and particularly Palaeolithic archaeology, has struggled to address the question of identity and its continual transformation in prehistory, relying instead on proxy measures such as lithic industries which, perhaps inevitably, all too often become reified and conflated with identity, and come to be seen *as* those identities. However, as I have demonstrated in this paper, rather than seeing archaeological assemblages, industries and 'cultures' as reified 'identities', material finds recovered from archaeological sites can be viewed as having formed part of the construction and continual negotiation of movement through the four-dimensional ecosystem. And it is this movement, the intersections with those of others, and the interactions that these afford, that constitutes the architecture of identity. The creation of the archaeological record acts to materialise and immemorate occasions of interaction with other denizens of the world and, from an analytical point of view, provide clues to their reconstruction or re-imagining: it is the sum total of these movements and interactions that can be considered constitutive of identities and personhood, in prehistory as today.

It has only been possible in this paper to consider one level of the site of Amalda. However, I have aimed to demonstrate here the ways in which an ecosystemic perspective undermines a simplistic equation of populations and their typologically defined lithic assemblages. Comparison of the patterns of ecosystemic interaction attested to by level VII with those from other levels at this site as well as from others elsewhere in the region reveals more subtle differences and similarities between populations of Neanderthals and 'modern' humans than those hypothesised as part of a post-hoc, accommodative 'just-so' story about prehistory, however well-couched in 'evolutionary' theory (Coward 2004). Rather than a series of discrete 'cultures' separated by points of 'transition', bounded events of change, an ecosystemic approach highlights the need for an analysis that reflects the potentialities of hominid and human lives. An ecosystemic approach thus emphasises a continuum of constantly altering matrices of movement, activity and interaction instead of compressing 'lumps' of time and experience into virtually meaningless (except in purely analytical terms) categories such as 'modern' and 'non-modern', which are really only secondary, proxy and purely descriptive terms for more subtle differences, effect rather than cause of changing identities and personhoods.

In this paper I have focused on subsistence issues in order to emphasise their underestimated potential for yielding much more than purely economic data. However, the real potential of an ecosystemic approach, and the methodology tentatively outlined here, lies in its ability to link apparently disparate parts of the archaeological record ('subsistence', 'lithics', 'symbolism' etc.) into an overarching whole, the habitual daily movements, activities and interactions of people in prehistory, thus providing a new basis for addressing the negotiation and enactment of identities and personhoods underlying change as seen in the archaeological record.

Acknowledgements

This research was funded by an AHRB grant and by small awards from the Dept. of Archaeology, University of Southampton. Clive Gamble and Rob Hosfield provided much help and advice throughout, and Annabel Field and Jenni Chambers kindly commented on early drafts of this paper – though I jealously reserve responsibility for all errors! With thanks also to all participants and discussions at the original TAG sessions.

References Cited

Alexandri, A. 1995. The Origins of Meaning. In I. Hodder, M. Shanks, A. Alexandri, V. Buchli, J. Carman, J. Last and G. Lucas (eds), *Interpreting Archaeology*, pp. 57-67. London: Routledge.

Allen, P. M. 1989. Modelling Innovation and Change. In S. E. van der Leeuw and R. Torrence (eds), *What's New? A closer look at the process of innovation*, pp. 258-80. London: Unwin Hyman.

Altuna, J. 1990. Caza y alimentación procedente de macromamíferos durante el Paleolítico de Amalda. In J. Altuna, A. Baldeón and K. Mariezkurrena (eds), *La Cueva de Amalda*, pp. 149-92. San Sebastián: Sociedad de Estudios Vascos, Sociedad de Ciencias Aranzadi.

Altuna, J., Baldeón, A. and Mariezkurrena, K. 1990. *La Cueva de Amalda (Zestoa, País Vasco): occupaciones Paleolíticas y Postpaleolíticas*. San Sebastián: Sociedad de Estudios Vascos.

Bailey, G. 1983. Economic Change in Late Pleistocene Cantabria. In G. Bailey (ed), *Hunter-Gatherer Economy in Prehistory*, pp. 150-65. Cambridge: Cambridge University Press.

Bailey, G. N. 1983. Concepts of Time in Quaternary Prehistory. *Annual Review of Anthropology* 12: pp. 165-92.

Bang, P. and Dahlstrom, P. 1974. *Collins Guide to Animal Tracks and Signs*. Glasgow: William Collins Son and Co Ltd.

Barrett, J. 1991. The archaeology of social reproduction. In J. Barrett, R. Bradley and M. Green (eds), *Landscape, Monuments and Society: the prehistory of Cranborne Chase*, Cambridge: Cambridge University Press.

Binford, L. R. n.d. Linking Ethnographic Information on Man-Bear Interaction to European Cave Bear Deposits.

- 1978. *Nunamiut Ethnoarchaeology*. New York: Academic Press.

- 1981. *Bones: ancient men and modern myths*. New York: Academic Press.

Borja, A. 1990. La Malacofauna de la Cueva de Amalda. In J. Altuna, A. Baldeon and K. Mariezkurrena (eds), *La Cueva de Amalda (Zestoa, País Vasco): Occupaciones Paleoliticos y Postpaleoliticos*, pp. 267-70. San Sebastian: Eusko Ikaskuntza.

Bourdieu, P. 1977. *Outline of a Theory of Practice*. Cambridge: Cambridge University Press.

Boyd, B. 1999. Animals as Technologies in the Epipalaeolithic Levant. Paper presented at the second Lampeter Workshop in Archaeology 24-27 September 1999: Embedded Technologies, reworking technological studies in archaeology, University of Wales Lampeter.

Boyle, K. V. 1990. *Upper Palaeolithic Faunas from South-West France: a zoogeographical perspective*. B.A.R. International Series 557. Oxford: British Archaeological Reports.

Brody, H. 1981. *Maps and Dreams*. Prospect Heights, Illinois: Waveland Press.

Butzer, K. W. 1986. Paleolithic Adaptations and Settlement in Cantabrian Spain. *Advances in World Archaeology* 5: pp. 201-52.

Carlstein, T. 1982. *Time Resources, Society and Ecology* Volume 1: preindustrial societies. London: George Allen and Unwin.

Cartmill, M. 1993. *A View to a Death in the Morning: hunting and nature through history*. Cambridge, Massachusetts: Harvard University Press.

- 2001. Taxonomic revolutions and the animal-human boundary. In R. Corbey and W. Roebroeks (eds), *Studying Human Origins: disciplinary history and epistemology*, pp. 97-106. Amsterdam: Amsterdam University Press.

Chazan, M. 1995. The Meaning of Homo Sapiens. In R. Corbey and B. Theunissen (eds), *Ape, Man, Apeman: Changing views since 1600. Evaluative Proceedings of the symposium, Leiden, The Netherlands, 28 June - 1 July 1993*, pp. 230-40. Leiden: Leiden University.

Churchill, S. E. 1993. Weapon Technology, prey size selection and hunting methods in modern hunter-gatherers: implications for hunting in the Palaeolithic and Mesolithic. In G. L. Peterkin, H. M. Bricker and P. Mellars (eds), *Hunting and Animal Exploitation in the Later Palaeolithic and Mesolithic of Eurasia*, pp. 11-24. Archaeological Papers of the American Anthropological Association No. 4. Washington: American Anthropological Association.

Clark, G. A. 1997. Through a Glass Darkly: Conceptual Issues in Modern Human Origins Research. In G. A. Clark and C. M. Willermet (eds), *Conceptual Issues in Modern Human Origins Research*, pp. 60-76. New York: Aldine de Gruyter.

- 2001a. Discussion: The logic of inference in transition research. In M. A. Hays and P. T. Thacker (eds), *Questioning the Answers: Re-solving fundamental problems of the Early Upper Palaeolithic*, pp. 39. B.A.R. International Series. vol. 1005. Oxford: British Archaeological Reports.

- 2001b. Observations of the epistemology of human origins research. In R. Corbey and W. Roebroeks (eds), *Studying Human Origins: disciplinary history and epistemology*, pp. 139-46. Amsterdam: Amsterdam University Press.

Conkey, M. W. 1987. Interpretive Problems in Hunter-Gatherer Regional Studies. In O. Soffer (ed), *The Pleistocene Old World: regional perspectives*, pp. 63-77. New York: Plenum Press.

Conkey, M. W. and Williams, S. H. 1991. The political economy of gender in archaeology. In M. D. Leonardo (ed), *Gender at the Crossroads of Knowledge: feminist anthropology in a post modern era*, pp. 102-39. Berkeley: University of California Press.

Coward, F. 2004. *Transitions, Change and Identity: the Middle and Upper Palaeolithic of Vasco-Cantabrian Spain*. Unpublished PhD thesis: University of Southampton.

Drell, J. R. R. 2000. Neanderthals: a history of interpretation. *Oxford Journal of Archaeology* 19(1): pp. 1-24.

Dupré, M. 1990. Análisis polínico de la cueva de Amalda. In J. Altuna, A. Baldeón and K. Mariezkurrena (eds), *La Cueva de Amalda (Zestoa, País Vasco): occupaciones paleolíticos y postpaleolíticos*, pp. 49-51. San Sebastián: Sociedad de Estudios Vascos.

Eastham, A. 1990. The Bird bones in the Cave of Amalda. In J. Altuna, A. Baldeón and K. Mariezkurrena (eds), *La Cueva de Amalda (Zestoa, País Vasco): Occupaciones paleoliticas y postpaleoliticas*, pp. 239-54. San Sebastián: Sociedad de Estudios Vascos.

d'Errico, F., Zilhão, J., Julien, M., Baffier, D. and Pelegrin, J. 1998. Neanderthal Acculturation in Western Europe? A critical review of the evidence and its interpretation. *Current Anthropology* 39 (2: Supplement: Special Issue: the Neanderthal Problem and the Evolution of Human Behavior): pp. S1-S44.

Field, A. 2002. *The Middle Pleistocene in Transition: lithic assemblages and changing social relations between OIS12 and 6 in Europe and Africa*. uncorrected draft PhD, University of Southampton.

Foley, R. 1984. Putting People in Perspective: an introduction to community evolution and ecology. In R. A. Foley (ed), *Hominid evolution and community ecology*, pp. 1-24. London: Academic Press.

Freeman, L. G. 1973. The significance of mammalian faunas from Palaeolithic occupations in Cantabrian Spain. *American Antiquity* 38(1): pp. 3-44.

Gamble, C. 2001. *Archaeology: the basics*. London: Routledge.

Gibson, J. J. 1979. *The Ecological Approach to Visual Perception*. Boston: Houghton Mifflin.

Gosden, C. 1994. *Social Being and Time*. Oxford: Blackwell.

Gosden, C. and Marshall, Y. 1999. The Cultural Biography of Objects. *World Archaeology* 31(2): pp. 169-78.

Graves, P. 1991. New Models and Metaphors for the Neanderthal Debates. *Current Anthropology* 32(5): pp. 513-40.

Graves-Brown, P. 1993. Ape and Essence. *Archaeological Review from Cambridge* 12(2): pp. 71-84.

Hallowell, A. I. 1960. Ojibwa ontology, behavior and worldview. In S. Diamond (ed.) *Culture in History: essays in honor of Paul Radin*, pp. 19-52. New York: Columbia University Press.

Heidegger, M. 1962 [1927]. *Being and Time*. Trans. J. Macquarrie and E. Robinson. Oxford: Blackwell.

Hodder, I. 1985. Post-processual Archaeology. In M. Schiffer (ed), *Advances in Archaeological Method and Theory*, pp. 1-25. vol. 8. New York: Academic Press.

Ingold, T. 1989. The Social and Environmental Relations of Human Beings and Other Animals. In V. Standen and R. Foley (eds), *Comparative Socioecology*, pp. 495-512. Special Publication No. 8 of the British Ecological Society. Oxford: Blackwell Scientific Publications.

- 1992. Culture and the perception of the environment. In E. Croll and D. Parkin (eds), *Bush Base: forest farm culture, environment and development*, pp. 39-57. London: Routledge.

- 1993a. The art of translation in a continuous world. In G. Pálsson (ed), *Beyond Boundaries: understanding, translation and anthropological discourse*, pp. 210-30. Oxford: Berg.

- 1993b. The Temporality of the Landscape. *World Archaeology* 25(2: Conceptions of Time and Ancient Society): pp. 152-74.

- 1996. Hunting and Gathering as Ways of Perceiving the Environment. In R. Ellen and K. Fukui (eds), *Redefining Nature: ecology, culture and domestication*, pp. 117-55. Explorations in Anthropology. Oxford: Berg.

- 2000 *The Perception of the Environment: essays in livelihood, dwelling and skill*, London: Routledge.

Jochim, M. A. 1998. *A Hunter-Gatherer Landscape southwest Germany in the late Palaeolithic and Mesolithic*. New York: Plenum Press.

Kurtén, B. 1968. *Pleistocene Mammals of Europe*. London: Weidenfekd and Nicolson.

Landau, M. 1992. *Narratives of Human Evolution: The Hero Story*. New Haven: Yale University Press.

Lewontin, R. C. 1982. Organism and Environment. In H. C. Plotkin (ed), *Learning, Development and Culture*, pp. Chichester: Wiley.

MacDonald, D. and Barrett, P. 1993. *Collins Field Guide: Mammals of Britain and Europe*. London: HarperCollins.

Mackie, Q. 2001. *Settlement Archaeology in a Fjordland Archipelago: network analysis, social practice and the built environment of western Vancouver Island, British Columbia, Canada since 2,000 BP*. B.A.R.

International Series 926. Oxford: British Archaeological Reports.

Mark, D. M. and Egenhofer, M. J. 1996. *Common-sense Geography: foundations for intuitive Geographic Information Systems*. Copies available from GIS/LIS'96 paper NG- I-21.

Mark, D. M., Egenhofer, M. J. and Hornsby, K. 1997. *Formal Models of Commonsense Geographic Worlds: report on the Specialist Meeting of Research Initiative 21*. National Center for Geographic Information and Analysis (NCGIA). Copies available from NCGIA Technical Report 1997-2.

Marks, J. 1997. Systematics in Anthropology: where science confronts the humanities (and consistently loses). In G. A. Clark and C. M. Willermet (eds), *Conceptual Issues in Modern Human Origins Research*, pp. 45-59. Chicago: Aldine de Gruyter.

Marriott, M. 1976. Hindu Transactions: diversity without dualism. In B. Kapferer (ed), *Transaction and Meaning: directions in the anthropology of exchange and symbolic behaviour*. Philadelphia: Institute for the Study of Human Issues.

McBrearty, S. and Brooks, A. S., 2000. The Revolution that Wasn't: a new interpretation of the origin of modern human behavior. *Journal of Human Evolution* 39: pp. 453-563.

Merleau-Ponty, 1962. *Phenomenology of Perception*. Trans. C. Smith. New York: Humanities Press.

Mithen, S. 1989. Evolutionary Theory and Post-Processual Archaeology. *Antiquity* 63: pp. 483-94.

Moore, H. 1995. The Problems of Origins; poststructuralism and beyond. In I. Hodder, M. Shanks, A. Alexandri, V. Buchli, J. Carmen, J. Last and G. Lucas (eds), *Interpreting Archaeologies: finding meaning in the past*, pp. 51-3. London: Routledge.

Muñiz, A. M. and Izquierdo, E. R. 1990. La Ictiofauna de la Cueva de Amalda. In J. Altuna, A. Baldeon and K. Mariezkurrena (eds), *La Cueva de Amalda (Zestoa, País Vasco): Occupaciones Paleoliticas y Postpaleoliticas*, pp. 255-66. San Sebastian: Eusko Ikaskuntza.

O'Brien, M. and Holland, T. 1992. The role of adaptation in archaeological explanation. *American Antiquity* 57: pp. 36-59.

Pellegrin, P. 1986. *Aristotle's Classification of Animals: biology and the conceptual unity of the Aristotelian corpus*. Berkeley: University of California Press.

Preucel, R. W. and Hodder, I. 1996. *Contemporary Archaeology in Theory: a reader*. Oxford: Blackwell Publisher.

Price, T. D. 2000. *Europe's First Farmers*. Cambridge: Cambridge University Press.

Proctor, R. N. 2003. Three Roots of Human Recency. *Current Anthropology* 44(2): pp. 213-39.

Quinney, P. S. 2000. Paradigms Lost: changing interpretations of hominid behavioural patterns since ODK. In P. Rowley-Conwy (ed), *Animal Bones, Human Societies*, pp. 12-9. Oxford: Oxbow Books.

Reitz, E. J. and Wing, E. S. 1999. *Zooarchaeology*. Cambridge: Cambridge University Press.

Relph, E. 2000 (1985). Geographical Experiences and Being-In-The-World: the phenomenological origins of geography. In D. Seamon and R. Mugerauer (eds), *Dwelling, Place and Environment: towards a phenomenology of person and world*, pp. 15-31. Malabar, Florida: Krieger Publishing Company.

van Reybrouck, D. 2001. On Savages and Simians: continuity and discontinuity in the history of human origin studies. In R. Corbey and W. Roebroeks (eds), *Studying Human Origins: disciplinary history and epistemology*, pp. 77-96. Amsterdam: Amsterdam University Press.

Roebroeks, W. 1995. 'Policing the Boundary'? Continuity of Discussions in 19th and 20th Century Palaeoanthropology. In R. Corbey and B. Theunissen (eds), *Ape, Man, Apeman: Changing views since 1600. Evaluative Proceedings of the symposium, Leiden, The Netherlands, 28 June - 1 July 1993*, pp. 173-9. Leiden: Leiden University.

Roebroeks, W. and Corbey, R. 2001. Biases and double standards in palaeoanthropology. In R. Corbey and W. Roebroeks (eds), *Studying Human Origins: disciplinary history and epistemology*, pp. 67-76. Amsterdam: Amsterdam University Press.

Schumann, B. 1997. Biological and Archaeological Classifications: boundaries, biases, and paradigms in Upper Paleolithic Research. In G. A. Clark and C. M. Willermet (eds), *Conceptual Issues in Modern Human Origins Research*, pp. 253-66. Chicago: Aldine de Gruyter.

Seamon, D. 1980. Body-Subject, Time-Space Routines, and Place-Ballets. In A. Buttimer and D. Seamon (eds), *The Human Experience of Space and Place*, pp. 148-65. London: Croom Helm.

Serjeantson, D. 2000. Good to eat *and* good to think with: classifying animals from complex sites. In P. Rowley-Conwy (ed), *Animal Bones, Human Societies*, pp. 179-89. Oxford: Oxbow.

Shanks, M. and Tilley, C. 1987. *Social Theory and Archaeology*. Oxford: Polity Press.

Simek, J. F. 2001. Discussion: space and time. In M. A. Hays and P. T. Thacker (eds), *Questioning the Answers: re-solving fundamental problems of the Early Upper Palaeolithic*, pp. 199-202. BAR International Series 1005. Oxford: British Archaeological Reports.

Stiner, M. C. 1994. *Honor Among Thieves; a zooarchaeological study of Neanderthal ecology*. Pinceton: Princeton University Press.

Strathern, M. 1988. *The Gender of the Gift: Problems with women and problems with society in Melanesia*. Berkeley: University of California Press.

Straus, L. G. 1991. Paradigm Found? A research agenda for study of the Upper and Post-Paleolithic in Southwest Europe. In G.A.Clark (ed), *Perspectives on the Past: theoretical biases in Mediterranean hunter-gatherer research*, pp. 56-78. Philadelphia: University of Pennsylvania Press.

- 1992. *Iberia Before the Iberians: The Stone Age prehistory of Cantabrian Spain*. Albuquerque: University of New Mexico Press.

Sturdy, D. A. and Webley, D. P. 1988. Palaeolithic Geography: or where are the deer? *World Archaeology* 19(3: New Directions in Palaeolithic Archaeology): pp. 262-80.

Sturdy, D., Webley, D. and Bailey, G. 1997. The Palaeolithic Geography of Epirus. In G. Bailey (ed), *Klithi: Palaeolithic Settlement and Quaternary Landscapes in Northwest Greece Volume 2: Klithi in its local and regional setting*, pp. 587-614. McDonald Institute Monographs. Cambridge: McDonald Institute for Archaeological Research.

Tansley, A. G. 1935. The use and abuse of vegetational concepts and terms. *Ecology* 16: pp. 284-307.

Thomas, J. 2002. Archaeology's Humanism and the Materiality of the Body. In Y. Hamilakis, M. Pluciennik and S. Tarlow (eds), *Thinking Through the Body: archaeologies of corporeality*, pp. 29-45. New York: Kluwer Academic/Plenum Publishers.

Tilley, C. 1994. *A Phenomenology of Landscape: places, paths and monuments*. Oxford: Berg.

van Valen, L. 1973. A new evolutionary law. *Evolutionary Theory* 1: pp. 1-30.

Viera, L. I. and Aguirrezabala, L. M. 1990. Estudio geológico del yacimiento prehistórico de la cueva de Amalda y su entorno. Determinación del materiel litológico excavado y possible procedencia del mismo. In J. Altuna, A. Baldeón and K. Mariezkurrena (eds), *La Cueva de Amalda (Zestoa, País Vasco): occupacionespaleolíticos y postpaleolíticos*, pp. 53-61. San Sebastián: Sociedad de Estudios Vascos.

Wagner, R. 1986. *Symbols that stand for themselves*. Chicago: University of Chicago Press.

West, D. 1997. *Hunting Strategies in Central Europe During the Last Glacial Maximum*. BAR International Series 672. Oxford: British Archaeological Reports.

Wobst, M. 1983. Palaeolithic archaeology - some problems with form, space and time. In G. Bailey (ed), *Hunter-Gatherer Economy in Prehistory*, pp. 220-5. Cambridge: Cambridge University Press.

---

[i] Pattern of anatomical representation is presented in the figures combined into anatomical 'regions' following Altuna's scheme (1990), with only two modifications: antler/horn is counted only on a presence/absence basis, and teeth are counted on the basis of MNI (e.g. if teeth NISP ≤ the number of teeth belonging to a single animal of that species, MNI = 1), as both of these elements commonly demonstrate anomalously high raw counts that would bias the ratio of head counts relative to postcrania (e.g. Stiner 1994). It is therefore possible that head counts for the Amalda data may be slightly underrepresented. For the same reason, sesamoids are not included in 'feet' counts.

[ii] As a comparison, 'normal' US army rucksacks ('approach march load') weigh somewhere in the region of 31Kg, with 'emergency' march loads weighing anything up to around 68kg (http://www.rdecom.army.mil/rdemagazine/200403/itl_nsc_combat.html)

[iii] It is estimated that bovids comprised c.40% of the total meat weight represented by the assemblage in level VII of Amalda - other species: red deer 17.9%; horse 17.2%; chamois 16.1%; ibex 7.8%; roe deer 1.1% (Altuna 1990).

[iv] Bearing in mind that adult male bovids weight between 800-900kg and females between 500-600kg, and stand about 180-195cm tall at the shoulder (Boyle 1990; MacDonald and Barrett 1993), this was probably considerably easier written than performed.

[v] Binford's meat, marrow, grease and 'general utility' indices, although widely used, are based on two sheep (one juvenile, one senile) and a single caribou (Reitz and Wing 2000). The indices are used here only for very general comparative purposes.

[vi] See e.g. Altuna (1990) and Straus (1992) for debate regarding the calculation of carnivore indices from NISP or MNI figures.

DARWIN VS. BOURDIEU – CELEBRITY DEATHMATCH OR POSTPROCESSUAL MYTH?
A PROLEGOMENON FOR THE RECONCILIATION OF AGENTIVE-INTERPRETATIVE AND ECOLOGICAL-EVOLUTIONARY ARCHAEOLOGY

Felix Riede

University of Cambridge

Abstract

A number of years ago, William Davies (2000), rather euphemistically, described the relationship of Palaeolithic specialists with postprocessualism as 'pragmatic'. Whilst it is true that not much of the postprocessual 'people'-centred archaeology of the last two decades has had significant impact on Palaeolithic archaeology, there are clearly good reasons for this: Vicious taphonomic distortions, an extremely coarse-grained stone-and-bone-only archaeological record as well as uncertainties about the cognitive states of pre-modern hominines mitigate against interpretations that go beyond the economic and ecological.

I would like to argue that to some degree this lack of integration between postprocessual theory and Palaeolithic archaeological practice is rooted in a mostly unconscious selective reading of key sources by both postprocessualists as well as Palaeolithic archaeologists. With a series of quotations and a case study from the Late Palaeolithic of Denmark I demonstrate that agentive approaches to technological skill are reconcilable with evolutionary thinking. Further, by drawing on recent developments in ecological modelling and evolutionary theory, I will show that traditional data on raw material economy and site location can be used to examine individual strategies of 'landscape learning' and enculturation. Again, I will draw on a case study from the Northern European Late Palaeolithic. To deny the biological dimensions of human (and hominin) existence would be folly. Postprocessual archaeologists are well advised to engage more fully and openly with evolutionary theory and to discontinue the bad practice of caricaturing Darwinian evolution as deterministic. Indeed, Darwinism, if wisely adapted, provides a powerful framework in which to examine the ultimate causes and processes of prehistoric culture change.

Introduction: Social and Biological Constructivism

A number of years ago, William Davies (2000, 5) remarked rather euphemistically that the relationship of Palaeolithic specialists with postprocessualism can be described as 'pragmatic'. Most archaeologists working in the Palaeolithic period perhaps feel rather safe from the post-modern critique of the last 25 years behind the barrier of vicious taphonomy, staggering time-depth and non-modern cognition, which separates most of early prehistory from later periods. However, this preoccupation with taphonomy, ecology and auxiliary scientific methods has engendered a (usually implicit) philosophical approach closer to that of a much older archaeology (Jones 2002). Operating in a strictly empiricist framework and drawing mainly on human behavioural ecology and evolutionary theory for explanatory models, most Palaeolithic archaeologists feel that postprocessualism has nothing to offer to them. Andrew Jones (2002, 1) has argued that contemporary archaeology encompasses "two cultures" of archaeological thinking, the interpretative and the scientific. In a similar vein, the historian of science David Hull (1988; 2000) has undertaken a citation analysis of a small field within the biological sciences (systematics) and has been able to show how even this subfield slowly split into two yet smaller divisions. This divide is reflected in the increasingly exclusive and self-referential citation practices of both groups. Returning to archaeology, even a cursory browsing of the bibliographies found in postprocessual and Palaeolithic archaeology texts demonstrates that there is almost a complete 'citation rift' between these two areas of research.

In many respects the present paper follows on from both Hull and Jones. From Hull, I take the source-critical approach; from Jones I take the ambition to reconcile these two divergent cultures, for I would argue that Palaeolithic archaeology can still do with yet another measured dose of social archaeology and that postprocessualists, despite their protestations, are ill-advised to ignore the lessons of deep prehistory and evolutionary theory. Yet, this is not an exhaustive citation analysis, which although surely highly revealing in its own right, would go beyond the bounds of this all too brief paper. Instead, this paper is divided into two parts. In the first, source-critical part I will focus on a single text, Shanks and Tilley's (1992) 'Re-Constructing Archaeology'. I am, of course, fully aware that this text does not represent the state-of-the-art of postprocessual thinking, but it is heavily used in both undergraduate as well as graduate teaching in Britain and it has certainly influenced the attitudes of many presently practicing archaeologists. At this point it is important to note, that I emphatically do not want to criticise postprocessualism as such, but rather I aim to criticise its ill-informed and outright dismissal of evolutionary and ecological models for the explanation of human behaviour and the archaeological record. I would argue that texts such as the one critiqued here were instrumental in producing this widespread and unjustified antipathy towards biology-inspired explanations of human behaviour. A general anti-scientific stance is common in post-modern writings, but has been shown forcefully to be unfounded (Sokal and Bricmont 1998). Yet, it seems that in some *archaeological* circles this criticism has gone unnoticed. By no means all, but many postprocessual texts perpetuate strongly non-scientific sentiments, partly referring to propositions that themselves have been shown to be unfounded (e.g. Latour, Derrida; see Sokal and Bricmont 1998).

In the second part of this paper I will present a number of novel theoretical positions, coming from the social sciences as well as from biology that offer reconciliation between the interpretative and the evolutionary approach. Introducing 'apprenticeship' (Warnier 2001), 'landscape learning' (Meltzer 2002; 2003) and the 'niche construction' model (Laland *et al.* 1999; 2000; 2001 Odling-Smee *et al.* 2003), I will try to demonstrate how the two approaches are in fact converging in modes of analysis, if not vocabulary.

The view presented in this paper rests on two pillars. One is the agentive approach, based generally on the writings of Bourdieu (1977) and Giddens (1984) and, more specifically, on the archaeological works of Leroi-Gourhan (1984 [1964]) and the French *chaîne opèratoire* school as well as more recent agentive approaches

Neo-Darwinian Tenets	**Biology**	**Archaeology**
Gradual Micro-Evolution	Chance genetic change (e.g. Kimura 1983; Ridley 2004). Backed by mathematics and computer simulation (Dawkins 1991).	Innovation, invention and stylistic change based on 'replicative success' (Leonard & Jones 1987; Shennan 1989a).
Punctuated Macro-Evolution	'Revolutions' of ecological systems e.g. mass extinction and the emergence of new species, e.g. Stanley 2000).	'Revolutions' and large-scale changes in social structure, e.g. Prentiss & Chatters (2003).
Social Behaviour	Common in many animals, across all phyla; animal sociality intricate and complex (Dawkins 1989; 1991; 1996)	Human Behavioural Ecology: Boone & Smith (1998); sexual selection: Kohn & Mithen (1999); herding & dairying (Mace & Pagel 1994)
Tool-Use	Common in many animals; tools can be studied as both extra-somatic means of adaptation (e.g. Turner 2000) as well as cultural traditions (e.g. Avital & Jablonka 2000; McGrew 1992; Perry & Fragaszy 2003; Reader & Laland 2003).	Instrumental in human culture and existence; can be studied using evolutionary methods (e.g. Shennan 2002b; O'Brien & Lyman 2000; 2003a; 2003b).

Table 4.1. Neo-Darwinian theory and archaeology. This table summarises some of the salient features of neo-Darwinian theory as pertinent to this paper. Under the umbrella of this meta-theory of change, a plethora of mutually compatible approaches have developed each specific for the level of analysis. Ridley (2004) gives an up-to-date account for the biological sciences, Shennan (2002) for archaeology. Note in particular that natural selection as a blunt external force acting on organism mainly by killing them off has receded far into the background in modern evolutionary theory, being replaced by stochastic models of change as well as more nuanced models of multi-component selection within the immediate, often partly self-constructed environment. Evolutionary change will depend more on differential reproductive/replicative success rather than survival and places evolutionary processes squarely within the realm of social relations.

(Dobres and Robb 2000). The second pillar is contemporary evolutionary theory (Table 4.1). As the 'historians of the biological world' evolutionary biologists are well aware of the issues of historical contingency and the problems arising from it (Bintliff 1991). Recently, biologists have taken to examining in much more detail 'animal traditions', that is, regionally and temporally distinct behavioural patterns, often connected to the use of material items. And whilst some (e.g. Avital and Jablonka 2000; Boesch and Tomasello 1998; McGrew 1992), shy away from calling such traditions 'culture', others do not (Whiten *et al.* 1999; 2001; 2003). Much effort has recently been expended on recording and quantifying this kind of animal behaviour (see http://biologybk.st-and.ac.uk/cultures3/), but many primatologists engage in what would have to be called 'panthropological' (Whiten *et al.* 2003) thick description (e.g. McGrew 1992; de Waal 2001), much for the same reasons that ethnographers do (i.e. longevity of their subjects, richness and individuality of the social actions under observation). It has long been recognised (Byrne and Whiten 1988; Whiten and Byrne 1997) that primates (and probably other animals) live in a rich social world and under the framework of modern ethology they are given the *status of both social as well as evolutionary actors* (Avital and Jablonka 2000; Perry and Fragaszy 2004; Odling-Smee *et al.* 2003). The view that these two forms of action are indeed complementary is not new (Shennan 1989a), and recent developments afford a much tighter integration.

Using examples from the Late Palaeolithic of Southern Scandinavia (13,500 – 11,000 BP), I will endeavour to demonstrate that interpretative and evolutionary theory are commensurable at a variety of scales. I will argue that postprocessual archaeologists are well advised to engage more fully with evolutionary theory as it offers not only a richly conceptualised meta-theory of change over time, but also a host of powerful methodological tools that allow rigorous quantification. It is fascinating to observe that both anthropologists interested in material culture and practice as well as biologists have now firmly turned their gaze towards tools and technology as a rich informative nexus. Despite a slowly growing awareness however (see Mesoudi *et al.* 2004), the work of archaeologists has been largely ignored by biologists. With a tremendous record of 2.5 million years of technological change, archaeology has much to contribute to an evolutionary analysis of human cultural behaviour, as well as any investigation of how modern human practice/praxis has come to be as it is.

Part 1: Shanks and Tilley on...

...Evolutionary Theory
In their widely read 'Reconstructing Archaeology' Shanks and Tilley (1992) devote two-and-a-half pages to their definitive and comprehensive dismissal of the application of evolutionary theory to all things cultural. They (Shanks and Tilley 1992) begin with a, not incorrect, but certainly crude and incomplete summary of Darwinian evolution. Besides the fact that they do not offer the reader a single reference, this summary makes biological evolution look like a simple, indeed simplistic, and straightforward process in stark contrast to the complex and marvellous field described by others (e.g. Gould 2002; Dawkins 2004; Ridley 2004).

Shanks and Tilley (1992) then go on to claim that Darwinian evolution is inextricably linked to aspects of political domination, the bourgeoisie and Social Darwinism. Of course, there is no doubt that Darwinian evolution, at its inception, had been caught up in the ethical and conceptual quagmire that is Social Darwinism (Bowler 1986), but to claim, again without further references, that all Darwinian thinking is inherently imperialist and middle-class – an argument that has also been used against postprocessual approaches (Brodie 2001) – is not justified. Practicing biologists are extremely aware of these issues and take great pains to highlight the differences between the political abuse of an ill-understood version of evolution, i.e. Spencer's social evolution, which in turn has given rise to many later models of social evolution, and the modern synthetic theory of neo-Darwinian evolution (Mayr 1991; Ridley 2004). The social evolutionism of Spencer has its roots in a wholly different intellectual environment and Spencer and others merely adopted a kind of quasi-Darwinian terminology for their own political purposes in the wake of its rise to prominence in the biological sciences (Hudson 1996; Peel 1972). Darwinian evolution is clearly situated within a field of broader social currents, but here is not the place to go into the finer details. Suffice it to say, modern neo-Darwinian evolution is quite unlike – historically, conceptually and methodologically – the Social Darwinism of the late 19th and early 20th centuries.

Having outlined the kind of evolution that Shanks and Tilley evidently consider representative of neo-Darwinian evolution as a whole, and having expressed their doubts as to the moral and ethical standing of this theory in respect to human culture, they (Shanks and Tilley 1992, 55) state:

> It is by the very means of the concepts of the theory of modern evolutionary biology that we know that it simply cannot be applied to the development of human social organization except in such a problematic fashion as to completely undermine any value the attempt might have. Social relationships are not in any primary sense biological relationships and may not be explained except in the most reductionist scenario by the physical attributes of human beings relation to different adaptive situations.

I have already expressed doubts as to whether the term "modern evolutionary biology" can justifiably be used by Shanks and Tilley to best describe their vision of it, but what is worth pointing out here is that neo-Darwinian evolution is not inherently a theory of biology, although this is where it has first been formulated and where it is most fruitfully applied. Yet, evolution is a property of any information system given certain conditions. In his brilliant 'Analytical Archaeology' David Clarke (1968) recognised this and framed his geography- and biology-inspired archaeology in terms of information theory (Shennan 1989b). Philosophers of Biology as well as anthropologists have shown that *a range of evolutionary processes, be they biological or cultural* can be modelled rather accurately using evolutionary theory (e.g. Boyd and Richerson 1985; Dennett 1995; Durham 1991; Hull 1988; 2000). In addition, the field of genetics has vastly enriched evolutionary biology and increasingly a variety of interactive, quasi-social processes are being considered extremely important in the evolutionary process. Most importantly however, the impact of modern genetics has demonstrated that very little evolutionary change actually is adaptive in the strict sense. The obsession with adaptation is the legacy of early processual archaeology and any simplistic adaptationist explanation is well worth critiquing (e.g. Gould and Lewontin 1979 in biology; O'Brien and Holland 1992 in archaeology). Archaeologists using evolutionary theory today however, have been and are well aware of the trap of adaptationism (e.g. Dunnell 1978; 1995; O'Brien and Holland 1990; 1992) and recognise that neutrality and what the archaeologist Ben Cullen (2000, 100) called "heritage constraint" are powerful factors. The emergence of population genetics has seen the rise of neutral models of evolution (Kimura 1983), which do not at all invoke adaptation, but rather focus on more familiar historical constraints such as contingency, chance, and elements of population structure. It is these neutral microevolutionary models that perhaps present more interesting models for culture change and although they are at present only inadequately explored in this respect (but see Bentley *et al.* 2004; Brantingham 2003; Neiman 1995; Shennan 2000), they certainly find no mention in Shanks and Tilley's tirade.

...on Behaviour

Conveniently, they (Shanks and Tilley 1992, 55, emphasis in original) also call up the spectre of sociobiology:

> Sociobiologists, and for that matter a large number of archaeologists...write of human social *behaviour*....

Sociobiology was a curiously controversial and early form of human behavioural biology, which even in 1992, and certainly today is largely ignored by practicing biologists (Laland and Brown 2002). Due to the highly politicised debate that sociobiology engendered in its time, it still produces a feeling of unease akin to an allergic reaction in many social scientists. Sociobiology itself however, has moved on and spawned a range of other approaches (human behavioural ecology, dual-inheritance theory, and memetics), each of which has developed methods for studying human culture with more or less success (Laland and Brown 2002). Its inadequacy as a framework for archaeology has already been established nearly 20 years ago (Rindos 1985).

> '[B]ehaviour' is the reduction of meaningful practice to physical movement, immediate and commensurable...But we would argue that people do not behave in the sense that animals behave..., they act and the difference between behaviour and practice or action is of fundamental significance (Shanks and Tilley 1992, 55).

It seems puzzling that Shanks and Tilley are so eager to perpetuate the philosophically dubious dualism of behaviour and action, body and mind, nature and culture. The works of Bourdieu and Giddens and their archaeological extensions demonstrate aptly that physical actions do play a significant role in the constitution of human society. Many ethologists would argue very strongly that animals, in particular primates, behave very much like people. The work of Nico Tinbergen and his students (Dawkins *et al.* 1988), landmark publications such as *Machiavellian Intelligence I* and *II* (Byrne and Whiten 1988; 1997) and modern ethological studies on animal traditions (Avital and Jablonka 2000; Fragazy and Perry 2004; McGrew 1992; Reader and Laland 2003) have conclusively demonstrated that the world of primates and other animals is no less socially constructed than that of humans. To claim that there is a categorical difference between human and animal sociality does not do justice to the richness of animal life.

> Humans must be conceived as sentient social beings living in a symbolically structured reality which is, essentially, of their own creation.... To reduce action to behaviour rather than leading to valid explanations in fact directly eschews anything which might be properly termed explanatory (Shanks and Tilley 1992, 55-56).

I have argued that humans are not alone in being "sentient social beings" and that it indeed seems to be an ancestral feature of all hominins (Steele and Shennan 1996), but clearly the statement that humans live in a world of their own creation is significant. Much modern behaviour is purely self-referential in the sense that any one action or artefact would not make sense and would not function without its social or material cultural context. To a lesser degree this holds true for societies in the past, but the further we go into the past the more immediate becomes the relationship of material culture with an unmodified nature. The important point to note is, however, that modern evolutionary models, in particular the 'niche construction' hypothesis, also known as triple-inheritance theory, allows this modification process to be framed in a quantitative manner (Figure 4.1). It must be recognised that any action has both *social as well as ecological consequences* and contributes *on both levels* to the constant re-creation of the human niche: culture. Removing the artificial separation between action and behaviour puts the explanatory onus back onto the data and how it is handled. Neither purely evolutionary (e.g. O'Brien and Lyman 2000) nor purely interpretative (e.g. Dobres 2000; Wobst 2000) approaches to prehistory have yielded many satisfactory or robust explanations of the archaeological record (see Shennan 2002a and Brodie 2001; Killick 2002; Sillar 2002 respectively).

...on Selection

> We are left with the imagery of a plastic, malleable cultural dope incapable of altering the conditions of his or her existence and always subject to the vagaries of external non-social forces beyond mediation or any realistic form of active intervention... (Shanks and Tilley 1992, 56).

No evolutionary process works without a variation-generating mechanism. In cultural evolution this is

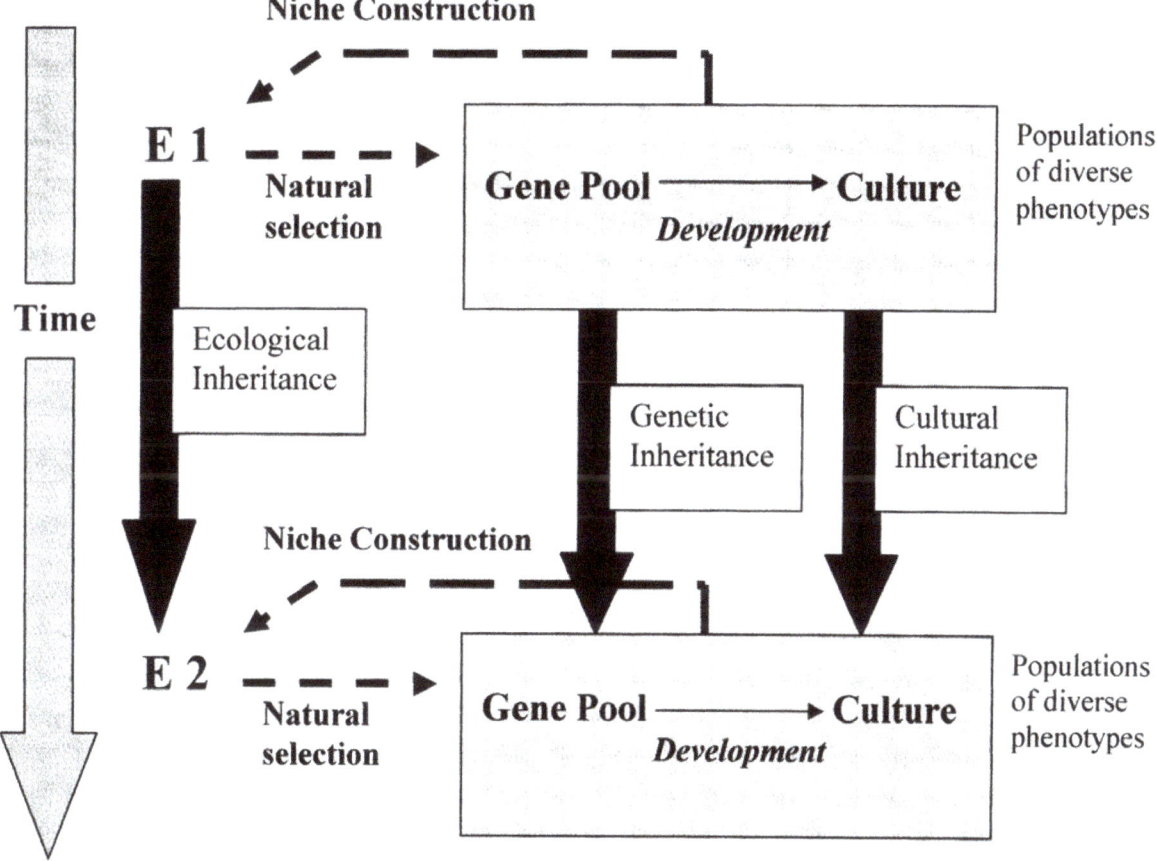

Figure 4.1 Odling-Smee et al.'s (2003) triple-inheritance model. Genetic, cultural and ecological inheritance are explicitly integrated into formal models of culture change. Genetic inheritance is fairly self-explanatory, although it should be noted that even in the biological world many kinds of information transmission within and between organisms take place (Barbieri 2003, Ridley 2004). Cultural inheritance covers such things as knapping skills, knowledge about seasonality, human and animal reproduction, myths and legends, etc. Ecological inheritance is comprised of those culturally modified physical aspects of the environment that are communal and outlast a single generation. Examples would be paths, modified settlement sites, tent structures, infant carriages, fire, hunting stands, artificial clearings and, in later periods, of course, fields, houses, monuments, etc. Modified from Laland et al. (2000, 136). See also www.nicheconstruction.com for further information on this model.

human inventiveness and human error (Eerkens 1998; 2000; Fitzhugh 2001; Mithen 1989; 1998). Human creativity takes on this role and this does in no way diminish its importance (Mithen 1989; 1991; 1998). It is merely recognised that the extent and execution of this creativity is ultimately limited by the constraints of tradition and a variety of other social and non-social factors. Agency theory clearly recognises this and stresses how incomplete information as well as lack of control over consequences condition human actions. The outcome of any one action cannot be tightly controlled precisely because it is partly shaped by *"the vagaries of external...forces"*, which must, of course, include other social beings.

> [A] biological evolutionary perspective, when transferred to the activities of human beings, collapses with the redundancy argument, i.e. that what people spend most of their time doing is completely redundant in terms of conferring any possible selective benefit. The sheer complexities of human social activities go substantially beyond the basic necessities of survival. Palaeolithic cave art is in no way explained by reference to cultural adaptations to climatic change...Human social action is the product of the symbolic praxis of people in and on the world, it is inherently meaningful and 99% of this action has no direct survival value in terms of conveying any definitive selective advantage. The archaeological record is, primarily, a record of style, i.e. ways of acting or accomplishing ends according to varying orientations to the world and with reference to individual and group social strategies and power relationships, which may not be assimilated or reduced to functional or adaptive necessity (Shanks and Tilley 1992, 56).

The foregoing has hopefully revealed this summary dismissal of evolutionary theory for what it is: uninformed and outdated. If neo-Darwinism is applied to material culture in the form of an abstract information theory, it is in the first instance uncoupled from the evolutionary dynamics of the human biological reproductive system. To Shanks and Tilley selective benefit seems to imply survival benefit, which as has been shown, plays only second violin in the evolutionary orchestra. The biological world is extremely complex, at least as complex as the human social sphere and the survival and evolutionary success of any one organism is contingent on a vast number of factors. The (unqualified and unexplained) statement that human social action is "inherently meaningful and 99% of this action has no direct survival value in terms of conveying any definitive selective advantage" might be correct, but has no weight as a criticism against evolutionary theory. Whether an action is meaningful or not, does not make it more or less evolutionarily relevant and, as pointed out repeatedly, selective advantage is no prerequisite for evolution to occur. The archaeological record, from perhaps the Late Palaeolithic onwards, is indeed *primarily* a record of stylistic changes, few of which will have had a measurable selective advantage. Selectively neutral change however, can still be firmly integrated into an evolutionary framework (Dunnell 1978; Neiman 1995; Lipo *et al.* 1997; Lipo 2001; Shennan 2000).

Nevertheless, it remains difficult to demonstrate which aspects of the archaeological record are stylistic and which are adaptive and again, an unqualified dismissal of an adaptive explanation in any given case seems rash. The selective context of most human action and material culture is itself a social one. More than ten years ago, Ben Cullen (1993a; 1993b; 1995; 1996a; 1996b) tried to express this quasi-ecological relationship between people and things with clumsy metaphors and an odd vocabulary. Rhetoric aside however, he was quite right in viewing human action as being partly constrained by the very items used and as viewing these items as wholly dependent on human action for their continued existence. New developments in practice theory as well as in biology have now given us a more suitable vocabulary to address the complex formative relationship of people to their environment (Warnier 2001 and Odling-Smee *et al.* 2003 respectively). In Part 2 I will present a brief case study from the Late Palaeolithic of Southern Scandinavia. Through this case study, I will explore how first human social action can be rendered archaeologically visible and how secondly, we can gain insights into the evolutionary context and consequences of these actions.

Part 2: Social Action in Evolutionary Context

In recent years there has been a gradual convergence with regards to studies of social action and behaviour in anthropology and biology. The importance of learned bodily schemata and the means of arriving at these – teaching, learning and the constraints of the material culture repertoire – are emphasised. In Part 2 of this paper, the dual analytical nexus of Warnier's (2001) notion of 'apprenticeship' and the 'niche construction' approach by Odling-Smee *et al.* (2003) will be used to suggest how social and evolutionary views of human life can be reconciled.

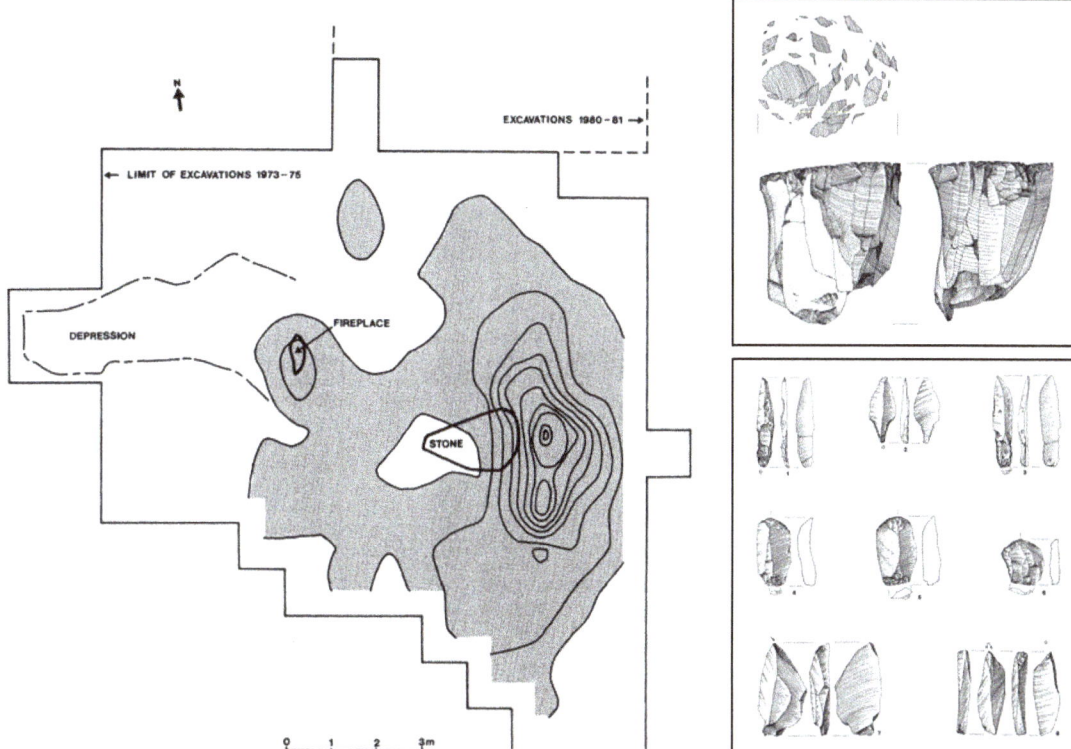

Figure 4.2 The Bromme site of Trollesgave. Here, two of the three lithic scatters are visible (as "isarithms"; see Fischer & Mortensen 1978). The refitted lithic material gives insights into the sensori-motoric conventions of the time and a similar pattern is extrapolated to hold true for the Hamburgian and Ahrensburgian periods (see, for example Hartz 1990 for a supporting study). The spatial distribution of the debitage has revealed a rich teacher-pupil setting (**A**) and the lithic material also includes a near-complete refitted core (**B**) as well as a range of classic Bromme formal tools (**C**). Adapted from Fischer (1989).

Warnier's (2001, 5) "praxeological" view of material culture builds on the prior work of Marcel Mauss, Paul Schilder and the French school of agentive anthropology. Through Leroi-Gourhan (1984 [1964]) this approach has been fruitfully transplanted into archaeology (e.g. Julien and Karlin 1994; Karlin *et al.* 1993; Pelegrin 1994), but, interestingly, in the English literature its application has focused almost exclusively on the psychological and social content of the manufacturing and use process (Schlanger 1994; 1995; Dobres 2000; Wobst 2000). A "praxeological" (Warnier 2001, 5) view of the *chaîne opèratoire* would instead shift the focus of attention to the socially transmitted and culturally specific ways of making and using material objects. It thus introduced, rather more explicitly, a diachronic perspective that reaches across generations. It is this added temporal dimension that allows an articulation with evolutionary models of social information transmission (e.g. Boyd and Richerson 1985; Odling-Smee *et al.* 2003). If situated in the recently proposed model of 'triple-inheritance evolution' the far-reaching importance of social traditions and their outcomes are recognised and both personal as well as communal material culture play important roles. Traditional quantitative models of cultural evolution (Cavalli-Sforza and Feldman 1981; Boyd and Richerson 1985) consider only the parallel tracks of biological and cultural information transmission and are well-suited to the study of change in short-lived personal gear composition and style (e.g. Bettinger and Eerkens 1999). Triple-inheritance theory however, aims to further incorporate the kinds of information and modifications that are communal and thus ecological (see www.nicheconstruction.com). Given that much archaeological data consists of ecological-type information (animal bones, environment, topography, tent structures, houses, fields, etc.), the promise of this approach is immediate. The triple-inheritance model posits that many animals impact so dramatically on their (and other animals') immediate environment, partly through learned behaviour, that these modifications must be taken into account, as ecological inheritance, when looking at organismal evolution (Odling-Smee *et al.* 2003).

The archaeological record constitutes an intricate palimpsest of hierarchically structured social information and action manifest in material culture. By "tacking" (Gamble 1999, 69) between the coarse-grained ('ecological') and the fine-grained ('cultural') we can not only maximise the information content gleaned from our datasets, but we can also hope to arrive at a more complete picture of what happened in the past. Here, I will thus address *i*) lithic reduction sequences, *ii*) caching, and *iii*) settlement patterns. By gradually proceeding from the small to the large scale I will try to demonstrate how we can describe and analyse a wide variety of archaeological evidence in social *as well as* evolutionary terms and how this can yield new insights into bio-social processes in the past.

2.a. Knapping 'Apprentices' at Trollesgave

The Late Palaeolithic site of Trollesgave in eastern Denmark is C-14 and TL-dated to c. 11,600 years BP (K-2641, K-2509; OcTL 601/32, OxTL 601/145, OxTL 601/31; Fischer 1996) and assigned to the Bromme culture based on this date as well as a typological and technological analysis of the flint material. The site has yielded upwards of 25,000 lithics, of which 1069 have been refitted. The raw material is local and the reduction strategy is typically wasteful (Fischer 1989; 1990). Both are characteristic aspects of the Bromme culture, which is dated to the Allerød warm phase. Its distribution is almost exclusively Southern Scandinavian and its formal inventory consists of large tanged points, scrapers and burins as well as a range of less well defined expedient tools (Andersson *et al.* 2004; Fischer 1985; Madsen 1992).

The refitting at Trollesgave has revealed not only distinct activity areas, but it has revealed a "school" (Fischer 1989, 33) of flintknapping: Three discrete knapping scatters cluster around a central fireplace, each characterised by a different level of knapping output, both in terms of quantity as well as quality (Figure 4.2). Furthermore, the richness of this situation is emphasised by the physical elevation of the teacher in comparison to of his/her pupils by sitting on a boulder. Here is not the place to speculate about the particular power relations expressed by this division of space created through the boulder and the secondary fireplace, but it does again emphasise the point that we are dealing with extremely fine-grained minute-by-minute, flake-by-flake human action.

However, we must not lose sight of the fact that these social actions, so wonderfully preserved at Trollesgave have also produced a classic Bromme lithic assemblage. The tuition given by the master knapper was evidently geared towards reproducing the culturally conditioned traditional range of tools, most likely using a set of standardised production methods. These include visible manifestations such as soft/hard-hammer percussion, right/left-handed knapping and uni-/bi-polar core use, but almost certainly also more subtle "motor algorithms" (Warnier 2001, 9) such as particular ways of swinging the hammer stone or of fixing the core. At Trollesgave we can follow how socially transmitted knowledge becomes manifest in material culture, subsequently acting both as an extension of its makers' phenotype (Dawkins 1989),

an external memory storage device (Renfrew and Scarre 1998) as well as an expression of *habitus* (Bourdieu 1977) and the active negotiation of social relations and structure. Through this repeated production and re-production of particular motor algorithms and their material manifestations – the "fossilised production process" (Fisher 1989, 41) – artefact lineages are created, which then can be modelled using evolutionary theory (Figure 4.3; Guglielmino *et al.* 1995; O'Brien and Lyman 2000; 2003a; Shennan 2002b).

Despite many insightful works (e.g. Clarke 1968; Cullen 1993a; Gandert 1950; Robson Brown 1995) workers have previously been dissuaded from phylogenetic analyses of artefact lineages due to the presumed occurrence of reticulation within and between these lineages. Today, however, a number of archaeologists maintain that although reticulation might indeed occur, it is far rarer than previously assumed and that its occurrence must be demonstrated rather than presumed a priori (Bellwood 1996; O'Brien and Lyman 2000; 2003a). Furthermore, evolutionary biologists have come to terms with genetic reticulation, quite common in the plant kingdom, and have devised a battery of techniques able to deal quantitatively with extracting phylogenetic signatures from reticulating lineages (e.g. Brooks and McLennan 1991; Page 2003). Based on production-related attribute analysis, an evolutionary approach to diachronic artefact change is not only more explicit than traditional typological schemes, but can also yield interesting new insights into the pattern and process of culture change (O'Brien, Darwent and Lyman 2001; but see also Shennan 2000).

2.b. Ecological Inheritance in Human Biological and Cultural Evolution

Odling-Smee *et al.* (2003) make 'ecological inheritance' central to their extended evolutionary theory. It is explicitly recognised that organisms through many of their behaviours partly create their own niches. This established an immediate feedback relationship between a given organism and its environment, including other organisms as well as abiotic factors. Of course, 'ecological engineering' (Jones *et al.* 1997) or 'niche construction' (Odling-Smee 1988; Laland *et al.* 1999; 2000; 2001; Odling-Smee 2003) is particularly extensive in the human lineage and can be expected to have played a significant role in shaping hominin ancestral environments. However, it seems that archaeologists of any persuasion have not adequately taken account of this. Indeed, it is perhaps the landscape archaeologists who have come closest to a full appreciation of this, but there still is a large rift between those studying the social transformation of the humanly modified environment (e.g. Ashmore and Knapp 1999; Bradley 2000; Exon 2000; Stoddart 2000; Tilley 1991; 1994) and those who stress the ecologically beneficial or destructive

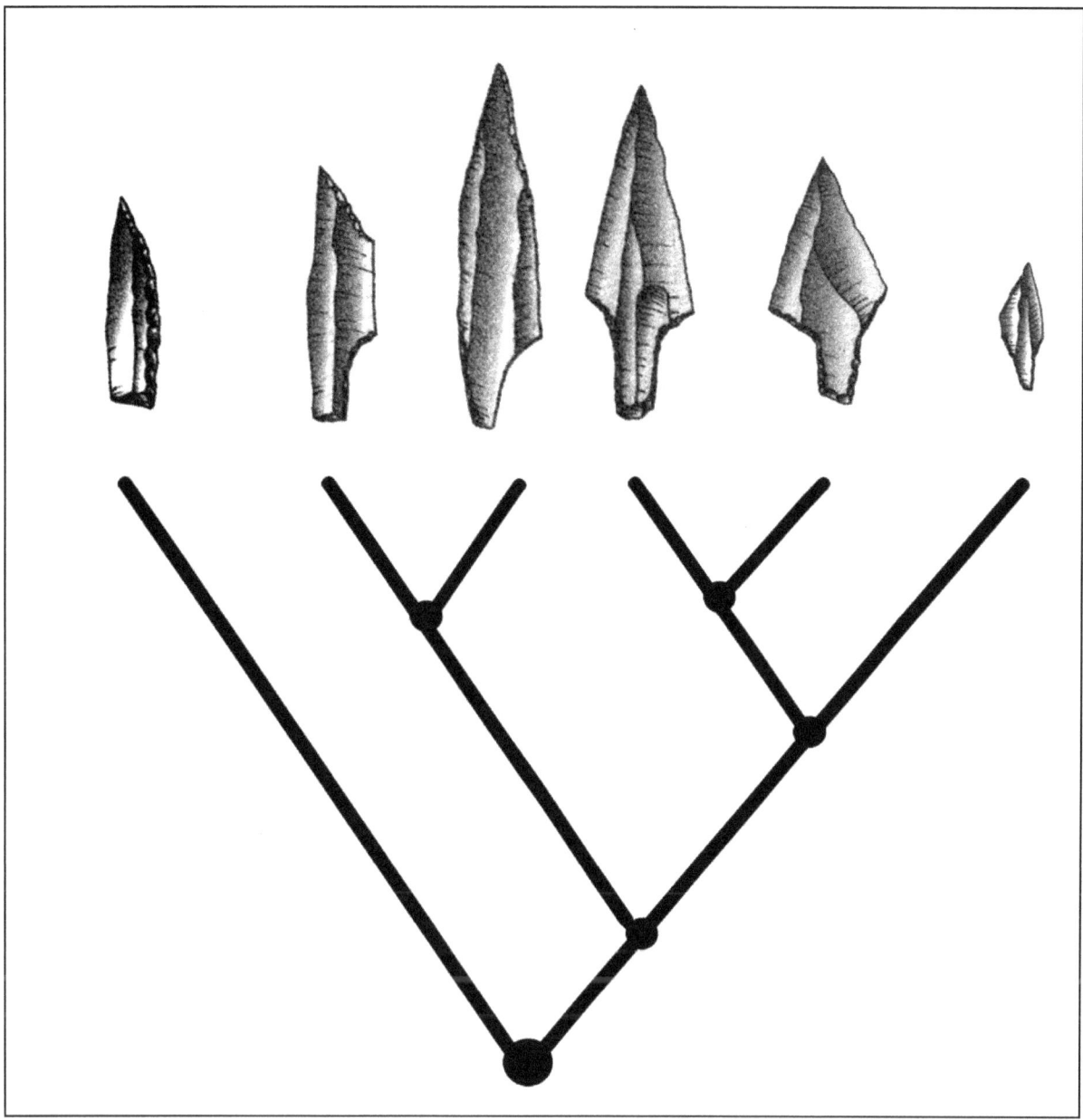

Figure 4.3 A hypothetical phylogenetic rendering of Late Palaeolithic armatures. The cladistic method, recently successfully applied to archaeological and other cultural data (Mace & Pagel 1994; O'Brien & Lyman 2000; 2003a; O'Brien et al. 2002; Tehrani & Collard 2002) creates nested hierarchies of relatedness. A lineage such as the above could be based on a range of quantitative and qualitative attributes used to distinguish lithics (e.g. Fischer 1985). Artefacts redrawn from Andersson & Knarrström (1999).

modification practiced by past human groups (Albarella 2001; French 2003).

Working in the context of the earliest colonisation of the Americas, David Meltzer (2002; 2003) has successfully applied a 'landscape learning' approach. It is an ethnographic truism that hunter-gatherers are experts when it comes to their immediate environment, but in converse this means that in situations of primary explorations and colonisations we must assume nearly the opposite: hunter-gatherer landscape use must have been constrained not only by natural resources and their given configuration, but, crucially, also by peoples' knowledge about these configurations. This corresponds to Ingold's (1986) conceptual division of *resources* (which can be objectively plotted) and *affordances* (that sub-set of the available resources that is actually recognised by people as useful and usable). 'Landscape learning' puts great stress on the central role of information in the process of human landscape appropriation and transformation – and this, of course, brings us back to the evolutionary models of trans-generational information transmission.

Although Kelly (2003) has strong reservations about the archaeological visibility of 'landscape learning' in prehistory, there are several types of evidence that can be marshalled to the case. Primarily, these are (*a*) caching and (*b*) settlement patterns. Whilst caching has been most intensely debated in the context of early hominin evolution (see Potts 1994), it commonly occurs in later periods as well. A combined 'niche construction'/'landscape learning' view would maintain that the significance of caching as both an archaeological indicator of landscape knowledge (or rather, a lack thereof) as well as of active niche construction has been overlooked. Caching can, of course, simply be seen as a safety measure against unforeseen circumstances, but it can also be read as a direct indicator of peoples' willingness to permanently colonise a landscape (i.e. to return to the site at a later point) as well as an active and significant modification of the natural lithic resource distribution of the area. Returning to the case study, the evidence for caching is quite minimal, yet highly revealing. Caches occur at the Hamburgian sites of Teltwisch 1 (Tromnau 1975) and Borneck (Rust 1958) and consist of over 600 pieces of flint each. 99.2% and 99.4% respectively are blades and flakes, which constitute the basis for all other formal tool types in the Hamburgian (Andersson and Knarrström 1999; Andersson *et al.* 2004; Jensen 1999; Madsen 1992). Note that caching in the Hamburgian and the later Ahrensburgian colonisers in Southern Scandinavia is particularly interesting as flint is – particularly to the north of the Ahrensburg Tunnel Valley – extremely abundant and thus might betray the lack of knowledge about these flint resources.

According to the excavator there are no indications that we are dealing with a ritual deposition, but it seems highly likely that this effort was also accompanied with some symbolic activities. Equally, lithic caches are found in the colonising Clovis culture in North America (Bamforth 2002; Kelly and Todd 1988; Meltzer 2002) as well as in other possible colonising contexts such as Mesolithic Ireland (Finlay 2003) and the Canadian Arctic (Fitzhugh 2004). In contrast, in Mesolithic England (Clark 1954) and Germany (Gramsch 1987; 1990) we can see a shift from lithics as the most valuable resource towards organic raw materials in concert with the development of an extremely efficient exploitation of flint during that time.

In terms of settlement pattern the Late Palaeolithic of Southern Scandinavia also presents an interesting picture. Choice of site location was presumably strongly constrained by prey movements and terrain properties (view-shed, shelter from winds, dryness of the ground, mosquito infestation, etc.). People thus clung to the large river valleys (Bratlund 1994; 1996; Petersen and Johansen 1993; 1996). Yet, an interesting recent survey of the Ahrensburg tunnel valley has revealed that the site clustering goes beyond topographic contingencies. Rather restricted areas seem to have been targeted specifically, whilst other, presumably equally suitable, locales were ignored (Bokelmann 1996). This suggests that choice of site location was also dictated by tradition, i.e. a socially transmitted preference for particular ground. Interestingly, this is also commonly observed in many animals (Odling-Smee *et al.* 2003). It is this preference for certain terrain types, enhanced by the socially conditioned choice bias that produced a linear pattern of landscape use and a nested pattern of landscape familiarity (Figure 4.4).

It must be stressed here that the marginality with respect for human settlement of the Late Pleistocene landscape in Southern Scandinavia has probably been consistently underestimated (Mandryk 1993; 2003). Recently deglaciated, the land would have been treacherously wet, seasonally inundated by vast spring floods, dotted with dangerous dead-ice lakes and scoured by vicious winds. Safely moving about in such a landscape would have been strongly constrained by intimate landscape knowledge. While large-scale find distributions give evidence for an increasing familiarity with the landscape (Bratlund 1996), it must also be assumed that such a landscape learning process would have gone hand-in-hand with the naming of significant places (Gustafsson 1998) and their incorporation into stories and legends (Tolan-Smith 2003). In a similar vein, information about seasonality and animal behaviour often becomes externalised in rock art (Barton, Clark and Cohen 1994; Mithen 1988; 1991). If the landscape thus becomes a cultural property it, much like other elements of (material as well as non-material) culture, also takes on an active role in the way that culture is shaped over time (Boyd and Richerson 1985; Durham 1991; Laland *et al.* 1999; 2000; 2001). The approach adopted here does not endeavour to compromise the *meaning* of material culture, but stresses that a parallel evolutionary conceptualisation allows these aspects to be modelled quantitatively and used in the context of specific hypotheses (Riede 2005). It is noteworthy that many archaeologists have previously drawn attention to the way that settlement patterns are not only shaped by environmental parameters, but how they also answer to, and reflect, the need for social information transmission (e.g., Cashdan 1990; Gamble 1986; 1999; Wobst 1974; 1976). In particular, Mandryk (1993) has stressed how cultural success and biological success are contingent on such choice variables as settlement structure and group size, particularly in extreme environments when failure margins are slim. Through the 'niche construction' approach this connection – here between 'genetic' and 'ecological' inheritance, but by implication also to 'cultural' inheritance – becomes more explicit.

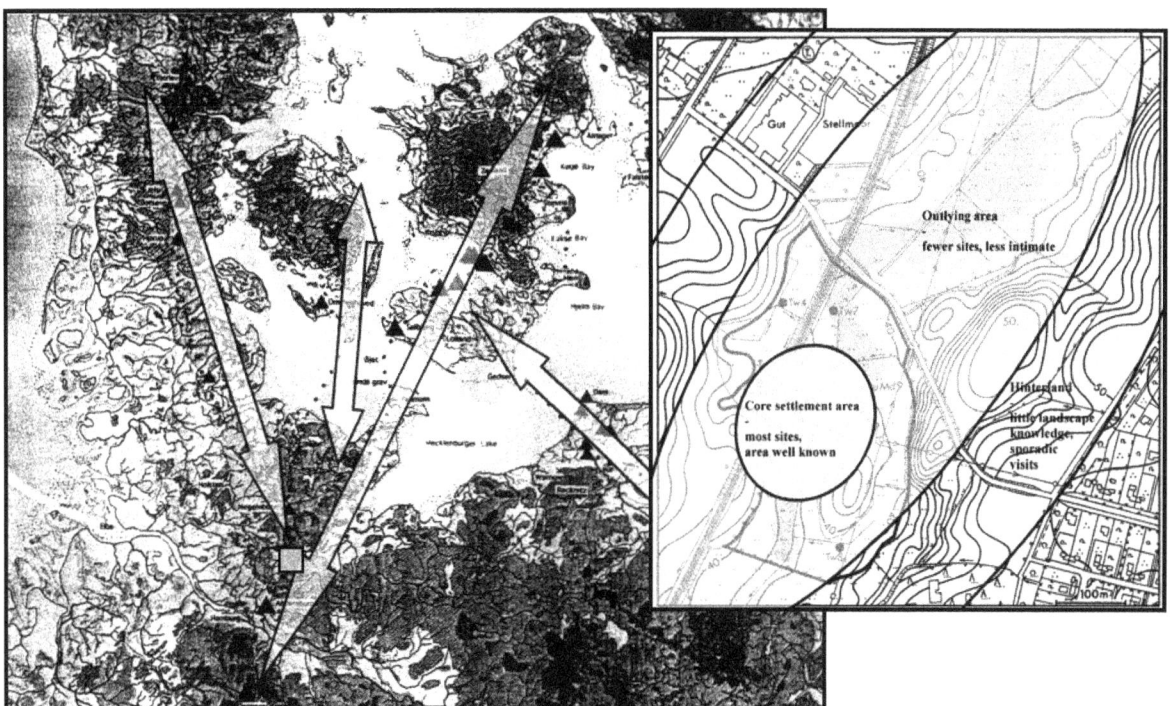

Figure 4.4 The linear settlement pattern of the Hamburgian and Ahrensburgian people consists of a nested set of landscapes, each of which differs in the degree of familiarity. This familiarity is not so exclusively determined by the availability of important resources in a given type of landscape (although it is clearly strongly channelled by these parameters (e.g. Sturdy 1975), but rather by cultural variables such as length of settlement and the degree of engagement with the landscape as well as ancestral cultural behaviour. Note that the nested zones indicated on the map of the Ahrensburg Tunnel Valley on the right are circles stretched lengthwise. They thus correspond well with the stylised circular exploitation zones often used in the palaeoeconomic studies of settled foraging groups (Higgs & Vita-Finzi 1972). Left: modified from Petersen & Johansen (1993, p.27). Right: Modified from Tromnau (1975,15).

Conclusion: The Human Niche Reconsidered

Odling-Smee *et al.* (2003, 380; my emphasis) have put forward...

>...two principal reasons why many human scientists have hitherto found it difficult to use evolutionary theory. One is that standard evolutionary theory appears to have little to offer them. Human scientists are predominantly interested in human behaviour and culture, rather than genes, and as a consequence they have little use for standard evolutionary theory. Our extended evolutionary framework may be more appealing to human scientists because it includes additional roles for phenotypes and *artifacts* in evolution. The other reason why human scientists have difficulty with evolutionary theory is that contemporary adaptationist accounts, as in evolutionary psychology, are frequently simplified to the point of distortion. Adding niche construction makes evolutionary theory more complicated, but for human scientists it may eliminate some of these egregious distortions.

In the last ten years there has been an explosion of literature applying one or another form of Darwinian evolution to human culture, both in archaeology (see Shennan 2002b; O'Brien 1996; O'Brien and Lyman 2003b) as well as in other fields of enquiry (see Laland and Brown 2002). Much like postprocessual archaeology however, this evolutionary archaeology remains rather self-referential and has thus had a limited impact on the general archaeological discussion. Whilst interest in Darwinian models of culture change is gradually increasing in the North American circle, British archaeology remains dominated by other approaches. Although the adoption of Darwinian principles to archaeological material has a long history in European archaeology (Montelius 1903; Årberg 1929; see also Riede 2003), the growth of a specifically British evolutionary archaeology has been retarded by the premature deaths of first David

Across = Period Down = Evidence	Hamburgian (Meiendorf IS), 12,6–12,000 BP	Bromme (Bølling/Allerød), 11,8-11,000 BP	Ahrensburgian (Younger Dryas), 11,-10,000 BP
Lithic Economy	Extremely efficient; light, multi-purpose tools; some important and mostly high-quality raw material	Wasteful; large and chunky tools; local raw material	Efficient; in part very large sturdy blades produced but also small, very slim ones; later, raw material regionalisation
Lithic & Meat Caching	Present	Absent	Present
Settlement System	Linear (South – North across ecological zones, but along similar topography)	Radial (North – South - West – East, within ecological zones)	Linear (South – North across ecological zones, with increasing diversification into other topographies)
Cultural Continuity	▶▶	▶	▶
Time (c. 12,500 – 10,000 BP)	▶		

Table 4.2 A summary table of the cultural processes during the Late Pleistocene in Southern Scandinavia. Time, at the bottom is continuous, but the cultural development is characterised by a real hiatus at the Older Dryas, the cold phase separating the Meiendorf Interstadial from the Bølling/Allerød. In later periods people were able to survive the more severe Younger Dryas due to a number of technological inventions (boats: Ellmers 1980, Clausen 2004; dogs: Baales 1992, Eriksen 1996) and a subsequently increased ability to construct their niche.

Clarke and, later Ben Cullen. Clarke (1968) re-phrased the New Synthesis (Mayr 1991) in archaeological terms but lacked the analytical tools of modern evolutionary biology, whereas Cullen (1993a; 1993b; 1995; 1996a; 1996b; 2000) emphasised the quasi-ecological relationship of human beings with material culture and the constraining as well as enabling aspects of tradition-based material culture.

To reiterate, evolution *per se* is by no means exclusively a phenomenon of the biological world, although it is here where it has been most fruitfully applied. Rather, it is a general property of any *information system*. Clarke (1968) realised this and later formal approaches to cultural evolution (e.g. Boyd and Richerson 1985) have taken this on board wholeheartedly. I hope to have demonstrated above that diachronic information, predominantly but not exclusively transmitted vertically from an older generation to its cultural descendant, is ubiquitous in cultural processes and indeed is strongly visible in the archaeological record. Many post-processual approaches as well as evolutionary theory put emphasis on the complex interplay between pattern and process, structure and action. The outright rejection of evolutionary theory with respect to human culture based on a gross misrepresentation of what constitutes modern evolutionary theory must be seen as unwise. The triple-inheritance model put forward by Odling-Smee *et al.* (2003) provides a basic framework for an integration of traditional archaeological concerns with rigorous quantitative models. Archaeology is in a prime position to investigate the increasing auto-catalytic human niche construction process and the effects of ecological engineering. It is immediately evident that increasingly the human niche itself becomes removed from environmental contingencies and that the success of certain cultural traits becomes a matter of cultural selection (Leonard and Jones 1987). However, the view put forward here, does not perpetuate the antiquated division of human/non-human or natural/cultural with respect to selection. In terms of process the two are identical and indeed it is difficult to even separate 'natural' and 'cultural' aspects of an environment that has been subjected to human modification for several million years.

The Late Palaeolithic of Southern Scandinavia has been selected as a case study because the process of niche construction, framed in terms of landscape learning and presumably going hand-in-hand with the ethnographically demonstrated naming of places, the creation of myths and legends, is strongly visible in the context of the colonisation of pristine environs. A wide range of traditional types of archaeological evidence (lithic reduction strategy, caching, and settlement pattern) have been used to elucidate the multiple facets of information transmission within a cultural system. In contrast to many traditional representations of the cultural development of the Late Palaeolithic societies in Southern Scandinavia, the analysis presented here would suggest that there is a significant cultural and arguably biological gap between the Hamburgian and later settlement in the area. The short-lived Older Dryas put an end to Hamburgian settlement, whilst the later Ahrensburgian culture survived even the more pronounced climatic downturn of the Younger Dryas. The collated evidence in Table 4.2 suggests that the technology and environmental engineering strategies of the Hamburgians were insufficient to deal with the changes wrought by the Older Dryas. The lack of non-pedestrian transport did not allow the linear social networks and the extreme long-distance mobility pattern to be maintained when climate worsened (Riede forthcoming).

While it is only quite recently that niche construction has become a more widely recognised aspect of evolutionary theory (Laland *et al.* 1999; 2000; 2001; Odling-Smee *et al.* 2003), it is recommended here that archaeologists in general, and post-processual archaeologists in particular, take notice of these developments. It answers the call for a "more closely reasoned" (Mandryk 1993, 39) approach that can simultaneously take account of small-scale behavioural traces such as lithic scatters as well as larger-scale signatures such as settlement patterns. Perhaps it is time to take another look at evolutionary theory.

References Cited

Andersson, M. And B. Knarrström 1999. *Senpaleolitikum I Skåne – en studie av materiell kultur och ekonomi hos Sveriges första fångstfolk*. Lund: Riksantikvarieämbetet.

Andersson, M. *et al.* 2004. *Stone Age Scania. Significant Places Dug And Read By Contract Archaeology*. Lund: Riksantikvarieämbetet.

Albarella, U. (ed.) 2001. *Environmental Archaeology: Meaning And Purpose*. London: Kluwer Academic Publishers.

Ashmore W. And A.B. Knapp (eds.) 1999. *Archaeologies Of Landscape*. Oxford: Blackwell.

Aunger, R. (ed.) 2000. *Darwinizing Culture: The Status Of Memetics As A Science*. Oxford: Oxford University Press.

Avital, E. And E. Jablonka 2000. *Animal Traditions. Behavioural Inheritance In Evolution*. Cambridge: Cambridge University Press.

Baales, M. 1992. Überreste Von Hunden Aus Der Ahrensburger Kultur Am Karstein, Nordeifel. *Archäologisches Korrespondenzblatt*, 22, Pp. 461 – 471.

Bamforth, D.B. 2002. High-Tech Foragers? Folsom And Later Paleoindian Technology On The Great Plains. *Journal Of World Prehistory*, 16(1), Pp. 55 – 98.

Barbieri, M. 2003. The *Organic Codes. An Introduction To Semantic Biology*. Cambridge: Cambridge University Press.

Barton, C.M., Clark, G.A. And Cohen, A.E. 1994. Art As Information: Explaining Upper Palaeolithic Art In Western Europe. *World Archaeology*, 26(2), Pp. 185 – 207.

Bentley, R.A. *et al.* 2004. Random Drift And Culture Change. *Proc.Roy.Soc.Lond.B*, 271, Pp. 1443 – 1450.

Bellwood, P. 1996. Phylogeny Vs. Reticulation In Prehistory. *Antiquity*, 70, Pp. 881 – 890.

Bevan, L. And J. Moore (eds.) 2003. *Peopling The Mesolithic In A Northern Environment*. Oxford: Bar (Is) 1157.

Boesch, C. And M. Tomasello 1998. Chimpanzee And Human Cultures. *Current Anthropology*, 39(5), Pp. 591 – 614.

Bokelmann, K. 1996. Ahrensburg, Kr. Stormarn. Baggersondagen Bei Vierbergen Im Ahrensburger Tunneltal. *Offa*, 53, Pp. 372.

Boone, J.L. And E.A. Smith 1998. Is It Evolution Yet? A Critique Of Evolutionary Archaeology. *Current Anthropology*, 39, Pp. S141 – S173.

Boyd, P. And P.J. Richerson 1985. *Culture And The Evolutionary Process*. Chicago: University Of Chicago Press.

Bourdieu, P. 1977. *Outline Of A Theory Of Practice*. Cambridge: Cambridge University Press.

Bowler, P.J. 1986. *Theories Of Human Evolution – A Century Of Debate, 1844 – 1944*. London: The John Hopkins University Press.

Bradley, R. 2000. *An Archaeology Of Natural Places*. London: Routledge.

Bratlund, B. 1994. A Survey Of Survey Of Subsistence And Settlement Pattern Of The Hamburgian Culture In Schleswig Holstein. *Jahrbuch Des Römisch-Germanischen Zentralmuseums Mainz*, 1994, Pp. 59 – 94.

Bratlund, B. 1996. Archaeozoological Comments On The Final Palaeolithic Frontiers In South Scandinavia. *In:* L. Larsson ed. *The Earliest Settlement Of Scandinavia And Its Relationship With Neighbouring Areas*. Acta Archaeologica Lundensia Series In 8°, No.24, Pp. 23 – 34.

Brooks, D.R. And D.A. Mclennan 1991. *Phylogeny, Ecology, And Behaviour: A Research Program In Comparative Biology*. Chicago: University Of Chicago Press.

Brodie, N. 2001. Social Worlds Of Technology. *Cambridge Archaeological Review* 11(1), Pp. 140 – 142.

Byrne, R.W. And A. Whiten (eds.) 1988. *Machiavellian Intelligence – Social Expertise And The Evolution Of Intellect In Monkeys, Apes, And Humans*. Oxford: Clarendon Press.

Cashdan, E. (ed.) 1990. *Risk And Uncertainty In Tribal And Peasant Economics*. Boulder, Colo.: Westview Press.

Cavalli-Sforza, L.L. And M. Feldmann 1981. *Cultural Transmission And Evolution: A Quantitative Approach*. Princeton: Princeton University Press.

Clark, J.G.D. 1954. *Excavations At Star Carr. An Early Mesolithic Site At Seamer Near Scarborough, Yorkshire*. Cambridge: Cambridge University Press.

Clarke, D.L. 1968. *Analytical Archaeology*. London: Methuen And Co.

Cullen, B.S. 1993a. *The Cultural Virus*. Unpublished Ph.D. Thesis, School Of Archaeology, Classics, And Ancient History University Of Sydney.

Cullen, B.S. 1993b. The Darwinian Resurgence And The Cultural Virus Critique. *Cambridge Archaeological Journal* 3(2), Pp. 179 – 202.

Cullen, B.S. 1995. Living Artefact, Personal Ecosystem, Biocultural Schizophrenia: A Novel Synthesis Of Processual And Post-Processual Thinking. *Proceedings Of The Prehistoric Society*, 61, Pp. 371 – 391.

Cullen, B.S. 1996a. Social Interaction And Viral Phenomena. *In:* J. Steele And S. Shennan Eds. *The Archaeology Of Human Ancestry. Power, Sex And Tradition*. London: Routledge.

Cullen, B.S. 1996b. Cultural Virus Theory And The Eusocial Pottery Assemblage, In H.D.G. Maschner ed. *Darwinian Archaeologies*. New York: Plenum.

Cullen, B.S. 2000. *Contagious Ideas. On Evolution, Culture, Archaeology, And Cultural Virus Theory. Edited By J. Steele, R. Cullen And C. Chippendale And Published Posthumously*. Oxford: Oxbow Books.

Cziesla, E. *et al.* (ed.) 1990. *The Big Puzzle: International Symposium On Refitting Stone Artefacts, Monrepos, 1987*. Bonn: Holos.

Davies, W. 2000. The Palaeolithic And Post-Processualism: A Pragmatic Approach?. *Archaeological Review From Cambridge*, 17(1), Pp. 5 – 17.

Dawkins, R. 1989. *The Selfish Gene*. Oxford: Oxford University Press.

Dawkins, R. 1991. *The Blind Watchmaker*. London: Penguin.

Dawkins, R. 1996. Climbing Mount Improbable. London: Penguin.

Dawkins, R. 2004. *The Ancestor's Tale: A Pilgrimage To The Dawn Of Evolution*. London: Weidenfels And Nicolson.

Dawkins, M.S. *et al.* 1988. *The Tinbergen Legacy*. London: Chapman And Hall.

Dennett, D. 1995. *Darwin's Dangerous Idea. Evolution And The Meanings Of Life*. Allen Lane: The Penguin Press.

De Waal, F. 2001. *The Ape And The Sushi Master. Cultural Reflections By A Primatologist*. London: Penguin.

Dobres, M.-A. 2000. *Technology And Social Agency*. Oxford: Blackwell.

Dobres, M.-A. And J. Robb (eds.) 2000. *Agency In Archaeology*. London: Routledge.

Dunnell, R.C. 1978. Style And Function: A Fundamental Dichotomy. *American Antiquity*, 43(2), Pp. 192 – 202.

Dunnell, R.C. 1995. What Is It That Actually Evolves?. *In:* P.A. Teltser ed. *Evolutionary Archaeology: Methodological Issues*. Tucson: The University Of Arizona Press.

Durham, W.H. 1991. *Coevolution: Genes, Culture, And Human Diversity*. Stanford: Stanford University Press.

Ebert, M. (ed.) 1929. *Reallexikon Der Vorgeschichte. Band 13*. Berlin: Verlag Walter De Gruyter And Co.

Eerkens, J. 1998. Reliable And Maintainable Technologies: Artifact Standardization And The Early To Later Mesolithic Transition In Northern England. *Lithic Technology*, 23(1), Pp. 42 – 53.

Eerkens, J. 2000. Practice Makes Within 5% Of Perfect: Visual Perception, Motor Skills, And Memory In Artifact Variation. *Current Anthropology*, 41(4), Pp. 663 – 668.

Ellmers, D. 1980. Ein Fellboot-Fragment Der Ahrensburger Kultur Aus Husum, Schleswig-Holstein?. *Offa*, 37, Pp. 19 – 24.

Eriksen, B.V. 1996. Regional Variation In Late Pleistocene Subsistence Strategies. Southern Scandinavian Reindeer Hunters In A European Context. *In:* L. Larsson ed. *The Earliest Settlement Of Scandinavia And Its Relationship With Neighbouring Areas*. Acta Archaeologica Lundensia Series In 8°, No.24, Pp. 7 – 22.

Eriksen, B.V. And B. Bratlund (eds.) 2002. *Recent Studies In The Final Palaeolithic Of The European Plain*. Højbjerg: Jutland Archaeological Society.

Exon, S. 2000. *Stonehenge Landscapes: Journeys Through Real-And-Imagined Worlds*. Oxford: BAR Publishing.

Finlay, N. 2003. Cache And Carry: Defining Moments In The Later Irish Mesolithic. *In:* L. Bevan And J. Moore Eds. *Peopling The Mesolithic In A Northern Environment*. Oxford: Bar (Is) 1157, Pp. 87 – 94.

Fischer, A. And B.N. Mortensen 1978. Report On The Use Of Computers For Description And Analysis Of Palaeolithic And Mesolithic Occupation Areas. *In:* K. Kristiansen And C. Paludan-Müller Eds. *New Directions In Scandinavian Archaeology*. Copenhagen: National Museum Publication, Pp. 7 – 22.

Fischer, A. 1985. Late Palaeolithic Finds. *In:* K. Kristiansen ed. *Archaeological Formation Processes. The Representativity Of Archaeological Remains From Danish Prehistory*. Copenhagen: Nationalmuseet, Pp. 81 – 88.

Fischer, A. 1989. A Late Palaeolithic "School" Of Flint-Knapping At Trollesgave, Denmark. Results From Refitting. *Acta Archaeologia*, 60:33-49.

Fischer, A. 1990. On Being A Pupil Of A Flintknapper Of 11,000 Years Ago. A Preliminary Analysis Of Settlement Organization And Flint Technology Based On Conjoined Flint Artefacts From The Trollesgave Site. *In:* E. Cziesla *et al.* ed. *The Big Puzzle: International Symposium On Refitting Stone Artefacts, Monrepos, 1987*. Bonn: Holos, Pp. 447 – 464.

Fischer, A. 1996. At The Border Of Human Habitat. The Late Palaeolithic And Early Mesolithic In Scandinavia, In L. Larsson (ed.) *The Earliest Settlement Of Scandinavia And Its Relationship With Neighbouring Areas*. Acta Archaeologica Lundensia Series In 8°, No.24, Pp. 157 – 176.

Fitzhugh, B. 2001. Risk And Invention In Human Technological Evolution. *Journal Of Anthropological Archaeology*, 20, Pp. 125 – 167.

Fitzhugh, B. 2004. Colonizing The Kodiak Archipelago: Trends In Raw Material Use And Lithic Technologies At The Tanginak Spring Site. *Arctic Anthropology*, 41(1), Pp. 14 – 40.

French, C. 2003. *Geoarchaeology In Action. Studies In Soil Micromorphology And Landscape Evolution*. London: Routledge.

Gamble, C. 1986. *The Palaeolithic Settlement Of Europe*. Cambridge: Cambridge University Press.

Gamble, C. 1999. *The Palaeolithic Societies Of Europe*. Cambridge: Cambridge University Press.

Gandert, K.-H. 1950. Typologie Und Typostrophismus. *In:* H. Kirchner ed. *Ur- Und Frühgeschichte Als Historische Wissenschaft. Festschrift Zum 60. Geburtstag Von Ernst Wahle*. Heidelberg: Carl Winter Universitätsverlag.

Giddens, A. 1984. The *Constitution Of Society: Outline Of A Theory Of Structuration*. Berkeley: University Of California Press.

Gould, S.J. 2002. *The Structure Of Evolutionary Theory*. Harvard: Belknapp Press.

Gould, S.J. And R. C. Lewontin 1979. The Spandrels Of San Marco And The Panglossian Paradigm: A Critique Of The Adaptationist Programme. *Proc R Soc Lond B Biol Sci.*, 205(1161), Pp. 581 – 98.

Gramsch, B. 1987. Zwei Mesolithische Knochenspitzen-Depots Von Friesack, Kr. Nauen. *Ethnographisch-ArchäOlogische Zeitschrift*, 28, Pp. 222 – 231.

Gramsch, B. 1990. Die FrüHmesolithischen Knochenspitzen Von Friesack, Kr. Nauen. *VeröFfentlichungen Des Museums FüR Ur- Und FrüHgeschichte Potsdam,* 24, Pp. 7 – 26.

Guglielmino, C.R. *et al.* 1995. Cultural Variation In Africa: Role Of Mechanisms Of Transmission And Adaptation. *Pnas,* 92, Pp. 7585 – 7589.

Gustafsson, P. 1998. The Earliest Stone Age Occupation Of Eastern Middle Sweden. *Current Swedish Archaeology,* 6, Pp. 47 – 62.

Hartz, S. 1990. Artefaktverteilungen Und Ausgewählte Zusammensetzungen Auf Dem Spätglazialen Fundplatz Hasewisch, Kr. Storman, Brd. *In:* E. Cziesla *et al.* ed. *The Big Puzzle: International Symposium On Refitting Stone Artefacts, Monrepos, 1987*. Bonn: Holos.

Higgs, E.S. And C. Vita-Finzi 1972. Prehistoric Economies: A Territorial Approach. *In:* E. S. Higgs And C. Vita-Finzi ed. *Palaeoeconomy*. Cambridge: Cambridge University Press.

Higgs, E.S. (ed.) 1975. *Palaeoeconomy. Papers In Economic Prehistory 2*. Cambridge: Cambridge University Press.

Higgs, E.S. And C. Vita-Finzi (ed.) 1972. *Palaeoeconomy*. Cambridge: Cambridge University Press.

Holm, J. And F. Rieck (eds.) 1992. *Istidsjægere Ved Jelssøerne. Hamburgkultur I Danmark*. Skrifter Fra Museumsrådet For Sønderjyllands Amt 5 (Haderlev).

Hudson, W.H. 1996 [1897]. *An Introduction To The Philosophy Of Herbert Spencer*. London: Routledge.

Hull, D. 1988. *Science As Process. An Evolutionary Account Of The Social And Conceptual Development Of Science*. Chicago: University Of Chicago Press.

Hull, D. 2000. Taking Memetics Seriously: Memetics Will Be What We Make It. *In:* R. Aunger ed. *Darwinizing Culture: The Status Of Memetics As A Science*. Oxford: Oxford University Press.

Ingold, T. 1986. *The Appropriation Of Nature. Essays On Human Ecology And Social Relations*. Manchester: Manchester University Press.

Jensen, J. 1999. *Danmarks Oltid. Stenalder 13.000 – 2.000 F.Kr.* Copenhagen: Gyldendahl.

Jones, C.G. *et al.* Positive And Negative Effects Of Organisms As Physical Ecosystem Engineers. *Ecology* 78, Pp. 1946 – 1957.

Jones, A. (2002). *Archaeological Theory And Scientific Practice*. Cambridge: Cambridge University Press.

Karlin, C. et al. 1993. Some Socio-Economic Aspects Of The Knapping Process Among Groups Of Hunter-Gatherers In The Paris Basin Area. *In:* A. Berthelet And J. Chavaillon Eds. *The Use Of Tools By Human And Non-Human Primates*. Oxford: Blackwell.

Karlin, C. And M. Julien 1994. Prehistoric Technology: A Cognitive Science?, *In:* C. Renfrew And E.B.W. Zubrow Eds. *The Ancient Mind. Elements Of Cognitive Archaeology*. Cambridge: Cambridge University Press.

Kelly, R.L. 2003. Colonization Of New Land By Hunter-Gatherers: Expectations And Implications Based On Ethnographic Data. *In:* M. Rockman And J. Steele Eds. *Colonization Of Unfamiliar Landscapes: The Archaeology Of Adaptation*. London: Routledge, Pp. 44 – 58.

Kelly, R.L. And Todd, L.C. 1988. Coming Into A Country: Early Paleoindian Hunting And Mobility. *American Antiquity,* 53, Pp. 231 – 244.

Killick, D.J. 2002. Reviewing M.-A. Dobres: Technology And Social Agency: Outlining A Practice Theory For Archaeology. *American Anthropologist*, 104(1), Pp. 348 – 350.

Kimura, M. 1983. *The Neutral Theory Of Molecular Evolution*. Cambridge: Cambridge University Press.

Kirchner, H. (ed.) 1950. *Ur- Und Frühgeschichte Als Historische Wissenschaft. Festschrift Zum 60. Geburtstag Von Ernst Wahle*. Heidelberg: Carl Winter Universitätsverlag.

Kohn, M. And S. Mithen 1999. Handaxes: Product Of Sexual Selection? *Antiquity*, 73 (3), Pp. 518 – 526.

Kristiansen, K. And C. Paludan-Müller (eds.) 1978. *New Directions In Scandinavian Archaeology*. Copenhagen: National Museum Publication.

Laland, K.N. et al. 1999. Evolutionary Consequences Of Niche Construction And Their Implications For Ecology. *Pnas*, 96, Pp. 10242 – 10247.

Laland, K.N. et al. 2000. Niche Construction, Biological Evolution, And Cultural Change. *Behavioural And Brain Sciences*, 23, Pp. 131 – 175.

Laland, K.N. et al. 2001. Cultural Niche Construction And Human Evolution. *Journal Of Evolutionary Biology*, 14, Pp. 22 – 33.

Laland, K.N. And G.R. Brown 2002. *Sense And Nonsense. Evolutionary Perspectives On Human Behaviour*. Oxford: Oxford University Press.

Larsson, L. (ed.) 1996. *The Earliest Settlement Of Scandinavia And Its Relationship With Neighbouring Areas*. Acta Archaeologica Lundensia Series In 8°, No.24.

Larsson, L. et al. 2003. *Mesolithic On The Move. Papers Presented At The Sixth International Conference On The Mesolithic In Europe, Stockholm 2000*. Oxford: Oxbow Books.

Leonard R.D. And G.T. Jones 1987. Elements Of An Inclusive Evolutionary Model For Archaeology. *Journal Of Anthropological Archaeology*, 6, Pp. 199 – 219.

Leroi-Gourhan, A.A. 1984 [1964]. Hand Und Wort, Band 1 And 2. [German Translation Of: *Le Geste Et La Parole, Tome 1and2. Technique Et Langue. La Mémoire Et Ses Rythmes*.]. Frankfurt A.M.: Suhrkamp.

Lipo, C.P. et al. 1997. Population Structure, Cultural Transmission, And Frequency Seriation. *Journal Of Anthropological Archaeology* 16, Pp. 301 – 334.

Lipo, C.P. 2001. *Science, Style And The Study Of Community Structure: An Example From The Central Mississippi River Valley*. Bar (Is) 918.

Mace, R. And M. Pagel 1994. The Comparative Method In Anthropology. *Current Anthropology*, 35(5), Pp. 549 – 564.

Madsen, B. 1992. Hamburgkulturens Flintteknologi I Jels (The Hamburgian Flint Technology At Jels). In: J. Holm And F. Rieck Eds. *Istidsjægere Ved Jelssøerne*. Haderlev: Skrifter Fra Museumsrådet For Sønderjyllands Amt 5, Pp. 93 – 132.

Mandryk, C.A.S. 1993. Hunter-Gatherer Social Costs And The Nonviability Of Submarginal Environments. *Journal Of Anthropological Research*, 49, Pp. 39 – 71.

Mandryk, C.A.S. 2003. Foreword. In: M. Rockman And J. Steele Eds. *Colonization Of Unfamiliar Landscapes: The Archaeology Of Adaptation*. London: Routledge, Pp. Xiii – Xv.

Maschner, H.D.G. (ed.) 1996. *Darwinian Archaeologies*. New York: Plenum Press.

Mayr, E. 1991. *One Long Argument. Charles Darwin And The Genesis Of Modern Evolutionary Thought*. London: Penguin.

Mcgrew, W.C. 1992. *Chimpanzee Material Culture*. Cambridge: Cambridge University Press.

Meltzer, D.J. 2002. What Do You Do When No One's Been There Before? Thoughts On The Exploration And Colonization Of New Lands. In: N. Jablonski ed. *The First Americans: The Pleistocene Colonization Of The New World*. Golden Gate Park: University Of California Press, Pp. 27 – 58.

Meltzer, D.J. 2003. Lessons In Landscape Learning. In: M. Rockman And J. Steele Eds. *Colonization Of Unfamiliar Landscapes: The Archaeology Of Adaptation*. London: Routledge, Pp. 222 – 241.

Mesoudi, A. et al. 2004. Perspective: Is Human Cultural Evolution Darwinian? Evidence Reviewed From The Perspective Of *The Origin Of Species*. *Evolution*, 58(1), Pp. 1 – 11.

Mithen, S.J. 1988. Looking And Learning: Upper Palaeolithic Art And Information Gathering. *World Archaeology*, 19(3), Pp. 297 – 327.

Mithen, S.J. 1989. Evolutionary Theory And Post-Processual Archaeology. *Antiquity*, 63, Pp. 483 – 494.

Mithen, S.J. 1990. *Thoughtful Foragers: A Study Of Prehistoric Decision-Making*. Cambridge: Cambridge University Press.

Mithen, S.J. (ed.) 1998. *Creativity In Human Evolution And Prehistory*. London: Routledge.

Mithen, S.J. 1991. Ecological Interpretations Of Palaeolithic Art. *Proceedings Of The Prehistoric Society*, 57(1), Pp. 103 – 114.

Montelius, G.O.A. 1903. *Die Typologische Methode.* Stockholm: Almqvist And Wicksell Int.

Neimann, F.D. 1995. Stylistic Variation In Evolutionary Perspective: Inferences From Decorative Diversity And Inter-Assemblage Distance In Illinois Woodland Ceramic Assemblages. *American Antiquity*, 60(1), Pp. 7 – 36.

O'brien, M.J. (ed.) 1996. *Evolutionary Archaeology: Theory And Application.* Salt Lake City: University Of Utah Press.

O'brien, M.J. And T.D. Holland 1990. Variation, Selection, And The Archaeological Record, In M.B. Schiffer ed. *Archaeological Method And Theory, Vol.2.* Tucson: University Of Arizona Press.

O'brien, M.J. And T.D. Holland 1992. The Role Of Adaptation In Archaeological Explanation. *American Antiquity*, 57(1), Pp. 36 – 59.

O'brien, M.J. And R.L. Lyman 2000. *Applying Evolutionary Archaeology. A Systematic Approach.* New York: Kluwer Academic/ Plenum.

O'brien, M.J. And R.L. Lyman 2003a. *Cladistics And Archaeology.* Salt Lake City: The University Of Utah Press.

O'brien, M.J. And R.L. Lyman (eds.) 2003b. *Style, Function, Transmission. Evolutionary Archaeological Perspectives.* Salt Lake City: The University Of Utah Press.

O'brien, M.J., J. Darwent And R.L. Lyman 2001. Cladistics Is Useful For Reconstructing Archaeological Phylogenies: Paleoindian Points From The Southeastern United States. *Journal Of Archaeological Science*, 28, Pp. 1115 – 1136.

Odling-Smee, F.J. et al. 2003. *Niche Construction. The Neglected Process In Evolution.* Princeton: Princeton University Press.

Page, R.D.M. (ed.) 2003. *Tangled Trees. Phylogeny, Cospeciation, And Coevolution.* Chicago: University Of Chicago Press.

Peel, J.D.Y. (ed.) 1972. *Herbert Spencer On Social Evolution.* Chicago: University Of Chicago Press.

Pelegrin, J. 1993. A Framework For Analysing Prehistoric Stone Tool Manufacture And A Tentative Application To Some Early Stone Industries, In A. Berthlet And J. Chavaillon Eds. *The Use Of Tools By Human And Non-Human Primates.* Oxford: Blackwell.

Perry, S. And D. Fragaszy 2003. (eds.) *The Biology Of Traditions: Models And Evidence.* Cambridge: Cambridge University Press.

Petersen, P.V. And L. Johansen 1993. Sølbjerg I – An Ahrensburgian Site On A Reindeer Migration Route Through Eastern Denmark. *Journal Of Danish Archaeology*, 10, Pp. 20 – 37.

Petersen, P.V. And L. Johansen 1996. Tracking Late Glacial Reindeer Hunters In Eastern Denmark. *In:* L. Larsson ed. *The Earliest Settlement Of Scandinavia And Its Relationship With Neighbouring Areas.* Acta Archaeologica Lundensia Series In 8°, No.24, Pp. 75 – 88.

Potts, R.B. 1994: Variables Versus Models Of Early Pleistocene Hominid Land Use. *Journal Of Human Evolution*, 27, Pp. 7 – 24.

Prentiss, W.C. And Chatters, J.C. 2003. Cultural Diversification And Decimation In The Prehistoric Record. *Current Anthropology*, 44(1), Pp. 33 – 58.

Reader, S.M. And K.N. Laland (eds.) 2003. *Animal Innovation.* Oxford: Oxford University Press.

Renfrew, C. And Scarre, C. (eds.) 1998. *Cognition And Material Culture: The Archaeology Of Symbolic Storage.* Oxford: Mcdonald Institute Monographs.

Rindos, D. 1986. The Genetics Of Cultural Anthropology: Toward A Genetic Model For The Origin Of The Capacity For Culture. *Journal Of Anthropological Archaeology*, 5, Pp. 1 – 38.

Ridley, M. 2004. *Evolution. 3rd Edition.* Oxford: Blackwell Science.

Riede, F. 2003. *Maglemosian Memes – An Evolutionary Archaeological Study Of Northern European Mesolithic Barbed Points.* University Of Cambridge: Unpublished M.Phil. Dissertation.

Riede, F. 2005. 'To Boldly Go Where No (Hu-)Man Has Gone Before': Some Thoughts On The Pioneer Colonisation Of Pristine Landscapes. *Archaeological Review From Cambridge*, 20(1), Pp. 20 – 38.

Robson Brown, K.A. 1995. *A Phylogenetic Systematic Analysis Of Hominid Behaviour.* University Of Cambridge: Unpublished Ph.D. Dissertation.

Rockman, M. And J. Steele (eds.) 2003. *Colonization Of Unfamiliar Landscapes: The Archaeology Of Adaptation.* London: Routledge.

Rust, A. 1958. *Die Jungpaläolithischen Zeltanlagen Von Ahrensburg*. Neumünster: Karl Wachholtz Verlag.

Schiffer, M.B. (ed.) 1990. *Archaeological Method And Theory, Vol.2*. Tucson: University Of Arizona Press.

Schlanger, N. 1994. Mindful Technology: Unleashing The *Chaîne Opèratoire* For An Archaeology Of Mind. *In:* C. Renfrew And E.B.W. Zubrow Eds. *The Ancient Mind. Elements Of Cognitive Archaeology*. Cambridge: Cambridge University Press.

Schlanger, N. 1995. *Flintknapping At The Belvédère: Archaeological, Technological And Psychological Investigations At The Early Palaeolithic Site Of Maastricht-Belvédère (Limburg, The Netherlands)*. University Of Cambridge: Unpublished Ph.D. Dissertation.

Shanks, M. And C. Tilley 1992. *Re-Constructing Archaeology. Theory And Practice. 2nd Edition*. London: Routledge.

Shennan, S. 1989a. Cultural Transmission And Cultural Change. *In:* S. Van Der Leeuw And R. Torrence Eds. *What's New? A Closer Look At The Process Of Innovation*. London: Routledge, Pp. 330 – 346.

Shennan, S. 1989b. Archaeology As Archaeology Or As Anthropology? Clarke's *Analytical Archaeology* And The Binfords' *New Perspectives In Archaeology* 21 Years On. *Antiquity*, 63, Pp. 831 – 835.

Shennan, S. 2000. Population, Culture History, And The Dynamics Of Culture Change. *Current Anthropology*, 41(5), Pp. 811 – 835.

Shennan, S. 2002a. Archaeology Evolving: History, Adaptation, Self-Organisation. *Antiquity*, 76, Pp. 253 – 256.

Shennan, S. 2002b. *Genes, Memes And Human History. Darwinian Archaeology And Cultural Evolution*. London: Thames And Hudson.

Sillar, B. 2002. Reviewing M.-A. Dobres: Technology And Social Agency: Outlining A Practice Theory For Archaeology. *Antiquity*, 76, Pp. 593 – 594.

Sokal, A. And J. Bricmont 1998. *Fashionable Nonsense. Postmodern Intellectuals' Abuse Of Science*. New York: Picador.

Stanley, S.M. 1998. *Macroevolution. Pattern And Process*. Baltimore: The John Hopkins University Press.

Steele, J. And S. Shennan (eds.) 1996. *The Archaeology Of Human Ancestry. Power, Sex And Tradition*. London: Routledge.

Stoddart, S. (ed.) 2000. *Landscapes From Antiquity*. Cambridge: Antiquity Publications.

Sturdy, D.A. 1975. Some Reindeer Economies In Prehistoric Europe. *In:* E.S. Higgs ed. *Palaeoeconomy. Papers In Economic Prehistory 2*. Cambridge: Cambridge University Press.

Tehrani, J. And M. Collard 2002. Investigating Cultural Evolution Through Biological Phylogenetic Analyses Of Turkmen Textiles. *Journal Of Anthropological Archaeology*, 21, Pp. 443 – 463.

Teltser, P.A. (ed.) 1995. *Evolutionary Archaeology: Methodological Issues*. Tucson: The University Of Arizona Press.

Tilley, C. 1991. *Material Culture And Text. The Art Of Ambiguity*. London: Routledge.

Tilley, C. 1994. *A Phenomenology Of Landscape: Places, Paths And Monuments*. Oxford: Berg.

Tolan-Smith, C. The Social Context Of Landscape Learning And The Lateglacial-Early Postglacial Recolonization Of The British Isles. *In:* M. Rockman And J. Steele Eds. *Colonization Of Unfamiliar Landscapes: The Archaeology Of Adaptation*. London: Routledge, Pp. 116 – 129.

Tromnau, G. 1975. *Neue Ausgrabungen Im Ahrensburger Tunneltal. Ein Beitrag Zur Erforschung Des Jungpaläolithikums Im Nordwesteuropäischen Flachland*. Neumünster: Karl Wachholtz Verlag.

Warnier, J.-P. 2001. A Praxeological Approach To Subjectivation In A Material World. *Journal Of Material Culture*, 6(1), Pp. 5 – 25.

Whiten, A. And R.W. Byrne (eds.) 1997. *Machiavellian Intelligence Ii: Extensions And Evaluations*. Cambridge: Cambridge University Press.

Van Der Leeuw, S. And R. Torrence (eds.) 1989. *What's New? A Closer Look At The Process Of Innovation*. London: Routledge.

Whiten, A. *et al.* 1999. Cultures In Chimpanzees. *Nature*, 399, Pp. 682 – 685.

Whiten, A. *et al.* 2001. Charting Cultural Variation In Chimpanzees. *Behaviour*, 138, Pp. 1481 – 1516.

Whiten, A. *et al.* 2003. Cultural Panthropology. *Evolutionary Anthropology*, 12(2), Pp. 92 – 105.

Wobst, H.M. 1974. Boundary Conditions For Paleolithic Social Systems: A Simulation Approach. *American Antiquity*, 39, Pp. 147 – 178.

Wobst, H.M. 1976. Locational Relationships In Paleolithic Society. *Journal Of Human Evolution*, 5, Pp. 49 – 58.

Wobst, M. 2000. Agency In (Spite Of) Material Culture. In: M.-A. Dobres And J. Robb ed. *Agency In Archaeology*. London: Routledge, Pp. 40 – 50.

Åberg, N. 1929. Typologie. *In:* M. Ebert ed. *Reallexikon Der Vorgeschichte. Band 13.* Berlin: Verlag Walter De Gruyter And Co.

Åkerlund, A. 2002. Life Without Close Neighbours. Some Reflections On The First Peopling Of East Central Sweden. *In:* B.V. Eriksen And B. Bratlund Eds. *Recent Studies In The Final Palaeolithic Of The European Plain.* Højbjerg: Jutland Archaeological Society, Pp. 43 – 48.

Åkerlund, A. *et al.* 2003. Peopling A Forgotten Landscape. *In*: L. Larsson ed. *Mesolithic On The Move*. Oxford: Oxbow Books, Pp. Xxxiii – Xliv.

Online Resources

Http://Biologybk.St-And.Ac.Uk/Cultures3/
-Last Consulted 03/05/2005
Http://Www.Nicheconstruction.Com
- Last Consulted 03/05/2005

WE'RE NOT WAITING ANY MORE…
OR
HUNTING FOR MEANING IN THE MESOLITHIC OF NORTH-WEST EUROPE

Hannah Cobb and Steven Price

Archaeology
School of Arts, Histories and Cultures
University of Manchester

Abstract

In recent years the landscape of Mesolithic studies has changed dramatically and studies of the period are now taking on a much greater interpretive theoretical stance. As a result the notion of an increasing social and ideological sophistication in the Neolithic contrasted to the paucity of such complexity and elaboration in the preceding Mesolithic is rapidly beginning to be eroded. Where only recently it was thought that the nature of the material record in the Mesolithic sentenced it to purely functional and economic approaches, explicitly interpretive approaches have begun to convincingly demonstrate how material culture played a central role in the creation of meaningful Mesolithic world views. Although in their infancy, these interpretive approaches to the Mesolithic have developed their own clear identity. They have not simply adapted Neolithic approaches to the study of hunter-gatherers but have sought to explore Mesolithic world views in their own right. This paper will bring together and discuss the growing body of such approaches toward the Mesolithic that explicitly take this stance. It will explore the new methodologies and theoretical stances that demonstrate how hunter-gatherer worldviews were actively and meaningfully created, in order to illustrate the multitude of new directions that these offer Mesolithic studies.

Introduction

> …for the past twenty years Mesolithic studies have been in a similar position: always threatening to step off the well-trodden path, but with no-one willing to make the great leap. At the same time, however,…signs of change are emerging (Young 2000a, 1).

Five years ago, Robert Young began a collection of papers entitled *Mesolithic Lifeways: Current research from Britain and Ireland* with a chapter entitled *Waiting for the great leap forwards* (Young 2000a). The above quote is taken from the first paragraph of this article, and the title of our chapter directly refers to Young's own introductory chapter title. We've chosen to begin with this quote because in only five years, since the publication of Young's volume, it is clear that what were emerging "signs of change" (*Ibid.*, 1) are already blossoming into radical new interpretations of the Mesolithic.

It was in the form of several conferences and publications in 2000 where the foundations of this movement were laid. Young's was of course one of these, and another, perhaps even more significant publication was Volume 17 (1) of the Archaeological Review from Cambridge. This collection of papers truly grasped the nettle and took the great leap to which Young referred (Young 2000a, 1), exploring a number of both Palaeolithic and Mesolithic sites and ideas through often explicitly interpretive theoretical perspectives. Similarly, the 6th International Conference on the Mesolithic in Europe, held in Stockholm in 2000, also provided a forum for more great leaps in the form of exciting and innovative ideas in papers by authors such as Cummings (2003), Finlay (2003a; 2003b) and Strassburg (2003). With such papers laying the foundations and taking those great leaps, there are now a number of academics who are not only in more senior positions (e.g Conneller, Finlay, Warren), but also include a number of today's Mesolithic doctoral students (e.g. Cobb, Kador, Little, Price), who are using a variety of clear and concerted interpretive perspectives in their research.

Taking the plunge, grasping the nettle, leaping forward

In his article, Young discussed the various areas into which Mesolithic studies are often subdivided, drawing on previous similar collections to illustrate that the predominant categories for study have been functional and ecological (Young 2000a, 2). Critically, Young explicitly acknowledged that "…our knowledge of Mesolithic social life … remains weak" (*Ibid.*), before examining how this is beginning to be rectified. For Young it was through an investigation of Mesolithic sites within their wider landscape contexts and through analysis of the impact Mesolithic peoples had upon their environment that such rectification could take place (*Ibid.*, 3-5). Yet through this discussion it is clear that such approaches alone could never provide the great leap required to move away from the well trodden path of Mesolithic studies.

It is clear that explicitly interpretive perspectives are required, perspectives that do not divorce the "social" from the "functional" and the "ecological" categories to which many studies still continuously adhere (i.e. Bonsall 1997; Price 2000; Saville 2004). Indeed, it is through the recognition that the category of "social" is simply untenable as an individual unit of analysis that new approaches have begun to move beyond traditional approaches to Mesolithic studies. Such approaches have explicitly recognised that what is social is clearly infused within all aspects of life, with Mesolithic understandings of material culture, environment and landscape all inseparable and ultimately deeply entwined with the creation and negotiation of personal identity. From such a recognition it remains only a short step to then examine the Mesolithic material record from an entirely different perspective.

By turning to different types of ethnographic analogy, a number of writers have suggested that Mesolithic identity and experience of the world may have differed fundamentally from how we experience it in the modern West. Accounts such as Marilyn Strathern's ethnography of the Hagen of the Western Highlands of Papa New Guinea have been instrumental in shaping such accounts. Both Finlay and Fowler have drawn on such ethnographies to provide diverse accounts of the formation of Mesolithic identity. Fowler (2004), for example, has studied the material record of the later Mesolithic of Scandinavia in relation to personhood in order to demonstrate alternative approaches to Mesolithic studies. He has argued that personhood is not limited to humans but can be held by animals and objects and that by considering these aspects we can go beyond models of cultural determinism or bounded individualists. Finlay (2003a) has made a similar point but in relation specifically to the social role of microlith production and use. Here she has suggested that the composite nature of tools comprised of microliths indicates that they may have been more than simply tools as understood in the modern West, but as both creating and being part of the active negotiation of social identities.

Hunting for Meaning

The papers in this section then, are critical parts of such new interpretive approaches to the Mesolithic. Indeed they were first presented within a session at the 2004 Theoretical Archaeological Conference. Yet the motivation for such a session and such papers originated from the recognition that although, as this paper has stressed, there is a growing interpretive movement in Mesolithic studies, such theoretical perspectives continue to be under-represented. Interpretive approaches, which have been established in studies of later chronological periods, are still more often than not, the minority in Mesolithic studies. Consequently it was the intention of the session to bring the Mesolithic into the wider theoretical discourse and highlight it as an area requiring greater recognition among the theoretical community. The papers in this section represent just some of those from the TAG conference, and forthcoming articles by participants that are not published here also further seek to highlight the issues raised in the session (Conneller Forthcoming, Davies 2005). All participants sought to critically examine not only how interpretive approaches are beneficial to examining the experience of the past, but all presented different research programmes which suggest different ways of going about this. Consequently we have tried to capture such innovative ideas and variety within the papers published in this section.

As such, Hannah Cobb argues that our preconceptions concerning how the Mesolithic should be understood, and our modern Western values need to be explicitly addressed, rather than simply unthinkingly applied to the past as universal truths. Steven Price argues that through examining the ways in which trees were used we can begin to see how people experienced their world and created diverse identities from interacting with it. Aimee Little addresses social aspects of hunter-gatherer inhabitation of the internal network of water systems in the northern Midlands of Ireland, from an ideological and cosmological perspective, examining hunter-gatherers as active agents in the transformation of space.

What the session, and this resulting publication, has demonstrated is that now, more than ever before, there is ample evidence that people in the Mesolithic were not mindless economic automatons but complex persons, interacting with each other and the world in meaningful ways. Places were attributed meanings over and above simple notions of economy and subsistence. Places became important through their association with meaningful things and meaningful people. Different people brought different ideas and experiences to different locales, and the memories of such differences and similarities were reinforced through action and deposition.

It is clear then, that Mesolithic studies are no longer waiting for the great theoretical leap forward. Through interpretive perspectives we have finally been able to move from the bounded path of traditional hunter-gatherer studies, towards new and exciting perspectives. In turn these are providing endless possibilities for understanding prehistoric hunter-gatherer communities and hunting for meaning in the Mesolithic of North-West Europe.

References Cited

Bonsall, C. 1997. Coastal Adaptation in the Mesolithic of Argyll. Rethinking the 'Obanian Problem'. *The Archaeology of Argyll.* G. Ritchie. Edinburgh, Edinburgh University Press: 25-37.

Conneller, C. (ed.) 2000 New Approaches to the Palaeolithic and Mesolithic. *Archaeological Review from Cambridge* 17:1

Conneller, C., in press. Mortuary practices. In Chantal Conneller and Graeme Warren (eds.) *The Mesolithic of Britain and Ireland.* Stroud: Tempus.

Cummings, V. 2003. The Origins of Monumentality? Mesolithic World-Views of the Landscape in Western Britain. In L. Larsson, H. Kindgren, K. Knutsson, D. Loeffler and A. Åkerlund (eds.) *Mesolithic on the Move: Papers presented at the Sixth international Conference on the Mesolithic in Europe, Stockholm 2000.* Oxbow Books, Oxford. pp 74-81

Davies, P., Robb, J.G. and Ladbrook, D. 2005. Woodland clearance in the Mesolithic: the social aspects. Antiquity Vol 79.

Finlay, N. 2003a Microliths and Multiple Authorship. In L. Larsson, H. Kindgren, K. Knutsson, D. Loeffler and A. Åkerlund (eds.) *Mesolithic on the Move: Papers presented at the Sixth international Conference on the Mesolithic in Europe, Stockholm 2000.* Oxbow Books, Oxford. pp 169-176

Finlay, N. 2003b Cache and Carry: Defining Moments in the Irish Later Mesolithic. In L. Bevan and J. Moore (eds.) *Peopling the Mesolithic in a Northern Environment.* BAR International Series 1157. BAR Publishing, Oxford. pp 87-94

Fowler, C. 2004. *The Archaeology of Personhood: An anthropological approach.* Routledge, London.

Price, T. D. 2000. The Introduction of Farming in Northern Europe. In T. D. Price (ed.) *Europe's First Farmers* Cambridge University Press: Cambridge pp 260-300

Saville, A. 2004. Introducing Mesolithic Scotland: The Background to a Developing Field of Study. In A. Saville (ed.) *Mesolithic Scotland and its Neighbours: The early Holocene Prehistory of Scotland, its British and Irish Context and some Northern European Perspectives.* Society of Antiquaries of Scotland: Edinburgh. pp 3-24

Strassburg, J. 2003. Rituals at the Meso 2000 Conference and the Mesolithic-Neolithic Terminological Breakdown. In L. Larsson, H. Kindgren, K. Knutsson, D. Loeffler and A. Åkerlund (eds.) *Mesolithic on the Move: Papers presented at the Sixth international Conference on the Mesolithic in Europe, Stockholm 2000.* Oxbow Books, Oxford. pp 542-546.

Warren, G., M. 2000. Seascapes: people, boats and inhabiting the later Mesolithic in western Scotland. In R. Young (ed.) *Mesolithic Lifeways: Current Research from Britain and Ireland.* Leicester Archaeology Monographs 7. University of Leicester, Leicester. pp 97-104.

Young, R. 2000a. Waiting for the Great Leap Forwards: Some Current Trends in Mesolithic Research. In R. Young (ed.) *Mesolithic Lifeways: Current Research from Britain and Ireland.* Leicester Archaeology Monographs 7. University of Leicester, Leicester. pp 1-12.

Young, R. (ed) 2000b. *Mesolithic Lifeways: Current Research from Britain and Ireland.* 1st ed. University of Leicester, Leicester.

MIDDEN, MEANING, PERSON, PLACE: INTERPRETING THE MESOLITHIC OF WESTERN SCOTLAND

Hannah Cobb

University of Manchester

Abstract

Of the British Mesolithic, perhaps one of the most prolifically and intensively studied areas over the last century has been the West of Scotland. These studies were characterised by typological debates in the earlier twentieth century, and in recent decades work on the area has become increasingly concerned with issues of economy and subsistence. Where such studies have considered people within these accounts it has been mostly their relation to their environment in an adaptive and economic sense that has remained a central concern, and very little attention has been afforded to the people who populated the region during the period outside of such Processual concerns. However, current research is beginning to illustrate the existence of meaningful ideological connections far beyond the previous economic and subsistence based interpretations that have ever been offered before. Consequently, this paper argues that by turning to alternative ethnographic accounts and examining aspects of personal identity a radical new interpretation of the Mesolithic experience of the world in Western Scotland is now possible.

Introduction

Midden, meaning, person and place; such concepts placed together appear relatively ethereal, abstract, and particularly out of place within a discussion of the Mesolithic of Western Scotland. Indeed, whilst the shell middens of the area have been covered extensively by research over the last century, the ephemeral nature of the archaeological record has frequently been cited as a critical factor that has restricted interpretations of meanings, places and personal identity in the Mesolithic period (Cummings 2003). It is the intention of this paper, however, to challenge this perspective. There is a growing body of work which has already begun to engage with such challenges, however this paper will both draw upon such earlier approaches and combine them with insights from an explicitly interpretive current research programme in order to address these various seemingly abstract ideas, and demonstrate how they can and should play a critical role in interpretations of the Mesolithic of Western Scotland.

In reassessing and reanalysing the data from the area, it is important to be clear that this paper does not represent an attack on prior, more processual based approaches. Indeed it will explicitly draw on the data from a lot of these earlier studies. Instead the intention of this paper is to take such data and to challenge the normative modern Western categories through which it has traditionally been constructed and analysed. It will explore alternatives to such, often dualistic, modern notions such as land and sea, and male and female, as well as ideas of the experience and interaction with the environment. The central intention of such a format is to make this paper more than programmatic. By doing more than just suggesting areas that need to receive interpretive treatment, and instead highlighting where interpretive approaches are leading such studies, it is the aim of this paper to open a dialogue which will identify not only areas that are still being overlooked, but areas that would benefit from being explored in different directions and by different theoretical stances. Ultimately then, it is the intention of this paper to suggest that without engaging in such a dialogue we might really be limiting ourselves and the potential for exploring new perspectives of this clearly exciting area.

Seeing People in Mesolithic Western Scotland

A pertinent place to begin is with a quote that comes from the most recent published volume about Mesolithic Scotland, *Mesolithic Scotland and its Neighbours* (Saville 2004a). The volume is edited by Saville, and his introductory paper, *Introducing Mesolithic Scotland*, does just that, illustrating the debates and themes that have driven and shaped research into the Scottish Mesolithic. Saville brings the main body of this introduction to a conclusion by saying that,

> Workers from many disciplines have begun to focus on the Early Holocene to achieve an understanding of the processes behind the formation of the environments and habitats in Scotland today. Mesolithic studies, by elucidating the anthropogenic factors involved, have a major role to play in this aspect of Quaternary investigation

and their future looks sound (Saville, 2004b: 17).

It may seem unusual to begin with a quote, which is, in essence, an ending. However this quote seems the most significant place to begin this paper because it is very much illustrative of the kind of research agendas that *are* dominating Mesolithic studies in Western Scotland at present. Indeed, this quote illustrates several essential points, which it is important to make and to be explicit about from the outset. Critically, whilst this section is entitled "seeing people", it is not the intention of this paper, nor any credible interpretive approach, to simply "put the people back in" to interpretations of the past. Indeed as this quote (and in fact a large part of the volume from which it is taken) demonstrates, the people are already firmly there. But what I want to take to task first in this paper is how people appear, and how they are discussed within these accounts. As such the above quote is a good place to begin, illustrating as it does that these perspectives perpetuate the notion of people in the Mesolithic as simply "anthropogenic factors" in wider systems.

Such a perspective is symptomatic of the underlying theoretical emphasis of accounts such as Saville's and those previous accounts, which his paper outlines. Most of these accounts seek explicitly to address the Mesolithic of Western Scotland from objective, empirical and positivist theoretical and methodological positions. Frequently they stress the ephemeral nature of the record and subsequently use this as justification of a reliance on data that can be quantitatively or empirically assessed in order to make interpretations of the past only from a rigorously objective position (e.g. Bonsall 1996, Saville 2004b, Wickham-Jones 2004). Yet, like many interpretive approaches that have been written over the past twenty years, this paper contends that such objectivity can never truly exist and therefore can never be achieved. All knowledge and meaning is situated within our own life experience, and as such can never be free of subjectivity. Consequently, no matter how rigorously objective the methodology, the categories into which data are classified and understood undermine such objectivity. They do so not only by relying on modern Western frameworks of reference to make such categories pertinent but by using only these frameworks to define such categories in the first place.

Consequently this kind of false objectification, which reduces people and their lived experience of Mesolithic Western Scotland to "anthropogenic factors", can be nothing but reductionist. Furthermore the experience of nature, the environment, and the interaction with sites and material culture are automatically sanitised by such reductionist epistemology. So whilst huge bodies of data exist regarding these aspects, there are clearly limitations in regarding the interaction between people and animals, or people and their environment in such functional terms,

and understanding humans as simply "anthropogenic factors" in wider systems. Indeed a number of people are now coming to stress that such perspectives really only serve to detract from the nature in which people experienced the world around them in the Mesolithic, and how they understood that world (c.f. Conneler 2001, Cummings 2003, Finlay 2003, Pollard, J., 2000, Pollard, T., 1996, Warren 1997, and all papers in this volume).

Experiencing places in the Mesolithic of Western Scotland

Shell middens provide a particularly good example of such reductionism. Indeed shell middens comprise many of the major Mesolithic sites in the area and a number have been excavated. Because of their high shell content, such sites offer superb levels of preservation of faunal materials and as such the last few decades have seen shell middens play a pivotal role in discussions of hunter-gatherer subsistence practices in Western Scotland. The animal bone assemblages in the middens have been used to suggest that primarily they represented a locale for not only intensive shellfish collection, but also sites for the primary butchering and processing of fish and sea mammals (Grigson and Mellars 1987). Whereas the distribution of skeletal parts of land mammals in the middens suggests that these may have largely been processed away from the middens, at the kill site, and only entered the midden context in a secondary sense because parts were brought to these sites for the working of bone tools and skins (*Ibid.*). Whilst it is not the intention of this paper to criticise what is the most likely functional explanation of the faunal remains in the middens, I do however, want to suggest that there are a number of aspects of this explanation that interpretive perspectives can take further.

Firstly, and critically, such an explanation for the nature of the faunal remains in the Oronsay middens is very much part of the same false objectification and sanitisation as an approach which regards people simply as anthropogenic factors. This explanation reduces the activities of hunting, fishing and gathering to a sterile, simple activity. The sheer experience of hunting, of butchery, of travelling by boat between islands, of working the skins and bones of dead animals, of gathering shell fish from the sea shore, of catching sea birds, of fishing, of collecting wood, of lighting a fire, of being hungry, of cooking and eating food, are all subsumed under terms such as "subsistence practices". Consequently these accounts paint the middens in such a sterile light that they could simply be perceived, as they were in 19th century Southern Scandinavia, like a kitchen; simply a locale for the processing of skins, fats, and meats for the next meal. In another respect they are portrayed very much like a modern workshop or utility area; an area in which tools, skins and bait for further expeditions were prepared. Mellars account suggests that at least one of the Oronsay middens was regularly

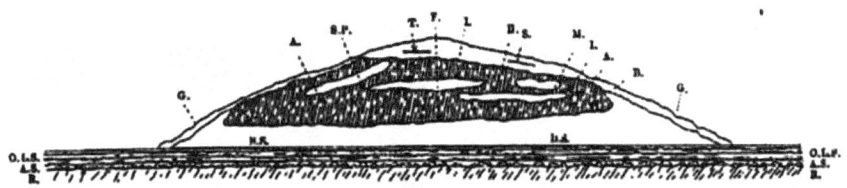

Figure 6.1: The much-reproduced, sanitised image of the shell midden of Caisteal nan Gillean I (After Mellars 1987: 119. Original Source Greive 1923: Figure 9)

levelled on top (Mellars 1987: 210), and this further encourages a sterile image, akin to wiping down the kitchen surface or sweeping the workroom floor at the end of the day. Frequently reproduced illustrations, such as those by Greive (Figure 6.1), serve only to compound such perspectives. Moreover these accounts have drawn on a number of ethnographies, such as Meehan's *Shell bed to shell midden*, which provide just as sanitised ethnoarchaeological accounts of site formation, and calorific values of shell fish as possible, to confirm this kind of functional, utilitarian perspective of the middens (e.g. Bonsall 1996, 1997).

Yet the reality of shell midden sites is far removed from such a sterile, and objective image. The smells of rotting fish, shellfish and animals, something we have all experienced, would have dominated shell midden sites. Similarly evidence from the analysis of shellfish size from a number of the middens, such as Ulva cave (Bonsall 1992: 12), suggests that quantities of seaweed were being brought into the middens too, and the smell of this rotting material would also have produced a powerful aroma. Equally a number of middens in Western Scotland have also yielded quantities of human bones, predominantly phalanges, and fragments of skull and vertebrae (Connock 1985, Connock et al 1992, Meikeljohn and Denston 1987). Such patterns of skeletal deposition suggest that human bodies were laid out on shell middens for excarnation and that the major bones were then removed from the middens (Cummings 2003, Pollard, J., 2000, Pollard, T., 1996). So in reality this amounts not to middens as Mesolithic equivalents of sanitised workshops, or even the still, and serene mounds that they are today, but as active growing and changing accumulations of the remains of animals, plant matter, fish, shell fish, and human occupation which would have been both a memorable experience of a specific place, and an experience that really aroused the senses. Moreover, depending on the activities taking place at these sites at any one time, and the prevailing wind direction, the sensual experience of such sites could well have been quite overwhelming.

Indeed it would not only have been the sense of smell that was aroused. Numerous pictures and illustrations, for example, demonstrate the powerful visual experience of the shell midden site of Caisteal nan Gillean I by illustrating both its imposing size and the way in which it appears very much framed by the island of Jura, and two of the highest peaks on the island, the Paps of Jura (e.g. Figure 6.2). Indeed such a visual experience would only have been enhanced in the past by a lack of blown sand and grasses, leaving the shells clear and visible against the surrounding land, sea and sky. Grieve's account of the middens, following these very early excavations sums up the visual impact of these sites only 100 years ago,

> The excavations at Caisteal-nan-Gillean have revealed that it is a place on which some of the ancient fisher folk of Oronsay dwelt, and they probably chose it as a place of residence because possessing two great advantages – namely, a dry soil and an extensive prospect seaward … in short, from Caisteal-nan-Gillean its inhabitants could watch for friend or foe, for food or storm (Grieve 1885: 59).

Clearly, as Grieve's account attests, the visual trends from a lot of these sites have certainly been noted much earlier than now. Indeed, several recent works have also explored the implications of such visuality upon the experience and understandings of the sites, drawing on the work of Barton *et al.* (1995) in discussing the middens as "persistent places" within the Mesolithic landscape (Cummings 2003, Pollard, J., 2000, Pollard, T., 1996). Such work has provided a number of clear arguments that, not only were notions of place in the Mesolithic particularly complex, but that this complexity has been underestimated, and is clearly embodied in shell middens (*Ibid.*). Recent research, however, has sought to take such theoretical perspectives further. By compiling Quick Time Virtual Reality panoramas, and *in situ* observations from a number of Mesolithic sites in the West of Scotland, such research has not only confirmed, but significantly contributed toward such discussions. It has shown that there is a real, observable and enduring trend for shell midden sites to visually reference major topographical features both on the same and on other islands (Cobb 2004: 150). It has also demonstrated that such visual references are also often associated with maritime navigation, raw materials, resources and areas where other contemporary, or slightly earlier sites were located (Cobb 2004).

Figure 6.2: Caisteal nan Gillean I in 1881, prior to excavation (After Mellars 1987: 171. Original source Grieve 1923: Figure 3)

I would like to suggest then, that if we think about the memories and experiences that these sites would have encompassed, as locales that were reused over hundreds, and in some cases thousands, of years, and then we think back to the typical way these sites are usually discussed, as part of a simple and mindless pattern of subsistence, it seems bizarre and utterly unrealistic to suggest they were such neat, sanitized, meaningless sites. Indeed with this in mind it seems even more unrealistic to suggest that meaning was not manifest and mediated through the use of space and material culture. Whilst some debate has already begun (for example Cummings 2003, Pollard, J., 2000, Pollard, T., 1996), it is clear that we need to further explicitly examine the roles of shell middens as significant places which both created and encompassed meanings about people and their relation to people in the past, present and future, as well as the wider world around them and their methods of understanding and interacting with that wider world. Consequently I will return to further address this subject towards the end of this paper.

Material Culture and Meanings in Mesolithic Western Scotland

Whilst landscape and place represent areas of growing theoretical concern with regards to the Mesolithic of Western Scotland, the contribution of many other areas in the production of meaningful relations and identities in the Mesolithic have seen much less consideration. Material culture from the period provides a particularly good example of this. Lithic and stone tool technology, for example, is still often classified, categorised and discussed as if it *alone* represents the Mesolithic populations of Western Scotland (e.g. Lacaille 1954). Of course there has also been a concerted movement away from such culture historically driven accounts, and indeed in many cases stone and bone tools, such as bevelled ended tools (Figure 6.3), have been reconstructed and used in experimental frameworks to establish their function (Barlow and Mithen 2000, Finlayson 1995, Mithen 2000). Indeed, functional approaches toward material culture through such experimental frameworks have played a central part in recent explanations of people's interactions with the Mesolithic environment and sites in western Scotland (*Ibid.*). The detailed work of the Southern Hebrides Mesolithic Project (SHMP) on inter-assemblage variability in chipped stone assemblages, for example, drew both on the extensive archaeological evidence that amounted from the project, as well as a number of experimental projects. Through this work Mithen has suggested that it is possible to identify,

> ...four major influences on inter-assemblage variability: cost-benefit decision making, artefact transport around the landscape, functional variability at an inter- and intra-site level and stylistic influences on knapping technique (Mithen 2000: 606).

Using interpretations of such aspects Mithen has suggested that hunter-gatherers in the southern Hebrides increasingly used quartz the further away they were from

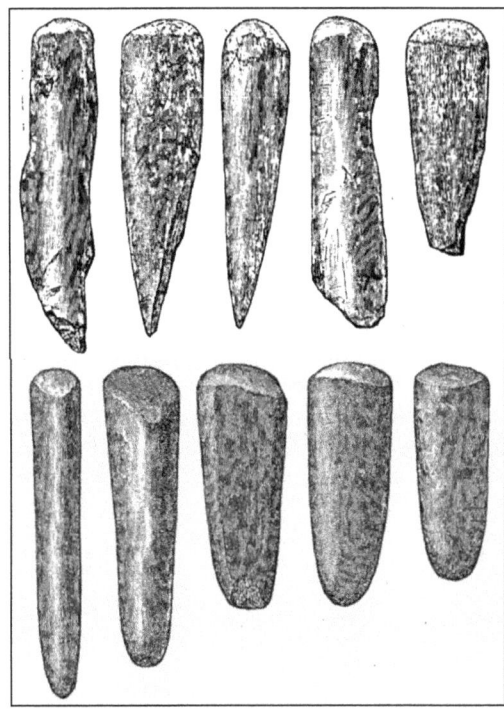

Figure 6.3 Bevelled ended bone tools (above) and stone tools (below) (After Anderson 1898: 309-310).

natural flint sources. Conversely he suggests that the closer they were to flint resources, the more wasteful hunter-gatherers were with their raw materials, working cores much less intensively than sites further away from such resources (Mithen 2000: 607). Variability in use wear analysis has also been used to illustrate functional differences between sites (*Ibid.*: 610) and the varying frequencies of microlith types amongst sites has also been drawn upon to support this (*Ibid.*: 611). Yet, as with the example of shell middens, what I would like to suggest is that maybe the picture isn't that simple. Maybe what people associated with tools and functions are not the same kind of associations we have today. Indeed, perhaps tools, like places, encompassed wider meanings. To examine such possibilities requires some discussion and deconstruction of how ethnographic analogy has largely been applied to interpretations of the archaeological record of Mesolithic Western Scotland. Prior approaches have applied ethnographic analogies to Mesolithic material culture in very much a Binfordian sense. By using ethnographic analogies and experimental work as tools to seek out similarities with contemporary hunter-gatherer communities, such work makes a number of assumptions. Many are on a relatively simplistic level, with proponents such as Mithen drawing directly on Binford's work with the Nunamiut Eskimo of north-central Alaska to suggest that between 8000 and 6500 BP the populations of the southern Hebrides engaged in foraging, rather than collecting, (Mithen 2000: 620). Similarly Bonsall, drawing upon ethnographies that explicitly examine shell fish collection, summarised in the work of Meehan (1982) and Wazelkov (1987), has

suggested that the Mesolithic middens of Western Scotland represent "special purpose processing camps associated with the exploitation of sea food resources" (Bonsall 1997: 191). In some cases work has taken anaolgies even further, in order to suggest more complex issues of social organisation. Again drawing on Meehan and Wazelkov, Bonsall goes on to suggest the gendered organisation of labour amongst Mesolithic shell fishing communities (*Ibid.*). Drawing upon very different analogies with the non-farming communities on the north-west coast of America, Finlayson has suggested that bevelled ended tools (common to so many Mesolithic sites in the West coast of Scotland) were hide working tools, and as such represent a high degree of social complexity, as the fine working and wearing of hides in such societies was a high status activity (Finlayson 1995: 262).

Of course this paper does not intend to suggest that we can interpret the past *without* analogies, either ethnographic or simply with our own life experiences. However the limitations of drawing solely upon ethnographic analogy to seek out similarities in the archaeological record have played a critical role in theoretical debate over the last two decades and cannot be over looked. Such debates have illustrated that rather than providing an objective "middle range" argument in themselves, ethnographies and subsequent analogies with these are inherently open to the flaws and unacknowledged, ever present subjectivities of the ethnographer's own experience (Hodder 1982, Wylie 1985). A concern with making analogical reasoning better has, over the last decade, come to conclude that it is simply untenable to use ethnographic analogy in the Binfordian sense, in terms of producing models to test and patterns to fit to. Instead recent work has stressed that we must acknowledge our own implicit assumptions and in turn draw upon ethnographic analogy as experience of difference in order to "think difference", as a starting point to allow us to interpret data differently (Tilley 1996: 2).

Taking such an approach on the use of ethnographic analogy, rather than drawing from ethnographies of shellfish gathering societies, or looking at ethnographic accounts of stone tool manufacture and function, my own research has turned to different ethnographies. Consequently it has explored ethnographies of the construction of personhood in Melanesia (such as Strathearn 1988) and Southern India (Busby 1997) to examine entirely different ways in which contemporary societies understand themselves, and conceptualise these relations through bodies, spaces and material culture. Drawing on these kind of ideas of fluidity of meanings and contextually defined personal identity, as well as Finlay's (2003) excellent application of the notions of multiple authorship to composite microlithic tools, what I want to suggest is that perhaps we should experiment with such notions in relation to Mesolithic Western

Scotland. So although usewear analysis might suggest that they had the same function, perhaps a bevelled ended tool made of stone and one made of bone had entirely different meanings. Indeed, if they were passed through different places, with different smells and different visual connections, which also had very different meanings, and were made and used by different people, perhaps they were not simply perceived as a bone or a stone bevelled ended tool, but as two entirely different objects.

Midden, Meaning, Person, Place
Drawing on such an approach and such ethnographies let us return to the Mesolithic shell middens of Western Scotland and in particular those on Oronsay. I have already mentioned that at the Oronsay middens there were clear differences between land and sea animals in the frequencies of skeletal parts that appeared in the middens. Here sea animals had much more complete skeletal remains, whereas land animals were predominantly represented by the bones of lower limbs and some tusks (Grigson and Mellars 1987). A further examination of this evidence suggests the existence of clear patterns discernable in the treatment of substances, with sea animals (and this includes not only fish, but cetaceans, seal and otter) associated predominantly with contexts of burning and with land animals and substances much less so. The traditional, and functional explanation offered for this, of the different kinds of butchery and working of animals that these patterns represent (*Ibid.*: 284), is a very plausible one and certainly not one which I would refute. However I would like to go further and suggest that the clear dichotomy in the record may relate to more than simply these functional explanations. Instead, I would like to suggest that specific substances from animals and humans, as well as naturally occurring items, such as different types of stone and wood, may have carried explicit symbolic associations. In turn these associations may have both influenced the identities of the persons handling such substances, and themselves have been actively transformed through working, use and deposition in specific locales, as well as through processes such as burning.

It has been suggested that the lack of larger human bones in the middens are primarily the result of bodies being excarnated upon the middens and then the bones disposed of elsewhere, perhaps in the sea (Pollard 1996). Such an explanation has seen the middens alone as transformative and symbolic locales. However I would suggest that whilst the middens on Oronsay provide the clearest evidence for the differential treatment of substances, such transformations continued through human use and symbolic association throughout all aspects of Mesolithic life, and that these were not simply confined to the middens. Through an examination of the visual setting and substances present at many Mesolithic sites in the area there is clear evidence to suggest that this was the case. Visual associations existed between sites and topographical features, as well as sites and other sites, both earlier and contemporary. On Oronsay, for example, the Priory Midden was directly aligned between the Paps of Jura and the Rhins of Islay, both topographic features that even today remain crucial navigational aids for sailors. Similarly the An Corran midden on Skye, over looks Raasay and the Applecross peninsula beyond, where other Mesolithic middens have been recorded (Hardy and Wickham-Jones 2002, 2003).

Critically my research has demonstrated that such visual connections did not exist in isolation, but were also reinforced through the presence of connecting substances and practices that involved the use and deposition of such substances at these sites (Cobb 2004). Both at Sanna Bay in the Ardnamurchan Peninsula, and at Camas Daraich on Skye, for example, Rhum Bloodstone has been found, and both sites have clear visual links to Rhum. In fact Camas Daraich is a very interesting example because had the site been located only a kilometre east or west it would have had wide views north, south and west, to the other Small Isles of Muck and Eigg, the Ardnamurchan Peninsula, the mainland, the north and west of Skye and beyond, to the Outer Hebrides. Yet due to its location, not only was Rhum the only visible island, but central to the view was Kinloch Farm (Figure 6.4), at which a contemporary and extensive Mesolithic Bloodstone processing site has been found (Wickham-Jones and Hardy 2001).

That the implications of such associations may have been intricately entwined with functional aspects is most likely, however it is clear that symbolic links between substance, places and persons clearly existed. Consequently my research indicates that complex relationships existed between understandings of land, sea, place and personal identity in the Mesolithic of Western Scotland. Moreover the treatment of substances at certain places in the area was actively used to cement and transform understandings of the world, tying peoples identities with those of the past, and with their environment around them. Such an interpretation points to the existence of very different conceptions of material culture and places than those that exist today. Subsequently the recognition of such factors demands that we go on to question further areas in which Mesolithic understandings of the world may have been significantly different, and yet which have so far only been fit into modern Western frameworks of understanding.

Deconstructing the duality of land and sea
Our own very dualistic modern Western understanding of the land and the sea for example, is clearly a modern conception that we unerringly assume also existed in the Mesolithic. This view is founded in an almost Cartesian dichotomy in which land and sea are inherently understood as forces in opposition with one another. In

Figure 6.4 The view of Rhum from the Mesolithic site of Camas Daraich, Skye (Source: Author).

this view the sea is clearly the inferior, the least known, and consequently a force to be conquered through exploration, and its wealth exploited. Many accounts have provided a concerted critique of this perception in relation to the interpretation of other chronological periods. In Mesolithic Western Scotland however, whilst it is clear that the sea was crucial as a medium for travel and a wealth of resources, it remains little more than a backdrop to most accounts, generally appearing only in relation to sites as a statistic of sea level, a resource to be exploited, or a cause of erosion or deposition. Of course some accounts have recognised this essentially modern perspective and tried to transcend it by discussing the importance of the sea as a medium for travel and therefore exchange and the maintenance of social networks (Warren 1997). Others have examined the value of the shoreline as a liminal place, which may have possessed transformative powers (Pollard, J., 2000, Pollard, T., 1996). For such accounts this explains the presence of human bone in the shell middens, and the underlying meanings and understandings of the middens themselves. However the shoreline can only be understood as liminal if land and sea are understood as two distinct and opposing identities, and consequently it is clear that this perspective still privileges the Western dualistic view of land and sea.

But how can we move beyond this and our own culturally embedded knowledge? My research shows a number of sites, not only middens, but also lithic scatters, often afforded the same privilege to the view of the sea as the view of the land beyond the sea, and often sites separated by the sea appear to have been linked both by visual relations and the presence of substances from each locations (Cobb 2004: 150). This suggests then, that the middens, and the shorelines that they occupied, were clearly only *one* context in which such important relations were played out, and that the meanings enacted and experienced at certain places and with certain substances only appear to have been possible through the visual situation of these sites within a wider context. Consequently other sites considered in this study that were not middens, nor were necessarily situated close to the shore, critically also demonstrated the presence of similar transformative and symbolic relations.

Questioning and Queer(y)ing Mesolithic community dynamics
A further area which again is continually assumed to have existed in the Mesolithic of western Scotland as it does today, are norms of gender and sexuality. Work in the last two decades has clearly demonstrated that both gender and sex are cultural constructions (for example Butler 1990, 1993, Conkey and Spector 1984, Dowson 2000, Schmidt and Voss 2000) and differ vastly in contemporary societies. Consequently such accounts have illustrated that to assume past gender roles and sexual norms mirrored those in the modern West is simply an untenable assumption. Yet these are notions that are continuously and uncritically projected back onto the Mesolithic. Of course such projections are never explicit, but when we discuss concepts such as exogamy and endogamy, at the heart of such discussions lies the presumption of heterosexual kinship relations as the social norm through which community networks were established. Similarly, when we assign our Mesolithic inhabitants differentiation in subsistence tasks based on biological sex, this is founded upon the simple assumption that, as is the norm for us today, biological sexual characteristics were commensurate with gender categories. Through such assumptions we clearly are placing our own understandings of normative western views of gender and sexuality unquestioningly onto the populations of Mesolithic Western Scotland. Yet if as the evidence reviewed here suggests, Mesolithic people constructed their understandings of themselves, land, sea, substances and material culture in much more fluid ways, then perhaps gender and sexual identities may also have

been understood incredibly differently (see Cobb forthcoming for a further discussion of this).

Conclusions
It seems pertinent to conclude by considering explicitly what this paper is advocating. Critically it is important to note that this paper suggests neither a full scale rejection of everything we know of the Mesolithic of Western Scotland so far, nor a radical image of homosexual, hippy, hunter-gatherers concerned only with experience and senses. Instead, what I am suggesting is simply that we can not only draw on the data that already exists, but we can combine this with new observations based upon developing interpretive theoretical stances and different ethnographic perspectives, as well as employing an explicit critical awareness of our own biases within interpretations. By doing this, it has been the intention of this paper to illustrate that not just myself, but a number of other people are already beginning to demonstrate that we *can* do more than simply describe human-environmental relations in a systems sense and we *can* do more than simply ascribe functional categories to material culture (c.f. Conneler 2001, Cummings 2003, Finlay 2003, Pollard, J., 2000, Pollard, T., 1996, Warren 1997, and all papers in this volume).

With regards to Western Scotland specifically, even from the early work of interpretive perspectives, it is clear that the modern western categories that we have neatly categorised everything in to so far require at the very least some revision. Sites can no longer be discussed simply in terms of their role in subsistence practices, or the ecological conditions that drove them. It is clear that the Mesolithic understanding of Western Scotland involved not simply a short term desire to seek out resources and shelter. Instead it was inhabited by a people who saw intricate connections between people, substances and places. Indeed it was the active role of these people in shaping, depositing and using substances and reusing places that at once connected places with memories and actively cemented such memories. Furthermore it is clear that not only did there existed important ideological connections between people, places, and material culture, but that these connections created, transformed and cemented Mesolithic personhood and the experience of the world in ways which we *can* begin to examine. In conclusion, then, it has been the aim of this paper to simply draw together some of these different perspectives that already exist and are already being developed and taken further, to demonstrate how a self-reflexive and concerted interpretative discussion can offer radical new perspectives and insights into middens, meaning, persons and places in the Mesolithic of Western Scotland.

Acknowledgments

I would like to thank Julian Thomas and Steven Price for their comments on earlier drafts of this paper, as well as Thomas Dowson for discussions regarding issues of Queer Theory and hunter-gatherers. I would also like to thank Nick Thorpe for comments made regarding the use of ethnographic analogy during the discussion following this paper at the TAG session. Hopefully in this paper I have clarified my perspective on issues raised there.

References Cited

Anderson, J. (1898). Notes on the Contents of a Small cave or Rock-Shelter at Druimvargie, Oban; And of hree Shell-Mounds in Oronsay. *Proceedings of the Society of Antiquaries of Scotland* 32(1898): 298-313.

Barlow, C., and Mithen, S. (2000). The Experimental Use of Elongated Pebble Tools. *Hunter-gatherer landscape archaeology: The Southern Hebrides Mesolithic project 1988 - 1998.* S. Mithen, J. Cambridge, McDonald Institute for Archaeological Research. 2: 513-521.

Barton, R., N., E., Berridge, P., J., Walker, M., J., C., and Bevins, R., E. (1995). "Persistent Places in the Mesolithic Landscape: An example from the Black Mountain uplands of South Wales." *Proceedings of the Prehistoric Society* 61: 81-116.

Bonsall, C., Sutherland, D., G., Lawson, T., J., and Russell, N. (1992). "Excavations in Ulva Cave, Western Scotland 1989: A Preliminary Report." *Mesolithic Miscellany* 13(1): 7-13.

Bonsall, C. (1996). The "Obanian Problem": Coastal Adaptation in the Mesolithic of Western Scotland. *The Early Prehistory of Scotland.* T. Pollard, and Morrison, A. Edinburgh, Edinburgh University Press: 183-197.

Bonsall, C. (1997). Coastal Adaptation in the Mesolithic of Argyll. Rethinking the 'Obanian Problem'. *The Archaeology of Argyll.* G. Ritchie. Edinburgh, Edinburgh University Press: 25-37.

Busby, C. (1997). "Permeable and Partible Persons: A Comparative Analysis of Gender and Body in South India and Melanesia." *Journal of the Royal Anthropological Institute (New Series)* 3: 261-278.

Butler, J. (1990). *Gender Trouble: Feminism and the subversion of identity.* London, Routledge.

Butler, J. (1993). *Bodies that Matter: On the Discursive limits of "Sex".* London, Routledge.

Cobb, H., L. (2004). *From Middens to Megaliths? A preliminary investigation into the possibility of using shell middens as a medium for interpreting the Mesolithic experience of the world.* Unpublished MPhil Thesis. Archaeology, School of Arts, Histories and Cultures. Manchester, University of Manchester.

Cobb, H., L. (Forthcoming). "Straight down the line? A Queer consideration of hunter-gatherer studies in North-Western Europe." *World Archaeology.*

Conkey, M., W and Spector J, D. (1984). "Archaeology and the Study of Gender." *Advances in Archaeological Method and Theory* 7: 1-38.

Conneller, C. (2001). Hunter-gatherers in the landscape; technical economies of the Vale of Pickering. *Ethnorahcaeology and Hunter-Gatherers: Pictures at an Exhibition.* K. Fewster, J., and Zvelebil, M. Oxford, BAR Publishing (BAR): 1-12.

Connock, K., D. (1985). Lorn Archaeological and Historical Society Rescue Excavation of the Ossuary Remains at Raschoille Cave, Oban: An Interim Report. Oban, Lorn Archaeological and Historical Society.

Connock, K., D., Finlayson, B., and Mills, C., M. (1992). "Excavation of a shell midden site at Carding Mill Bay near Oban, Scotland." *Glasgow Archaeological Journal* 17(1991-1992): 25-38.

Cummings, V. (2003). The Origins of Monumentality? Mesolithic World-Views of the Landscape in Western Britain. *Mesolithic on the Move. Papers Presented at the 6th International Conference in the Mesolithic in Europe, Stockholm, 2000.* L. Larsson, Kindgren, H., Knutsson, K., Loeffler, D., and Akerlund, A. Oxford, Oxbow Books: 74-81.

Dowson, T. (2000). "Why a Queer Archaeology? An Introduction." *World Archaeology* 32(2): 161-165.

Finlay, N. (2003). *Microliths and Multiple Authorship.* Mesolithic on the Move. Papers Presented at the 6th International Conference in the Mesolithic in Europe., Stockholm, 2000., Oxford: Oxbow.

Finlayson, B. (1995). *Complexity in the Mesolithic of the Western Scottish Seaboard.* Man and Sea in the Mesolithic: Coastal Settlement Above and

Below Present Sea Level., Kalundborg, Denmark 1993, Oxford: Oxbow Books.

Grieve, S. (1885). *The Great Auk or Garefowl (Alca impennislinn.): It's History, Archaeology and Remains.* Edinburgh, Grange Publishing Works.

Grieve, S. (1923). *The Book of Colonsay and Oronsay.* Edinburgh, Oliver and Boyd

Grigson, C., and Mellars, P., A. (1987). The Mammalian Remains from the Middens. *Excavations on Oronsay: Prehistoric Human Ecology on a Small Island.* P., A., Mellars. Edinburgh, Edinburgh University Press: 243-289.

Hardy, K., and Wickham-Jones, C. (2002). "Scotland's First Settlers: The Mesolithic Seascape of the Inner Sound, Skye and its Contribution to the Early Prehistory of Scotland." *Antiquity* 76(293): 825-834.

Hardy, K., and Wickham-Jones, C. (2003). *Scotland's First Settlers: an Investigation into Settlement, territoriality and Mobility During the Mesolithic in the Inner Sound, Scotland, First Results.* Mesolithic on the Move, Stockholm, 2000, Oxford: Oxbow.

Hodder, I. (1982). *The Present Past: An introduction to Anthropology for Archaeologists.* London, BT Batsford.

Lacaille, A., D. (1954). *The Stone Age in Scotland.* London, Oxford University Press.

Meehan, B. (1982). *Shell Bed to Shell Midden.* Canberra, Australian Institute of Aboriginal Studies.

Meiklejohn, C., and Denston, B. (1987). The Human Skeletal Material: Inventory and Initial Interpretation. *Excavations on Oronsay: Prehistoric Human Ecology on a Small Island.* P. Mellars, A. Edinburgh, Edinburgh University Press: 290-300.

Mellars, P., A. (1987). *Excavations on Oronsay: Prehistoric Human Ecology on a Small Island.* Edinburgh, Edinburgh University Press.

Mithen, S., J., Ed. (2000). *Hunter-gatherer landscape archaeology: The Southern Hebrides Mesolithic project 1988 - 1998.* Cambridge, McDonald Institute for Archaeological Research.

Pollard, J. (2000). "Ancestral Places in the Mesolithic Landscape." *Archaeological Review from Cambridge* 17(1): 123-138.

Pollard, T. (1996). Time and Tide: Coastal Environments, Cosmology and Ritual Practice in Early Prehistoric Scotland. *The Early Prehistory of Scotland.* T. Pollard, and Morrison, A. Edinburgh, Edinburgh University Press: 198-210.

Saville, A., Ed. (2004a). *Mesolithic Scotland and its Neighbours: the early Holocene Prehistory of Scotland, its British and Irish Context, and some Northern European Perspectives.* Edinburgh, Society of Antiquaries of Scotland.

Saville, A. (2004b). Introducing Mesolithic Scotland: the Background to a Developing Field of Study. *Mesolithic Scotland and its Neighbours: the early Holocene Prehistory of Scotland, its British and Irish Context, and some Northern European Perspectives.* A. Saville. Edinburgh, Society of Antiquaries of Scotland: 3-24.

Schmidt, R., A. and Voss, B., L. (2000). *Archaeologies of Sexuality.* London, Routledge.

Strathearn, M. (1988). *The Gender of the Gift: Problems with Women and Problems with Society in Melanesia.* London, University of California Press.

Tilley, C. (1996). *An Ethnography of the Neolithic: Early prehistoric societies in southern Scandinavia.* Cambridge, Cambridge University Press.

Warren, G., M. (1997). "Seascapes: Navigating the coastal Mesolithic of Western Scotland." *Assemblage* (2): http://www.shef.ac.uk/assem/2/2war1.html [online] (last accessed 12/12/2004).

Wazelkov, G., A. (1987). "Shellfish Gathering and Shell Midden Archaeology." *Advances in Archaeological Method and Theory* 10: 93-210.

Wickham-Jones, C., R. (2004). Structural Evidence in the Scottish Mesolithic. *Mesolithic Scotland and its Neighbours: the early Holocene Prehistory of Scotland, its British and Irish Context, and some Northern European Perspectives.* A. Saville. Edinburgh, Society of Antiquaries of Scotland: 229-242.

Wickham-Jones, C., R., and Hardy, K. (2001). Camas Daraich. The University of Edinburgh, Department of Archaeology Annual Report 2001, University of Edinburgh. 2004.

Wylie, A. (1985). "The Reaction Against Analogy." *Advances in Archaeological Method and Theory* 8: 63-111.

RECONSTRUCTING THE SOCIAL TOPOGRAPHY OF AN IRISH MESOLITHIC LAKESCAPE

Aimée Little

University College Dublin

Abstract

This paper is a report on research currently being undertaken in the northern Midlands of Ireland, where even though there is a strong history of Mesolithic finds recovery there has never been a comprehensive landscape study that aims to integrate all the bodies of evidence at a landscape-scale. The principal aim of this research is to investigate spatial and temporal variation in hunter-gatherer activities from a social perspective, and to illustrate how the material can be approached at a variety of scales and through a range of analytical techniques. Two examples of how this can be achieved are considered within this paper: firstly, by highlighting differences in the practice of deposition and secondly, by investigating the materialisation and meaning of lakeside platforms. In addition, the predominant pattern of river mouth site location in the area has been noted time and again and is often attributed to hunter-gatherers inhabiting the best 'fishing spots'. However, this 'fishy' settlement pattern has, until now, never been tested for potential biases affected through natural and human initiated change to the landscape. Different methodological approaches to interrogating these biases will be discussed, as will the need to integrate organic evidence, which is often overlooked, into the narrative construction process. It is argued that addressing biases in human and natural landscape change and placing new emphasis on the identification of inland sites is a critical step that needs to be taken if we are to rebalance the current geographical bias towards coastal sites in Ireland.

Introduction

In the northern Midlands of Ireland - in counties Cavan, Longford and Westmeath - a number of Mesolithic finds/sites have been identified in a variety of contexts: from single finds exposed along the foreshore to *in situ* material excavated from fen peats after a drainage scheme in the 1960's lowered the water table in a series of loughs connected to the River Inny. Despite this wealth of material, there has never been a comprehensive landscape study that encompasses lake, river and dry land locations in any truly meaningful way. It will be argued here that the significance of this internal network of water systems for hunter-gatherer societies has been overlooked in Irish Mesolithic research, creating a partial picture of a potentially much more socially dynamic landscape than has previously been realised.

This paper reports on the first stages of research addressing the social aspects of hunter-gatherer inhabitation in the northern Midlands from an ideologically and cosmologically grounded perspective, where hunter-gatherers are seen as active agents in the physical transformation of space into place. These acts of environmental transformation will be explored through a number of key themes, including: depositional practice, variation in the temporal and spatial contexts of activities, and the construction and meaning of platforms. Because of the unique environmental qualities of these wetlands, this research will consider the nature of site identification in this area and discuss the effects of peat growth and river drainage as biasing factors in the identification of Mesolithic sites. Emphasis will be placed on the importance of identifying alternative forms of evidence, namely organic material culture, which has in Ireland been historically overshadowed by a reliance on lithic datasets.

Setting the context

The research area selected for this project includes Loughs Sheelin, Derravaragh, Kinale, Iron, and Owel (Figure 7.1). All of these lakes, except Lough Owel, are linked by the River Inny system that flows from north-west to south-east and has a source somewhere near Lough Sheelin. After passing through the loughs, and sometimes collecting drainage from them, the River Inny finally connects up with the River Shannon (Mitchell 1972, 160). The most notable archaeological feature of this landscape is the distribution of Late Mesolithic sites on all of the loughs, "generally at the point of entry or exit of the river" (*Ibid.*) and the fact that they are generally located on higher ground (Woodman 1978, 162), although there is a significant absence of Mesolithic sites on Lough Owel.

An additional factor contributing to the distribution pattern of sites in the area is the conditioning preservational relationship between quaternary deposits

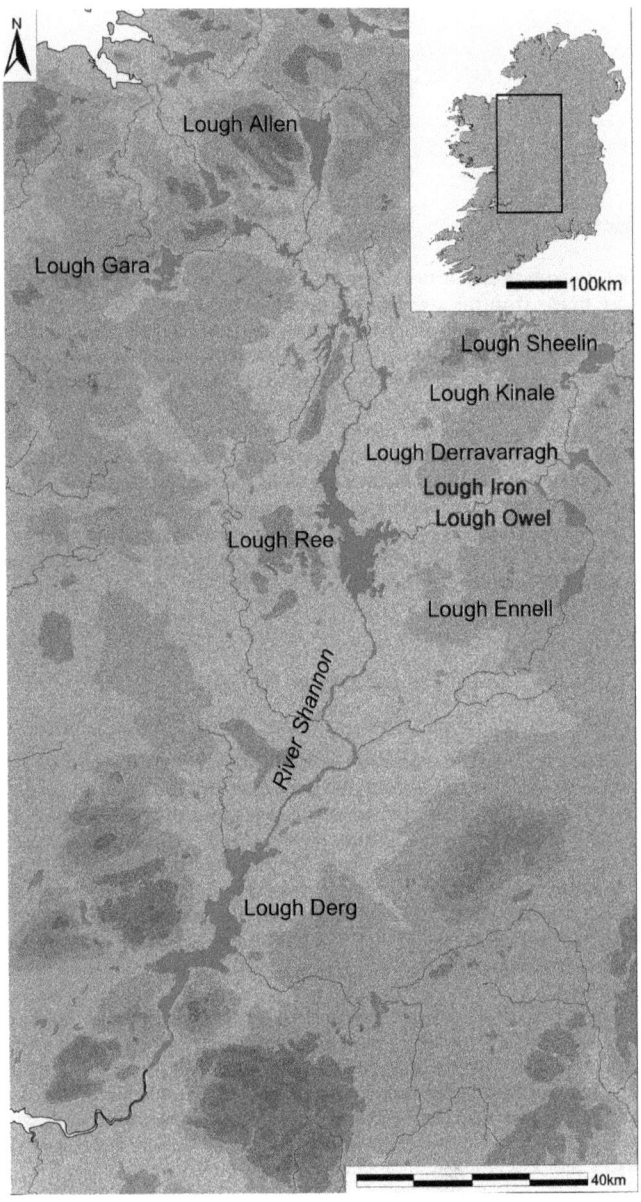

Figure 7.1 Map of study area (courtesy of Aidan O'Sullivan)

and archaeological material, meaning that in some locations material is still submerged beneath raised bog (Woodman 1978, 162). The size of these lakes would have been much larger to what they are today. For example, Lough Derravaragh is only a fragment of its original size compared to what it was during the early post-glacial time as "marginal reed swamps then built fen-peat out into the open water, and when the fen-peat had reached sufficient thickness, *sphagnum*-moss and its associates invaded the fen and gradually built up domed raised-bogs" (Mitchell 1972, 160). It was during this time of initial peat formation that hunter-gatherers inhabited the area, with evidence of their occupation becoming embedded in the fen-peats that, over the years, have either been buried further or eroded away. This erosion is largely due to human initiated changes to the landscape that started to take place when the water level of the lakes was artificially lowered by a drainage scheme that took place in the 1960's (Figure 7.2). This scheme had a huge impact on the exposure of finds and sites in the area and lowered the water level in some loughs by up to 6 metres (OPW files). The majority of the eroded material could then be seen scattered along the flood plain and has been recovered in recent years by archaeologists, including: Frank Mitchell (1970 and 1972) Joseph Raftery (1972) and Gabriel Cooney (1987).

Although there have been numerous single finds, larger surface scatters and material still *in situ* within fen-peat deposits, (e.g. the sites of Clonkeen (Cooney 1987, 62-4) (Figure 7.3), and Corralanna (Moore *et al.* 2003)) recorded in the northern Midlands, only two excavations of Mesolithic sites have taken place in this region: Mitchell's excavation at Site 1, Clonava (1972) and more recently the Discovery Programme excavated a Late Mesolithic platform at Derrya townland at Lough Kinale. This site would been "at the centre of the lake system" and similarly to Clonava, would have been located on an island during the Mesolithic (Fredengren 2004, 29)

It is important that sites like Clonava Island and Derrya Island are understood within their original context, especially when considering the considerable difference between the landscape of the Late Mesolithic compared to the one we experience today. A hunter-gatherer inhabiting or moving through the area would have been surrounded by extensive areas of fen through which many open channels would have run. It was through these channels that the River Inny entered the lakes (Mitchell and Ryan 2003), creating a wetland environment rich in aquatic and plant resources that would have attracted a range of water and land based activities (Mitchell 1972; Woodman 1978; Cooney 1987, Cooney and Grogan 1999; O'Sullivan 1998; McCartan 2000); opening up endless possibilities for social encounters.

Even though the evidence in the area is primarily Late Mesolithic, Early Mesolithic settlement cannot be ruled out, as it is likely that this area would have been peppered with lakes "that would have been attractive to Mesolithic man" and evidence of this may now be covered by the raised bogs which started forming during the Later Mesolithic" (Woodman 1978, 161). Understanding the development of peat deposits in the area and the chronological implications of this need to be prioritised within research agendas, as this natural environmental change - alongside the human initiated change caused during drainage works – has massive implications for identifying, recovering, recording and interpreting the material from the area in the future.

Figure 7.2 Late Mesolithic material eroding out of a bank of the River Inny (courtesy of Aidan O'Sullivan)

Looking at the recent past; an historical account of Mesolithic research in the northern Midlands

Until the middle of the twentieth century Mesolithic settlement in Ireland was seen as a North Eastern phenomenon, an assumption made on the availability and importance of flint deposits only readily available in this part of the island (Woodman 1978, 142; 2003, 9). However finds recovery processes have compounded this geographical bias; because the recovery of artefacts has largely been due to surface visibility and the enthusiasm of the collector, there has historically been a greater recovery rate in the north east of the country, which is known for its distinctive grey Antrim flint deposits and has a long tradition of flint tool collection by local enthusiasts (Woodman 1978). Conversely, in the northern Midlands artefact recovery has been hindered by the fact that the raw materials available, chert and limestone, are less easily recognisable and because the majority of sites have been submerged under large areas of raised peat bog.

There is a dramatic change in stone tool technology in Ireland from the Early (7000 BC) to Late Mesolithic (6200-6000 BC), with microlith forms being replaced by a broad blade hard hammer 'Bann flake' industry. The Isle of Man is the only other place identified where a similar process takes place (McCartan 2003, 335). The transition from microlith to broad blade technology is still poorly understood (Woodman and Anderson 1990). However, what is even more of an enigma than the change in lithic technology is that the Bann flake is unique to Ireland, and is commonly accepted as an indigenous development resulting from geographical and cultural insularity (O'Sullivan 1998).

In addition to the argument for technological change as an insular development, the most commonly accepted reason in Ireland for this shift in technology has been that it represents a functional response to an increase in woodworking; possibly related to the manufacture of fish weirs and a general increase in a reliance on fishing (Woodman 1978, 168; Anderson 1993, 17; Woodman and Anderson 1990, 385). This, in conjunction with the "the presence of so many sites on the main rivers" (Woodman 1978, 168), has created an emphasis on the "economic value" of the northern Midland lakes and waterways, leading to the integration of sites from this area into a site catchment model, with the northern Midlands argued to have been inhabited on a seasonal basis (Woodman 1978). Within this model, the northern Midland settlement pattern represents a seasonal shift in resource exploitation, with salmon and eel migrations being the economic purpose for inhabiting the area.

However, this method relies on the environmental and geographical contexts of sites and it works on the premise that "hunter-fisher communities usually rely extensively on food supplies to be found close to their base camp" (1978, 170). As Mount Sandel is still considered as the only 'base-camp' from the Irish Mesolithic (Cooney and Grogan 1999, 19), the proposed models, which rely on set parameters determined by the seasonal availability of food resources, are only really useful for considering the types of resources that would have been exploited at this time. Moreover, even though this model attempts to make links between coastal and inland areas, the relationship between the two is never explored in anything other than diagrammatic and economic terms.

Cooney and Grogan (1999, 19) have challenged the usefulness of Woodman's model within an Irish context, and have suggested that because of its inflexible nature, sites such as Clonava Island at the northwest end of Lough Derravaragh have been overlooked. Using the material excavated at Clonava by Mitchell (1972), as an example of a site that could be categorized as a specialized function camp, "a place that would have had potential as a more substantial base for settlement" (Cooney and Grogan 1999, 19) and the fact that "the majority of Mesolithic sites similarly occur in the best locations to exploit resource-clustering on a year-round basis" (*Ibid.*, 21), they argue that there was an increase in sedentism from the Early to Late Mesolithic. In a later publication Woodman defended an earlier discussion on Late Mesolithic settlement patterns (Woodman and Anderson 1990), asserting that Cooney (2000), Kimball (2000) and Fredengren (2002) had in fact misinterpreted his argument. Rather than saying that the Late Mesolithic

Figure 7.3 Late Mesolithic finds from Clonkeen, a Late Mesolithic site on the River Inny

was characterized by low density and high mobility settlement he pointed out that "we could not presume that the Early Mesolithic was followed by a period of increased population levels and sedentism" (2003, 15). Ultimately, while both sides have succeeded in identifying weaknesses in the other's proposed settlement models for the Late Mesolithic, neither model challenges the accepted (economically determined) norms of Mesolithic settlement, or attempts to address the variety of social factors active in structuring settlement patterns across the country.

The situation in Ireland with regard to Mesolithic finds distribution has improved steadily over recent years and we now have relatively impressive distribution maps for the period. Yet, even though we can now "*Push Back the Boundaries*" (Woodman 2003) of Mesolithic settlement, with Early and Late sites recorded at inland and coastal regions, we still have no real appreciation of how these sites relate in either a temporal or spatial sense. While there has been some attempt to investigate the relationship between inland and coastal communities through the importation of material (Griffiths and Woodman 1987; Woodman and Anderson 1990; Woodman *et al.* 1999, 141), research projects like Strangford Lough (McErlean *et al.* 2002), Lough Swilly (Kimball, 1998 and 2000) and Ballylough (Zvelebil and Green 1992) have followed a predominantly coastal theme, and are yet to integrate their discoveries with those found at inland locations.

As a result of this geographical bias we currently have a fragmented understanding of Mesolithic settlement, with a predominantly coastal focus, that reveals very little about the continuity of hunter-gatherer landscape inhabitation. It is argued here that until research interests shift the focus inwards our understanding of the depth and range of hunter-gatherer narratives on this island will be limited to seaside accounts of Mesolithic life. Significantly this is where a landscape-scale study of the northern Midlands can be seen as the critical 'inland link', a crucial step towards a more balanced view of settlement and an opportunity to move away from the traditional reliance on lithic datasets to construct human narrative.

So why is it that the large majority of contemporary projects addressing Mesolithic settlement in Ireland are still targeting coastal locations? One reason is the comparative ease of identifying lithic material in coastal landscapes over Midland ones where Mesolithic material has been submerged under layers of peat bog. Additionally, Late Mesolithic sites - which are the most common type of site for this period in the area - carry their own sets of problems. Woodman *et al.* (1999, 139) have drawn attention to this by highlighting some of the issues involved in identifying Late Mesolithic finds; pointing out that many of the locations that the artifacts are found in, such as marine or riverine contexts, are not settlement sites and that the material is often not *in situ*: "we have few actual sites to investigate, just lots of information about general localities" (Woodman 2003, 13).

The key issue in terms of present day biases towards the northern Midlands is not with the material itself, as the 'archaeological wealth' of the area has been noted time and again, it can be found in the paucity of attention given to this region, and the fact that there has never been a landscape study here which aims to integrate all the bodies of evidence. This situation has huge implications for studies of the Irish Mesolithic at large. As Nyree Finlay has pointed out, "many of the areas that may have been settlement foci, such as the interior lakes, have not been the subjects of intensive study since artifact collections in the 1950s" (2003, 88). Because of this, the nature of settlement during the Irish Late Mesolithic is still unresolved. Since there has been a historical trend for research to focus on coastal areas, with the focus shifting occasionally up river valleys and into the interior (although mostly from a coastal direction), such as the work in the Barrow Valley, Co. Kilkenny (Zvelebil *et al.* 1996) and in the field-walking carried out by Anderson (1991) in the south-west of the country, we now have not only a lopsided portrait of the geographical world of Ireland's hunter-gatherers but of the material and ideological ones as well. This situation can readily be seen reflected in the narrow range of social narratives constructed about life at this time.

Thus the unique preservational qualities of the northern Midland bogs can be seen as having a considerable role to play in the development of alternative narratives for the period, with greater opportunities to understand the manufacture, deposition and meaning of non-lithic objects and the types of activities that were carried out with their use. The potential of Irish bogs for preserving archaeology *in situ* - especially organic material dating to the Mesolithic - has been noted time and again (O'Sullivan 1998, 44; Murray 2002, 16; Moore, 2003, 124; Fredengren 2004, 28), although, somewhat surprisingly, Ireland has a limited amount of organic remains compared to that recovered from European occupation sites (O'Sullivan 1998, 44). Consequentially, there has been limited discussion within the archaeological literature on what would have been a much more multi-media experience of the material world during the Mesolithic. Furthermore, O'Sullivan (*Ibid.*, 45) has pointed out that Irish lakeshore archaeology in general has been severely neglected, with very few methodical studies carried out that attempt to identify subsoil organic structures or artifacts and as a result, "we know very little about the organic material culture of these Mesolithic lakeshore sites" (*Ibid.*, 59).

Although O'Sullivan's statement is rings true on a number of levels, in that evidence of organic remains in Ireland is still inadequate, it should be noted that a small but significant number of organic finds have been recovered from the northern Midland region and with a more systematic approach to the archaeology of these peatlands the chances of recovering additional finds is bound to increase.

Organic finds from inland lake shores include a possible portion of a log boat at Lough Neagh, dated to 5470 – 5246 cal BC and a possible Mesolithic fish weir from Toombridge (Woodman 2003, 12). During Mitchell's excavations at Clonava Island, Lough Derravaragh, a wide range of edible plant remains were found alongside lithic material, wood, hazelnuts and charcoal (Mitchell 1972, 165). Other reports of wooden artefacts of a probable Mesolithic date can be found in the NMI topographical files, for example a Bann flake was said to have been found in Scurlockstown, Co. Westmeath in 1954: "10" below surface during ploughing of boggy land" with "traces of what appears to have been a wooden handle...the finder has now no idea of the shape or length of the handle". In the townland of Kilgolagh a bone pin, another piece of worked bone and a wooden pin were found in association with lithic material of a late Mesolithic date within the spoil from the drainage of the River Inny (NMI files). Although the bone point is said to be similar to ones recovered in the Bann Valley, the wooden pin "has no definite Mesolithic parallels" (Woodman 1978, 316). This method of 'dating by association' is one of many problems that arise when considering organic finds and is an especially problematic exercise when considering the limited knowledge of organic find 'typologies' that we currently have for the Irish Mesolithic and greater Europe. In Ireland there is an urgent need for a publication that reviews *all* evidence for organic material culture from the Mesolithic period, which addresses the issues involved in identifying, recording, dating and conserving these types of finds.

An inter-related problem to the absence of organic finds is the peculiar lack of direct evidence for fishing activities. This is particularly unusual in the northern Midlands, where in light of the argument for the northern Midland settlement pattern representing fishing activities, there is virtually no archaeological evidence for this fishing activity taking place. This 'missing link' in the archaeological record is referred to time and again within the literature and can certainly be seen as an island-wide problem. Even at Ferriter's Cove where the faunal evidence suggested that fishing was a major activity carried out at the site it was observed that given "the role of fish there is one intriguing anomaly, namely the comparative lack of fishing equipment" (Woodman *et al.* 1999) In fact, except for a fish weir from Toombridge that was "never given the attention it deserved because no one could believe that it could be that early" (Woodman 2003, 12) there is no other artifactual evidence of fishing related activities. Why is this? One major reason for this is that organic Mesolithic finds (compared to lithics) have never been a research priority; there has, therefore, been only a small amount of archaeological investigation that would uncover this type of evidence. Woodman and Anderson have drawn attention to this situation by suggesting that,

> perhaps most of the other equipment used was like the fish traps made from wood and the only method by which the Later Mesolithic of Ireland will be fully understood will be through the excavation of a water logged site where the full range of Later Mesolithic artefacts will be recovered for the first time (1990, 387).

Testing the 'fishy' settlement pattern

The spatial relationship between lithic assemblages and good fishing spots - namely at the mouth of the River Inny as it enters Loughs Sheelin, Kinale, Derravaragh, and Iron - has been used as further supporting evidence for a settlement pattern based on a seasonal round of economically determined activities during the Late Mesolithic. However, this argument, which is already somewhat problematic in that it is shaped almost entirely by economic concerns, is further weakened by the fact that the biasing agents, which are likely to have contributed to the current picture of site distribution, have never been addressed in detail (Spikins, 1999). Not only is there surprisingly little cognisance of this fact within the literature, until now there has been no attempt to interrogate the northern Midland settlement pattern methodologically and document the nature and scale of biases active here.

Historically the majority of evidence for hunter-gatherer inhabitation in the area has come from shoreline surveys carried out in 1960's and 70's following the drainage of the River Inny, revealing large quantities of worked chert along the shoreline and within sections of fen peat (Mitchell 1972; O'Sullivan 1998, 48; Cooney and Grogan 1999, 15). The overwhelming pattern generated as a result of these post-drainage artefact collection episodes has been one of river mouth site location. In order to test this 'fishy' settlement pattern and develop methodologies that are not simply going to reinforce current find distribution trends, it will first be necessary to assess the degree and rate of impact modern land use has had on identifying Mesolithic sites in the area by reconstructing landscape change through time, particularly seeing as "different land-use practices can have a marked effect on the *visibility* of sites" (Spikins 1999, 21). The primary focus will be to unearth the possible non-economic reasons for hunter-gatherers choosing to inhabit one particular location over another. In the following section I will bring attention to a number of methodological approaches that are being undertaken to address these biases and which will in turn contribute to a deeper understanding of the diversity and richness of settlement patterns present in the area.

Reconstructing the pre and post river drainage water levels of the loughs by overlaying 6" *Geological Survey of Ireland* maps with the *Ordanance Survey of Ireland* 1:50 000 *Discovery Series* maps was the first methodological step taken (Figure 7.4), as it was necessary to illustrate how dramatically the environment has changed as a result of these drainage episodes. This information has formed the foundation upon which a more detailed range of methodologies have been constructed which aim to pull apart, critique, and identify weaknesses in the current settlement model. The creation of maps like this, with the aid of GIS, has been useful for plotting known find/site spots and for creating a physical reference point for discussing the present picture for site location in relation to exposed shorelines. In addition, knowledge of the contour of past shorelines has been a key factor in shaping ongoing survey programmes.

The majority of these survey exercises will target non-river mouth locations around the loughs that have been affected by the drainage scheme, identifying areas of erosion where lithic and organic material might remain *in situ*. Because of the potential to simply reinforce known settlement patterns, specifically the location of sites at river mouth locales and waterside locations in general,

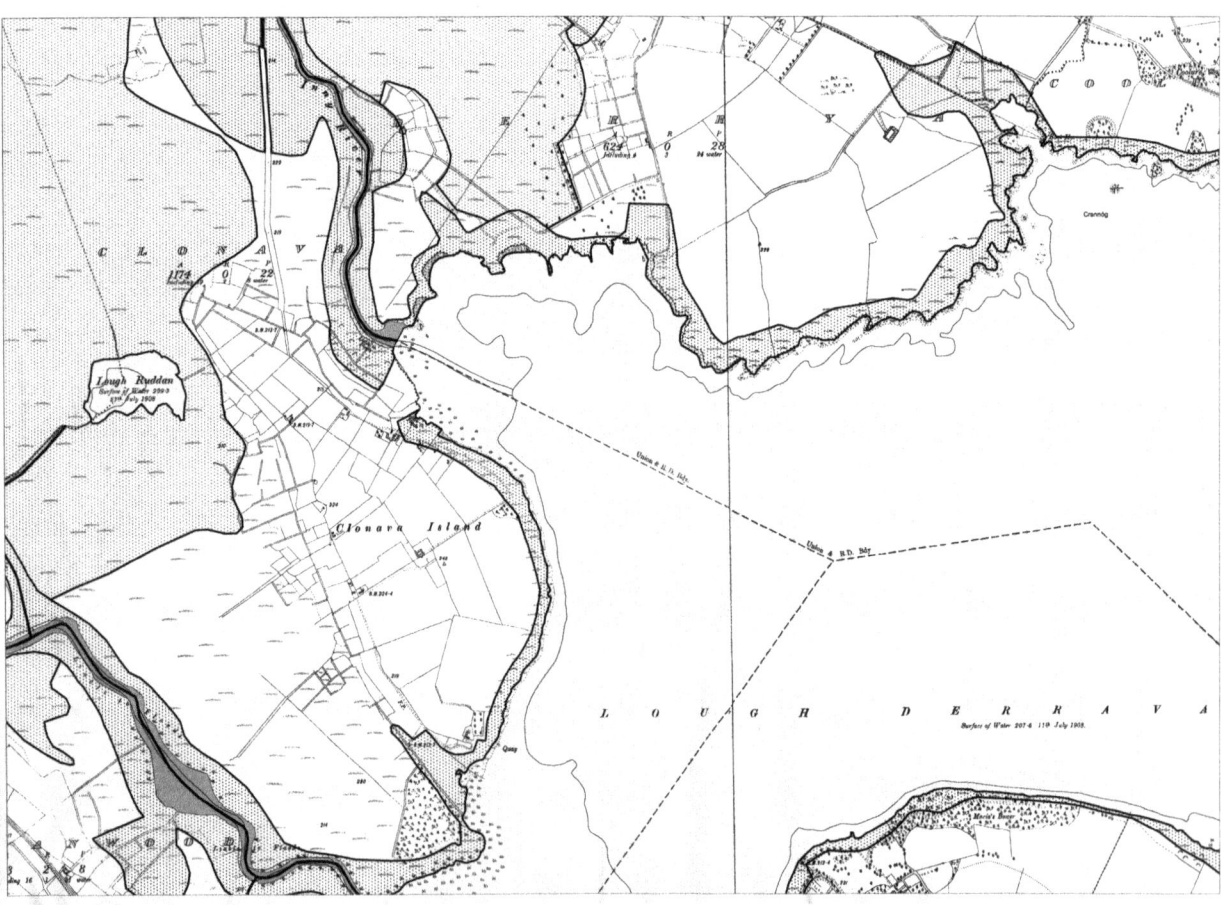

Figure 7.4. Map of Clonava Island showing pre-and post-drainage water levels (map: courtesy of Vincent Hussey, OPW, Trim)

alternative approaches to surveying will also be undertaken, as a shift in the geographic focus of surveys from the shoreline needs to be the first practical step taken if we are to change the lingering perception that hunter-gatherer activities in the area were inextricably connected to water. It is important to note that if there are sites in this region that are located in non-waterside settings then they have potentially been biased two-fold: firstly in that, as previously stated, they are inland, and historically Mesolithic research has been coastal. Secondly, they are not located near water and privy to the same environmental changes (either natural or human initiated change) that have exposed the majority of sites in the area. Similarly lakes, such as Lough Owel, that have not been affected by drainage and have no evidence for Mesolithic activity may also have been overlooked in the past and need to be included in current research agendas. Addressing these biases through systematic methodologies is therefore essential to illuminating a fuller picture of what was likely to have been a landscape of sociability during the Mesolithic.

It is in this respect that Lough Owel deserves closer consideration. This lough is interesting because not only is it *not* connected to the River Inny and therefore it has not been affected by the drainage scheme, it also presently has no evidence for Mesolithic activity. This lough was included in the study area as a comparative exercise, as a way of testing the impact of the drainage scheme on find and site visibility. During a recent survey carried out by the author, a single piece of prehistoric worked chert was recovered from the townland of Farranistic, on the southern shoreline of the lough.

One way to access "the spaces between the loughs" is to identify other topographical features within the landscape that may have been foci of activity. As such, the integration of a layer of geological data on bedrock and chert outcrops, which are a well-known feature of this landscape, into a GIS finds distribution map is one alternative avenue that is being taken to investigate patterns and associations between material and potentially social topographical points in the landscape. In addition, plots that are being prepared for aforestation in non-waterside locations within the study area will be monitored. This process involves the construction of mound drains spaced up to 8ms apart and up to 45cms in depth. The resulting spoil from these drains can then be 'picked through' for archaeological material. Similarly, fields that have been stripped down to their formal ground level after peat harvesting could hold a great deal of archaeological potential and need to be systematically surveyed for evidence of finds and/or surface features. Furthermore, other areas that may have attracted inhabitation such as the dry areas or 'lake islands', like Clonava, that would have been present during the Mesolithic (McCartan 2000, 15) also need to be identified and surveyed.

The Irish Archaeological Wetland Unit has started this process by using maps that illustrate the extent of the wetlands in early prehistory and which have been used to provide an environmental context for the site at Corralanna. Corralanna, said to be of "considerable significance" (Moore *et al.* 2003, 129) because of the vast quantities of worked chert, quartzite hammerstones, hazelnuts and wood fragments which were visible on the surface of the bog and compressed within peat sods' (Figure 7.5), is a rare example of a site that has recently been recorded within this study area, and is not located on the modern day river system. However, by reconstructing the wetland/dryland environment surrounding the site, the IAWU were able to demonstrate that Corralanna was probably located on an area of dry land adjacent to a small tributary connected to the River Inny. In a landscape such as this - where extensive fens and open water channels would have played a dominant role in orientating and structuring peoples movements, influencing their choices of places to inhabit - the reconstruction of the Mesolithic environment plays a critical role not only in orientating fieldwork, but also in contextualizing the material within its original landscape setting.

Figure 7.5. Worked chert from Corralanna embedded in peat sod (photo: courtesy of Aidan O'Sullivan)

Making more of deposition

> ...Specific places in the landscape are physically enculturated by the transformation or deposition of artifacts and the construction of material structures (Jordan 2003b, 183)

For the remainder of this paper I will explore the ways in which material from the northern Midlands can be approached from a range of scales. By introducing a multidisciplinary approach to the material and varying the scale of analysis from 'nested' scales to larger environmental reconstructions I will demonstrate that there is huge potential here for discussing social narrative on a number of different levels. Clonava Island at the northwest end of Lough Derravaragh is one place that has revealed a range of evidence for hunter-gatherer inhabitation, although the nature and meaning of this occupation is poorly understood. Using the material from Clonava as a case study I will work through a number of research questions that could be asked of this material and discuss the different methodological approaches that can be taken to interpret Clonava and other sites in the area. At the microscale, understanding patterns and associations between deposits of bone and stone and will be used to illustrate how this material can be given a social context (Torrence 2001, 74). Broader macroscale approaches to the reconstruction of the Mesolithic environment will then be drawn on as a way of placing this material within a landscape scale setting.

Depositional practice in the Irish Mesolithic has seen very little research and consequentially we have no real understanding of how and why people deposited objects. There are two major reasons underpinning the lack of attention given to 'depositionary activities' (Conneller 2001, 9) during the Irish Mesolithic; the primary one is that research concerns have ultimately been geared towards economic interpretations of a site and have failed to appreciate other tacit (and perhaps even explicit) meanings behind the activities associated with the use and discard of objects and/or waste (Warren 2001). Secondly, in Ireland, the way material was deposited has played only a secondary role to the objects themselves. These problems clearly extend beyond the shores of Ireland and can be seen as an endemic part of European hunter-gatherer studies, even though other phases of prehistory acknowledge that "the formal burial of objects...and their structured spatial and compositional arrangement is commonplace" (Pollard 2001, 315). One obvious cause of this dilemma is the nature in which Mesolithic sites are identified and recorded. For example, many of the finds recovered from the northern Midlands came from spoil created during the river drainage works and have no recorded provenance beyond the townland level. Problems relating to an inadequate level of detail on the exact location of a find and its depositional context have therefore caused some limitations on the amount of interpretive analysis carried out in the area. However, we must ask ourselves if this is in fact the real issue? It is suggested here that the real problem lies not with the evidence itself, but with the kinds of research questions that are being asked and the narrow range of methodologies that are being developed to answer these questions.

In this respect thinking through the processes of deposition and understanding biasing agents that may have lead to a find's recovery is of utmost importance if we are going to gain insights into the ways hunter-gatherers set about structuring their environment, and in developing arguments for ritualised hunter-gatherer landscapes. Moreover, by paying closer attention to different depositional arrangements it becomes possible to engage with specifics of data on a more 'intimate' level (Finlay 2003, 87) and develop narratives that focus on the social implications leading to material finding a final resting place. In the following paragraphs I will work through some examples drawn from ethnographic literature as well as recent archaeological projects where space is defined through the embedded practice of deposition. In these cases arguments have been made that, whether discard has occurred as a result of everyday 'mundane' activities or deposited as part of more symbolic acts of veneration, the archaeological signatures are pronounced and readable. A closer look will then be given to evidence from the northern Midlands and the different types of methodological approaches that could be taken in order to construct a more socially meaningful narrative.

An ethnographic example of meaningful depositional practice can be seen through the differentiation in animal bone deposits at Siberian Khanty Yurt sites. The Yurt which is described by Jordan (2003b, 200) as "a space in which people conduct meaningful lives, is a vast workshop in which material culture is created, used, transported, and deposited" and can be spatially defined as having three parts: a 'clear' inner area where the dwelling structures are located, a 'clear' river bank area that sees only deposits of hazel nut shells and 'little else', and thirdly a peripheral arc that surrounds the settlement and contains a variety of items which are "deposited according to different conceptual frameworks" (2003b, 201). Although there is a paucity of faunal evidence from the Midlands, other evidence, such as the nature and variation of lithic deposits could be an alternative way of appreciating the act of deposition and the organisation of space.

Warren (2001, 94) suggests that in later Mesolithic Scotland "the hints of pattern in the deposition of stone tools are not strong but we might associate these with repeated mundane activities and the principles that generated them with tacit meanings, the associations and resonances drawn from daily life: where rubbish is placed, how it was associated with various activities, and perhaps various people". It is interesting to note that in the Vale of Pickering a number of small-scale, low-density scatters excavated around Lake Flixton have revealed a pattern of "thoughtful discard" practices (Conneller and Schadla-Hall 2003). At these sites many of the tool-using activities (reflected in the nature of the assemblages, which are dominated by utilised flakes and blades) are apparently isolated from the knapping stations and are either located at the waters edge, or in the water itself. Conneller and Schadla Hall (*Ibid.*, 100) have interpreted this occurrence as possible evidence for people deeming it appropriate to "undertake particular tasks away from the knapping stations or longer lasting activity areas on the drier ground".

At the Irish Early Mesolithic Midland site of Lough Boora, Co. Offaly (Ryan 1980), faunal remains, consisting almost entirely of calcined bone fragments were interpreted as having been exposed to a prolonged burning after the meat was removed, indicating that this "was not part of the normal food preparation procedure" (Van Wijngaarden-Bakker 1989, 126). The evidence suggested that "the bones must have undergone extensive heating for a considerable time while in a fresh state" and that they "were deliberately discarded into the fire" (*Ibid.*). Refuse discard is said to have occurred at the same place that preparation and consumption were carried out. Unfortunately there are no social interpretations of the faunal evidence from this site, as the research objectives were focussed on site taphonomy and seasonal indicators. A reinterpretation of this particular set of data might include ways of thinking about the process of 'discard' and the meaning embedded into the deliberate deposition of waste products into the hearth. Although this is just one example of a distinctive act of deposition and obviously needs further developing, the point is that, whether or not this is evidence of a mundane act of rubbish disposal or a more symbolic act with ritualistic associations, the true potential of this data has not been realised from a social perspective.

In recent years there has been a number of exciting discoveries in Ireland in which Mesolithic finds have been recovered from what could be described as more formal deposits, such as the caches of axes at Ferriter's Cove (Woodman *et al* 1999), caches of stone tools with unretouched and retouched forms found mostly in the northeast (Finlay 2003, 90), and a stone axe recovered from a cremation pit at Hermitage, Co. Limerick (Collins and Coyne 2003). In the northern Midlands there is also considerable variation in the types of objects deposited, the quantity, their context, and their relationship to other finds as well as features such as hearths and platforms. For example, at Derragh 1 at Lough Kinale an unusually high number of stone axes were found scattered across the ground surface that may be the remnants of a cache (Woodman and Anderson 1990, 385; O'Sullivan 1998, 51). To date, lithic material has been identified at lake and riverside locations in the form of:

- The large assemblage of stone axes found at Lough Kinale (Woodman 1978 see also O'Sullivan 1998, 51)
- Material found in association with wooden structures (Mitchell, 1972; McCartan 2002; Fredengren 2004)
- In association with organic material, such as charcoal, wood, nuts, seeds and bone (Mitchell 1972)
- And in varying sized assemblages (Woodman 1978; Cooney 1987; O'Sullivan 1998; see also Fredengren 2004 for recent findings)

One area that has the potential to reveal a great deal about the practice of deposition and can be approached from a number of analytical levels is Clonava Island, located towards the northwest end of Lough Derravaragh. This is a knoll-reef of calcite mudstone with numerous chert outcrops that would have formed a large 'island' (c.2 km in length) surrounded by bog, open water, fens, and reed swamps in early post-glacial times (Mitchell 1972, 162; O'Sullivan 1998, 59). For people inhabiting, or perhaps moving through this area, Clonava would have been a prominent landmark in what would otherwise have been extensive wetlands (Figure 7.6). The fact that three sites were recorded on the island by Mitchell could be seen as testament to its visual prominence within the landscape and the view from parts of the island of the hill of Knockeyon – a potential source of chert and the highest hill in the area – might suggest that the inter-visibility of the island with other important landmarks may also have been a key factor in choosing to inhabit Clonava. The location of the island between the inlet and outlet of the River Inny would also have meant that it was centrally located within the river system and therefore centrally located within the wider social landscape.

At Clonava, and in the immediate environs, there is a great deal of variety in material and in the depositional contexts in which material is found: clusters of seeds of edible plants were identified *in situ* at Site 1, some of which were charred, lithic material that was evident on the surface of the foreshore included a diverse range of typical Late Mesolithic forms and a large amount of debitage. In the townland of Derrya, just to the east of the entry point of the river, additional Late Mesolithic material was noted within an irregular surface of eroding fen peat (Mitchell 1972, 169-170). The evidence thereby suggests that this was a place where a variety of day-to-day activities were carried out. Although O'Sullivan (1998, 57) has drawn attention to some of the economic activities that may have been performed here by asking whether the material represents "lithic production and procurement sites or were they hunting camps associated with lakeshore hunting, fishing and fowling? Or were they both?" what is yet to be developed, however, is a methodological framework that will do justice to the material and support a series of research questions that

Figure 7.6. View of Lough Derravaragh from Clonava Island

draw out the social (rather than economic) reasons for inhabiting Clonava.

With this in mind, it is worth reconsidering the results from Mitchell's excavation of Site 1 at Clonava that revealed a layer of wood overlying debitage, with larger lithic pieces collected from the surface (1970, 7). A similar pattern of vertical deposit formation can be seen in a number of Danish dwelling pits; where debitage has managed to fall through floors made up of bark, branches and twigs, larger pieces have been prevented from doing so (Grøn 2003, 695). Previously Site 1 has been interpreted from a functional perspective as an 'industrial site' (Woodman 1978, 321), however the depositional arrangement of the lithic material suggests something else and an alternative interpretation of Site 1 at Clonava could be made that would suggest this was a more likely a place of 'dwelling', where a different range of activities might be expected to take place, as opposed to those specifically associated with 'industrial' tasks.

However, as Conneller and Schadla-Hall have pointed out, this interpretation is also limiting: site descriptions that are built on "models of what constitutes a base camp – or even a ritual site – are too narrow and restrict interpretation" (2003, 103). Furthermore, making distinctions between social and working spaces is also questionable, as how polarised were these activities in the past? Conneller's (2000, 146) view of the landscape as a '*taskscape*' (Ingold 1993) is a useful one to take here, as it works to deconstruct "the dichotomy between people and the environment" and, importantly, suggests that the "taskscape represents the entire assemblage of tasks that constitute the act of dwelling for us, and their mutual resonance" (Conneller 2000, 146). A reinterpretation of Site 1 based on typological and depositional relationships would therefore potentially involve not only a shift in the 'function' of the site, it would be a way of highlighting and expanding upon the varied temporal and spatial relationships involved in *all* the acts of dwelling – instead of limiting the interpretation to evidence for 'industrial activities'.

Another question on deposition and temporality arises when looking at the evidence from Clonava, but this time on a larger landscape scale. The lithic assemblages from the island are relatively small and have been interpreted as "the repair and preparation of tools rather than any large-scale production" (O'Sullivan 1998, 57). This temporary settlement pattern would fit into the commonly accepted model of Late Mesolithic settlement, where it is argued that most sites "were occupied for a limited time and perhaps with a limited set of intentions" (Woodman and Anderson 1990, 381). Furthermore, Mitchell noted at the time of the excavation of Site 1 at Clonava that there was a large amount of fire cracked sandstone and heaps of chert and limestone along the flood-plain, which he interpreted as evidence that "a large number of fires had been lighted at various points from time to time during casual visits and there had not been a primary occupation-centre here" (1972, 162). The overall picture generated by these interpretations is therefore one of Clonava representing the material remains of hunter-gatherers who occupied the island for only *short* quantities of time but perhaps returned over a *long* period of time.

So what does the material deposited at Clonava mean in terms of time frames, and how do we go about accessing and making sense of what those time frames meant, from a social perspective? Are these lithic assemblages (from the surface and buried under peat deposits), the wooden structure at Site 1 with associated deposits of wood, charcoal, and hazelnuts, and the hearths mentioned by Mitchell, simply the result of a single palimpsest of activity? Or does this material reflect something else? Perhaps the island was inhabited on a year-round basis, or perhaps this was a landscape with a long history of activity - a place that hunter-gatherers 'routinely reoccupied' (Conneller and Schadla-Hall 2003, 101).

One example of an approach that has been used to establish phasing and the repeated use of a site can be seen in Spikins' *et al* (2002) work at March Hill Carr. In this case GIS was used at two sites (Early and Late Mesolithic) to link artefact distributions to recorded stratigraphy. This kind of approach is particularly useful in that it attempts to identify *physical* evidence for the repeated use of space through differentiating phases of occupation, which Spikins *et al*. point out, could potentially be used to identify "persistent places" (Barton *et al*. 1995) within the Mesolithic landscape. However, while this method has obvious advantages, it depends on a site being excavated and therefore has limited applications in situations that do not permit this methodology, such as this one. It has therefore been necessary to develop alternative approaches to investigating temporal and spatial patterns in material deposits. One technique that has potential in this respect is geophysical survey. A recent project carried out on a prehistoric site in Co. Monaghan used high-resolution geophysical survey to successfully identify even the most ephemeral features (O'Connor 2004). Gaffney and Gater (2004, 120) likewise recommend that "geophysical techniques can be used in a variety of situations to help archaeologists who are investigating Palaeolithic or Mesolithic sites and that the most obvious technique is the use of magnetometery to identify areas of burning".

Thinking back to Mitchell's comments alluding to evidence of fire cracked rock along the flood-plain, probably remnants of hearths, a survey of this kind could be used not only to test the presence of burning on the island but also to investigate the spatial patterns manifest in different types of tool production and their relationship to what was likely to have been a social place in the landscape: the 'fireplace'. Significantly, a recent ethnographic study on patterns in cave deposits discovered that all hunter-gatherer hearths except for ovens have multiple purposes, which include:

> cooking, sleeping by, giving warmth and light and acting as the point around which people relax, chat, interact socially or perform ceremonies (Galanidou 2000, 247).

The importance of hearths and their interconnectedness with the performance of a variety of social meaningful activities can be seen at a number of sites, which have already been discussed in this paper. Spikins *et al* (2002, 1237) observed that the artefact refit patterns from March Hill Carr "appeared to relate to distinctive activity patterns around the hearths" and at Ferriter's Cove a number of discrete activity areas were identified that appeared to "have focussed on particular hearth complexes where artefacts and organic remains cluster" (Woodman *et al*. 1999, 154) and a different variety of deposits, relating to a different series of activities, were identified as taking place further away from the heat of the hearth. As was mentioned earlier, at Lough Boora the placing of bone waste products into the hearth would suggest that not only were particular sets of activities undertaken by the fireside, but that hearths have the potential to reveal more about ritualised acts of deposition.

In this respect, while a reanalysis of the lithics from Clonava will play a central role in the investigation of the temporal and spatial patterning of social activities carried out on the island, alternative techniques like geophysical survey need to be developed in order to relieve what has been a traditional reliance on lithic datasets for constructing human narrative. By honing in on some of the finer-scale relationships between features (such as the possible hearths and wooden structure mentioned by Mitchell), the deposits, and finds and approaching the material found at Clonava at a 'nested scale' it may then be possible to view the temporal and spatial changes in activities that took place here as part of a complex web of socially grounded decisions made within an island context.

Mitchell's pioneering work at Clonava (1972) and his use of palaeoenvironmental studies, including the analysis of palaeobotanical remains found within the fen-peats to reconstruct the Mesolithic environment at Clonava and some of the economic activities that took place here, offers another opportunity to look at this material; this time from a broader landscape-scale perspective, which places these more 'nested' or 'intimate' acts of deposition within their contemporaneous environmental setting.

Constructing ideological platforms

> At the landscape level it is curious given the environmental focus of the ecological paradigm that there has been little written on constructions of the Mesolithic landscape (Finlay 2000, 75).

In this lake region we have evidence for the construction of platforms and the artificial enhancement of 'natural islands'. Importantly, the act of platform construction - where layers of brushwood and mud marls were used to construct a level and dry 'living' surface in the boggy areas surrounding the Loughs – is itself another example of how the landscape may have been structured through repeated acts of deposition. At Moynagh Lough, in Co. Meath, hunter-gatherers stabilised and enhanced natural clay knolls with mud, stones and brushwood, which would have formed dry areas, 'platforms' or 'artificial islands' within the former lake (Bradley 1991, 7). Recently Christina Fredengren from the Discovery Programme excavated a brushwood platform dating to the Late Mesolithic, which was located on a 'natural island' at Derragh Lough and associated with a large assemblage of Late Mesolithic stone tools, including several polished stone axes (Fredengren 2004; see also McCartan 2000).

Platforms such as those identified in the Midlands are not an uncommon feature of the Mesolithic landscape, with similar examples identified at British and European sites. The most famous example of a birchwood platform (Clark 1971, 1) can be seen at the site of Star Carr, that Clark emphasised "represented nothing more than a stabilisation of the swamp surface through the throwing down of birch brushwood, stones and wads of clay" (*Ibid.*, 9). A similar approach to negotiating a semi-waterlogged environment was taken at the Williamson's Moss site in Eskmeals, coastal northwest England. Here excavation revealed a Mesolithic platform that had been constructed with a foundation made from a 'lattice' of oak branches and multiple layers of birch brushwood, creating a dry habitation area in a low-lying, waterlogged environment that would have been prone to periodic flooding (Bonsall *et al.* 1990, 190).

Although recently this site has been heavily critiqued (Clare *et al.* 2001, 88) for discrepancies in dates because "one of the timbers forming the 'lattice' was 500 yrs earlier than the bark considered to have been flooring on the platforms". This, combined with fact that there were no artefacts found in direct association with the platforms and that "the waterlogged ground seems an unlikely place for human occupation" (Bonsall *et al.* 1986, 187-190 cited in Clare *et al.* 2001, 88) has been used to undermine the authenticity of the site. An alternative argument is then made in which biogenic deposits are said to have contributed to the formation of the 'platform'. For this reason, if we are to gain a better appreciation of these structures, and their wider landscape context, then more time needs to be given to investigating the process of deposition involved in their construction and maintenance.

There are several key questions that arise when thinking about the manufacture and meaning of these platforms. Surprisingly, in Ireland, patterns and associations between different materials deposited on these 'artificial islands', whether it is stone, wood, bone, or dumps of charcoal has had only minimal research from an ideological perspective. How were platform spaces structured? Was there a sense of differential placement of material culture? What types of contextual relationships between people and objects took place here compared to those that took place in other parts of the landscape? The latter question is perhaps the most critical, as we still have no *real* appreciation of the role of these platforms within the wider Mesolithic landscape.

Christina Fredengren (2002) gives a good discussion on the broader ideological and cosmological symbolism of platforms and works through some of the key problems in identifying and dating "small platform crannogs" (*Ibid.* 112) at Lough Gara, Co. Sligo, which are mentioned in antiquarian texts and the up to 2000 lithics found along the foreshore. Responding to the claims that, post-drainage, 110 to 300 (Fredengren 2002, 130) small crannogs dating to the Stone Age were identifiable during shoreline surveys of the lough, Fredengren develops a series of narratives that look at a range of reasons for how the sites may have come into being (the majority of these sites have been dismissed as Mesolithic in date by Woodman (1978), for showing no irrefutable evidence for a connection between the so-called 'crannogs' and the artefacts), and looks at the deeper social significance of these sites if the claims are to be accepted.

The low height of the crannogs at Lough Gara (c. 0.5m) meant that they would be 'open for activity' for only half the year and during the remainder they would have been inundated. Temporal and spatial patterns between the sites are teased out via the understanding and acceptance of a seasonal round of activities, where the stone platforms are seen as a "place that people returned to year after year after year" (Fredengren 2002, 135) and therefore became "places of intensity" (*Ibid.*, 118) within the landscape. Furthermore the restricted space of these islands (no more than 5-10m) is seen as having social implications, being more 'exclusive spaces' than natural islands (*Ibid.*, 136). By challenging the rationality grounding economical determinations for platform construction, in that "to build an island, even a small platform, is not the easiest way to fish" (*Ibid.*, 135), Fredengren argues that alternative interpretations that place greater significance on the monumentality of these spaces and their role in identity formation need to be considered.

At Moynagh Lough hunter-gatherers artificially enhanced two knolls with steep sides that would have provided dry areas of ground within the original lake (Bradley, 1991, 7). The knolls were then covered with a white layer of lacustrine mud. Bradley points out that this redeposited mud was "almost completely sterile and its presence is difficult to explain" (Bradley 1991, 7). This act of collecting white mud marls and then redepositing these over brushwood would have made a profound visible impact on those approaching the structures. The creation of artificial 'white islands' could be interpreted in a variety of ways. From a functional perspective these marls may have been used to create a level living surface, and as Bradley notes, "raised the knolls above the lake waters" (*Ibid.*). Another interpretation is that they performed a monumental role within the landscape. However, just how useful a term *monumental* is in describing the role of these artificial islands within the wider landscape is a whole new debate, one that is beyond the remit of this paper. Furthermore I believe that, rather than seeking to identify acts of monumentality – where interpretations often work at such a grand scale that they exclude the possibility of distinguishing other smaller or 'intimate' social exchanges, such as would be necessary in the construction of a platform - it is more productive to engage with the *specifics* of the material and develop frameworks that "bridge the gap between creative interpretations and the prehistoric material evidence" (Jordan 2003a, 130).

The fact that hunter-gatherers were physically modifying their environment when traditionally "the hunter-gatherer (almost by definition) may be supposed to inhabit a natural rather than an artificial environment" (Ingold 1996, 187) seems, in this case, a useful starting point for initiating a discussion on the ways in which people in the Mesolithic set about transforming the landscape. Part of the process of engaging with the specificity of this data needs to be the development of a suite of more meaningful research questions, such as: Exactly how many of these platforms exist? Is it possible to identify patterns in their construction and location? What time frames are associated with these structures? Do they represent repeated visits or were they part of a longer lasting palimpsest of lakeside activity? Looking at the manufacture of platforms; from the initial gathering of material to their deposition in a vertical sequence of layers, is another useful way of illuminating different temporal frames associated with the act or acts of manufacture and could be seen as representational act of community collaboration.

Through the nature of their construction and their location these artificial islands suggest hunter-gatherers had an intimate and shared knowledge of the local landscape; it was through these repeated acts of deposition that spaces became radically *physically* transformed, and even the most basic distinction of these platforms as being 'inhabited spaces' versus 'non-inhabited' spaces serves as a good 'ideological platform' for thinking about the role of material culture and deposition in structuring and transforming the landscape.

Conclusion

In conclusion, the northern Midlands have been overlooked within Irish Mesolithic research agendas in the past. Not only does this landscape hold the potential to pursue alternative lines of evidence from the traditional reliance on lithic data sets, it provides the critical inland link in an otherwise coastally dominant understanding of settlement patterns. Here the absence of hunter-gatherer narratives has been coupled with the physical loss of the Mesolithic environment. For this reason it is proposed that before attempting to "reconstruct the *social topography of this lakescape*" a reconstruction of the impact of modern land use on finds recovery and distribution must first be a priority. By drawing on two themes (depositional relationships and the construction of platforms) as a way of illuminating the temporal and spatial variation of hunter-gatherer activities, I have highlighted the need to rethink current deterministic models and shift our perceptions so that people in the Irish Mesolithic are seen as active agents in the *physical* transformation of space into place.

Acknowledgements

Graeme Warren, Mark Gordon, Blaze O'Connor, Aidan O'Sullivan, Rob Sands, Aidan O'Donoghue.

References Cited

Anderson, E. 1991. Kilcummer Lower, Co. Cork – flint scatter. In I Bennett (ed.), Excavations 1990: summary accounts of archaeological excavations in Ireland. Wordwell, Bray. 3-4.

Anderson, E. 1993. The Mesolithic in Munster: fishing for answers. In E. Shee Twohig and M. Ronayne (eds.), *Past Perceptions: the Prehistoric Archaeology of South- West Ireland*, Cork University Press. Cork. 16-24.

Barton, R.N.E., Berridge, P.J., Walker, M.J.C. and Bevins, R.E. 1995. Persistent places in the Mesolithic landscape: an example from the Black

Mountain Uplands of South Wales. *Proceedings of the Prehistoric Society* 61, 81-116.

Bonsall, C., Sutherland, D.G., Tipping, R.M. and Cherry, J. 1986. The Eskmeals Project: late Mesolithic settlement and environment in north-west England. In C. Bonsall (ed.), *The Mesolithic in Europe.* 175-205.

Bonsall, C., Sutherland, D., Tipping, R., and Cherry, T. 1990 The Eskmeals Project: Late Mesolithic settlement and environment in north-West England. In C. Bonsall (ed.) *The Mesolithic in Europe: papers presented at the Third International Symposium Edinburgh*. John Donald Publishers Ltd. Edinburgh. 175 –205.

Bradley, J. 1991. Excavations at Moynagh Lough, Co. Meath. *Journal of the Royal Society of Antiquaries of Ireland* 111, 5-26.

Christensen, C. 1999. Mesolithic boats from around the Great Belt, Denmark. In B. Coles, J.Coles and M.S. Jørgensen (eds.) *Bog bodies, sacred sites and wetland archaeology; proceedings of a conference held by WARP and the National Museum of Denmark, in conjunction with Silkeborg Museum, Jutland, September 1996.* Short Run Press, U.K, 47-50.

Clare, T. Clapham, A.J., Wilkinson, D.M. and Haworth, E.Y. 2001. The Mesolithic and Neolithic landscapes of Barfield Tarn and Eskmeals in the English lake district: some new evidence from two different wetland contexts. *Journal of Wetland Archaeology* 1, 83-105.

Clark, J. G. D. 1971. *Excavations at Star Carr: an Early Mesolithic Site at Seamer Near Scarborough, Yorkshire.* Cambridge University Press, Cambridge.

Collins, T. and Coyne, F. 2003. Fire and water, Early Mesolithic cremations at castleconnell, Co. Limerick. *Archaeology Ireland* 17 (2) 24-27.

Conneller. 2001. Hunter-gatherers in the landscape; technical economies of the Vale of Pickering. In K.J. Fewester and M. Zvelebil (eds.), *Ethnoarchaeology and hunter-gatherers: pictures at an exhibition.* British Archaeological Reports International Series. 955, 1-11.

Conneller, C. 2000. Fragmented space? Hunter-gatherer landscapes of the Vale of Pickering. In *Archaeological Review from Cambridge.* 17: 1 139-150.

Conneller, C. and Schadla-Hall, T. 2003. Beyond Star Carr: the Vale of Pickering in the 10th Millennium BP *Proceedings of the Prehistoric Society* 69, 85-106

Cooney, G. 1987. *North Leinster in the earlier prehistoric period: a settlement and environmental perspective.* Unpublished Ph.D. thesis, University College Dublin.

Cooney, G. 2000. *Landscapes of Neolithic Ireland.* Routledge. London.

Cooney, G. and Grogan, E. 1999 *Irish prehistory: a social perspective.* Wordwell, Dublin.

Finlay, N. 2000. Deer prudence. *Archaeological Review Cambridge* 17 (2) 1-8.

Finlay, N. 2003. Cache and carry: defining moments in the Irish later Mesolithic. In L. Bevan and J. Moore (eds.) *Peopling the Mesolithic in a northern environment.* British Archaeological Reports International Series; 1157, 87 – 94.

Fredengren, C. 2002. *Crannogs.* IWordwell, Bray.

Fredengren, C. 2004. The cutting edge. In *Archaeology Ireland,* 18 (4) 28-31.

Gaffney, C. and Gater, J. 2004. *Revealing the buried past: geophysics for archaeologists.* Gloucester.

Galanidou, N. 2000. Patterns in caves: foragers, horticulturalists, and the use of space. *Journal of Anthropological Archaeology* 19, 243-275.

Griffiths, D. and Woodman, P.C. 1987. Cretaceous chert sourcing in north-east Ireland: preliminary results. In G. de G. Sieveking and M.H. Newcomer (eds.), *The human uses of flint and chert,* 249-52. Cambridge University Press. Cambridge.

Grøn, O. 2003 Mesolithic dwelling places in south Scandinavia: their definition and social interpretation. *Antiquity.* Vol. 77, number 298, 685 – 708

Hingley, R., Ashmore, P., Clarke, C. and Sheridan, S. 1999. Peat, archaeology, and palaeoecology in Scotland. In B. Coles, J.Coles and M.S. Jørgensen (eds.) *Bog bodies, sacred sites and wetland archaeology; proceedings of a conference held by WARP and the National Museum of Denmark, in conjunction with Silkeborg Museum, Jutland, September 1996.* Short Run Press, U.K.104-114.

Ingold, T. 1996. Social relations, human ecology, and the evolution of culture: an exploration of the concepts and definitions. In A. Lock and C. Peters (eds.) *Handbook of Human Symbolic Evolution.* Claredon Press, Oxford. 178-203.

Jordan, P. 2003a Investigating post-glacial hunter-gatherer landscape enculturation: ethnographic analogy and interpretive methodologies. In Larsson, L., Kindgren H., Knutsson, K., Loeffler, D. and Åkerlund, A. (eds.) *Mesolithic on the move: papers presented at the Sixth International Conference on the Mesolithic in Europe, Stockholm 2000,* Oxford: Oxbow, 128-138.

Jordan, P. 2003b *Material Culture and Sacred Landscape: the anthropology of the Siberian Khanty.* Oxford: Alta Mira Press

Kimball, M.J. 1998 *The Lough Swilly archaeological survey: investigations into the Neolithic transition in eastern Donegal, Ireland.* Unpublished Ph.D thesis, University of Wisconsin-Madison

Kimball, M.J. 2000 Variation and context: ecology and social evolution in Ireland's Later Mesolithic. A. Desmond, G. Johnson, M. McCarthy, J. Sheehan, E. Shee Twoigh (eds.) *New agendas in prehistory: papers in commemoration of Liz Anderson.* Wordwell, Bray. 31-48.

McCartan, S. 2000. The utilisation of island environments in the Irish Mesolithic: agendas for Rathlin Island. In A. Desmond, G. Johnson, M. McCarthy, J. Sheehan, E. Shee Twoigh (eds.) *New Agendas in Irish Prehistory: Papers in Commemoration of Liz Anderson.* Wordwell, Bray. 15-30.

McCartan, S. 2003. Mesolithic hunter-gatherers in the Isle of Man: adaptations to an island environment? In Larsson, L., Kindgren H., Knutsson, K., Loeffler, D. and Åkerlund, A. (eds.) 2003 *Mesolithic on the move: papers presented at the Sixth International Conference on the Mesolithic in Europe, Stockholm 2000,* Oxford: Oxbow, 331–339.

McErlean, T., McConkey, R. and Forsyth, W. 2002. *Strangford Lough: an archaeological survey of the maritime cultural landscape.* Blackstaff Press Ltd, Belfast

Mellars, P., and Dark, P. 1998. *Star Carr in context.* Cambridge University Press, Cambridge.

Mitchell, G.F. 1970. Some Chronological Implications of the Irish Mesolithic. *Ulster Journal of Archaeology* 33, 3-14.

Mitchell, G.F. 1972 Some Ultimate Larnian sites at Lake Derravaragh, Co. Westmeath. *Journal of the Royal Society of Antiquaries of Ireland* 102, 160-73.

Mitchell, G.F. and Ryan, M. 2003. *Reading the Irish landscape.* Town House, Dublin.

Moore, C., Murray, C., Stanley, M., and McDermott, M. 2003. Bogland surveys in Ireland: forty shades of brown. In J. Fenwick (ed.) *Lost and Found: Discovering Ireland's Past.* Wordwell, Bray. 123-138.

Murray, C., Stanley, M., McDermott, C., and Moore, C. 2002. Sticks and stones: Wetland Unit survey 2002. In *Archaeology Ireland,* 16 (4) 16-19.

O'Connor, B., 2004. 'Places in the prehistoric landscape: exploring Irish rock art through high-resolution geophysical survey and test excavation'. Paper presented at the British Academy and Royal Swedish Academy of Letters History and Antiquities Symposium: Rock Carvings of North and West Europe: Documentation, Investigation and Presentation, British Academy, April 2004. London.

O'Sullivan, A. 1998. The archaeology of lake settlement in Ireland. *Discovery Programme Monographs 4.* Royal Irish Academy. Dublin.

O'Sullivan, A. and Daly, A. 1999. Prehistoric and coastal settlement and wetland exploitation in the Shannon estuary, Ireland. In *Bog bodies, sacred sites and wetland archaeology: proceedings of a conference held by WARP and the National Museum of Denmark, in Conjunction with Silkeborg Museum, Jutland, September 1996.* WARP 177-184.

Pollard, J. 2001. The aesthetics of depositional practice. *World Archaeology* 33 (2) 315-333.

Raftery, J. 1972. National Museum of Ireland: archaeological acquisitions in the year 1969. *Journal of the Royal Society of Antiquaries of Ireland* 103, 17-213.

Ryan, M. An early Mesolithic site in the Irish midlands. *Antiquity* 80, 46-7.

Spikins, P. 1999. *Mesolithic northern England: environment, population and settlement.* In British Archaeological Reports, British Series 283.

Spikins, P., Conneller, C., Ayestaran, H., Scaife, B. 2002. GIS Based Interpolation Applied to Distinguishing Occupation Phases of Early Prehistoric Sites. In *Journal of Archaeological Science* 29, 1235-1245.

Torrence, R. 2001. Hunter-gatherer technology: macro- and microscale approaches. In C. Panter-Brick. R. H. Layton and P. Rowley-Conwy (eds.), *Hunter-gatherers: an interdisciplinary perspective.* Biological Symposium Series. Cambridge. 73-98.

Van Wijngaarden-Bakker, L.H. 1989. Faunal remains and the Irish Mesolithic. In C. Bonsall (ed.), The Mesolithic in Europe: papers presented at the third international symposium, 125-33. Edinburgh.

Warren, G. 2001. Marking space? Stone tool deposition in Mesolithic and early Neolithic eastern Scotland. In K.J. Fewster and M. Zvelebil *Ethnoarchaeology and hunter-gatherers: pictures at an exhibition.* British Archaeological Reports, International Series. Oxford. 955, 91- 99.

Woodman, P.C. 1978. *The Mesolithic in Ireland: hunter-gatherers in an insular environment.* British Archaeological Reports, International Series 58. Oxford.

Woodman, P.C. 2003. Pushing back the boundaries. John Jackson lecture 2003. *Occasional Papers in Irish Science and technology* No. 27. 1-18.

Woodman, P.C. 2004. Some problems and perspectives: reviewing aspects of the Mesolithic period in Ireland. In A. Saville (ed.), *Mesolithic Scotland and its Neighbours: the early Holocene prehistory of Scotland, its British and Irish context and some Northern European Perspectives.* 285-297.

Woodman, P.C. and Anderson, E. 1990. The Irish Later Mesolithic: a partial picture. In Vermeersch and P. Van Peer (eds.), *Contributions to the Mesolithic in Europe,* 377-87. Leuven.

Woodman, P.C., Anderson, E. and Finlay, N. 1999 *Excavations at Ferriter's Cove 1983-95: last foragers, first farmers in the Dingle Peninsula.* Wicklow.

Zvelebil, M., and Green, S.W. 1992. Looking at the Stone Age in South-East Ireland: the Work of the Bally Lough Archaeological Project. *Archaeology Ireland* 6 (1) 20 -23.

Zvelebil, M., Macklin, M.G., Passmore, D.G. and Ramsden, P. 1996. Alluvial archaeology in the Barrow Valley, southeast Ireland: the Riverford Culture revisited. *Journal of Irish Archaeology* 7,13-40.

CAN'T SEE THE TREES FOR THE WOOD: THE SOCIAL LIFE OF TREES IN THE MESOLITHIC OF SOUTHERN SCANDINAVIA

Steven Price

University of Manchester

Abstract

Within Mesolithic studies the symbolic role of plants is rarely addressed, with the emphasis placed firmly on economic factors such as resource availability and environmental reconstruction. In these cases the landscape becomes a backdrop to human activity, providing resources and predictions of fauna, thus reducing wood to a raw material to be exploited and is supposed to have been perceived in an economic and scientific stance much as is common today. This model, whilst recognising the technological properties of different woods, ignores the diversity of different tree species and the qualities that they bring to a place; in short, how they are lived with and experienced. Within many societies (including our own) forests, different tree species, and even individual trees hold a much greater significance to people than as raw materials to be exploited as and when they are needed, and indeed, our category of 'tree' is not a universal nor obvious one. Thus, this paper will address these issues and examine how people in the Mesolithic of Scandinavia categorised wood through an examination of how different types of trees are and are not used.

Introduction

The title of this paper has come from the recognition that current archaeological approaches to the Mesolithic prioritize wood as a raw material over the trees from which it is derived. Where trees are recognised it is to make up the ecological environment and consequently reduce them to merely forming the background to human action (Austin 2000, 44). These approaches give the forest priority over and above the trees which make it up and so create a single unit comprising the environment or at most a 'place' within the landscape. What these approaches ignore however, is the individuality of different species and the different qualities that they afford. 'The forest' has become a generic object with the implicit assumption that all trees are identical and consequently so are all forests. The reality however, is much different, as the collection of individual species creates a unique experience affording different modes of behaviour and different experiences for the senses. The identification of individual species has been to reconstruct the natural environment to the detriment of how different trees were experienced (i.e. Ballantyne 2004; Jochim 2000; Price 1985; Robinson 2000). To lump all species of tree together as just a generic forest is to ignore the unique structuring conditions which different species and individual trees offer. This idea of a passive environment has emerged from the separation of humanity and nature, with the presumption of humanities transcendence over nature. Consequently, nature has become synonymous with passive raw material to human activity (Ingold 2000, 63).

It is proposed here that the interconnectedness of trees and people goes much further than archaeologists usually consider. To see trees as just making up the environment and forming a stable resource overlooks the great depth of interweaving within the lives of people and trees. Mesolithic people were not single minded economic entities, but were immersed within their world, a world in which they held active relationships with material things.

Symbolic Trees

The current state of affairs regarding the treatment of plants in prehistory is slowly beginning to be addressed, with an acknowledgment of their symbolic importance, although these mainly come from Neolithic studies (Austin 2000; Hastorf and Johannessen 1994; Moore 2003). With regards to Mesolithic studies the perception of trees as static entities and fixed landscape features has been questioned by Moore (2003), who noted that the colonisation of trees in the early Holocene was remarkably fast, with changes apparent within a persons lifetime. The role of trees in prehistoric life needs to be addressed moving away from portraying them as only economic resources, with consideration taken towards demonstrating their relationship with people and how these may have been materially manifest in the construction of society (*Ibid.*, 143).

Whilst the recognition of the symbolic importance of trees has not gone unnoticed in anthropology, it is often downplayed in favour of their practical uses as a raw material or food resource. What has been demonstrated however, is that trees have played and continue to play a considerable role in articulating social concerns and symbolic values. Indeed, as Ingold has pointed out, in many accounts of hunter-gatherer societies the landscape is considered to be alive and people have to maintain relationships with different kinds of powers within the landscape, much as they do with people (2000, 66-67).

In many societies, different types of trees and plants are recognized and used according to how they are perceived. Tree symbolism has long been acknowledged among the native groups of the northwest coast of North America with reference to the cedar. Despite this studies have tended to examine technology in great detail without a serious examination of tree symbolism. Mauzé (2001) has noted that the diverse species of trees growing in the region are used to create a rich material and symbolic world, with elaborate distinctions between species and varieties within species (*Ibid.*, 235). Here, trees are considered to be people and as such they are not thought of as mere materials. Wooden objects are consequently regarded as living things, a point evidenced in myths with wooden objects, such as doorways and house posts, portrayed as living creatures (Goldman 1975, 192). Many taboos also surround the use of trees. Canoe makers undergo a period prayer and fasting before finding the right tree to be felled; if bark is required care is taken to ensure that enough is left for the tree to survive; and when planks are needed, rather than felling a tree they are split from a standing one (Mauzé 2001, 241). One of the common themes apparent in the origin myths is the belief that people come from wood, (rather than stone) and that this is why people, like trees, are mortal and shall die. This tree/person analogy is also apparent in the origin myths of the Koyukon people of Alaska, who believe that some trees were transformed from human women, evidenced by their bark. The story tells that when three women were told that their husband had died, the first woman was so distraught that she pinched her skin and changed in to the spruce with its rough and pinched bark, the second cut her skin with a knife, becoming the poplar with its deeply cut bark, and the third pinched herself until she bled, turning into the alder whose bark is used to make red dye (Nelson 1983, 51-52).

The cedar is also significant to the Khanty people of Siberia which, along with birch, is believed to grow in the upper world (Jordan 2001, 33). For this reason cedar wood is chosen to create the physical presence of local guardian spirits in the form of carved idols. Whilst the influence of these spirits is sensed in many different spheres of activity, their physical presence is only at the holy site; a place where hunting, fishing and gathering are prohibited as everything in the area is owned by the spirits and are not places for casual visits (*Ibid.*, 33). At the site the idols are placed in low open-fronted or stilted houses, where they are cared for by a young active hunter, who is responsible for providing food for the visits which occur four times a year and granting access to visitors. This role is held for 3 years before being passed on. The idols themselves are carved by elders from another community and are remade once the carver has died, an act which is often accompanied by blood sacrifices (*Ibid.*, 34). The significance of the cedar here then is obviously as more than a raw material, and is engaged in complex relationships to do with the regeneration, reincarnation and the reiteration of social ideas and values.

Another theme which is apparent is the recurrence throughout many societies of the correspondence between trees and human bodies. Within Zafinimena society particular types of wood are considered equivalent to the corpse of a royal, manifest in how they are both dealt with. After decomposition on the mainland, the royal corpse is returned to the island and placed below the royal burial compound where it is washed with mead, so that "the flesh turned to water and fell from the bones...thus 'drying' the body" (Feeley-Harnik 1991, 445). Similarly, the trees cut to make the inner-most fence around the royal tomb (the *menaty*) were described as being 'washed' when they are stripped of leaves, branches and bark to expose the heartwood (*teza*). Many restrictions surround the use and choice of which heartwood can be used. Only those which are red, white or yellow can be selected and some types of tree are considered dangerous and can not be used, such as *Ficus*, as although it is praised for its conquering habits in the surrounding villages, it is for this reason that it is prohibited in royal constructions. Further, only trees which are dead but still standing can be used whereas living trees are prohibited (*Ibid.*, 444). The heartwood is then further treated in a similar way to the royal corpse as both are only allowed to be taken up into the burial compound once work at the drying bed has been completed and then they must be positioned directly into their proper place. Thus, "workers in the menaty service handled the trees like royal bodies and they handled the teza like royal corpses" (*Ibid.*, 445).

Tree-Person identity can also be taken further with parts of the tree recognized as parts of the human body and vice versa. Among the Aluund of Southwestern Zaire the roots of a tree are considered to be the penis, the sap is the semen and the trunk is the womb. The fruit is the result of the coming together of the root and the trunk and is considered the offspring (De Boeck 1994, 461). However, not all trees share these characteristics. The *mulooz* tree is an exclusively male tree as it grows the tallest and has a characteristic white sap, likened to sperm. Most importantly, however, it is said to have one large root which penetrates deeply into the earth, suggestive of insemination. The *musaal* tree, conversely, is 'the tree of mother-hood' noticeable for its red bark and wide-ranging branches, in contrast with its short roots. The *kapwiip* tree is the 'elder' of the trees having extremely hard wood which is red on the inside and covered with a layer of white wood under the bark (*Ibid.*, 461-462). Thus the differently perceived attributes of trees are likened to human features, with different trees selected as important for various experiences and qualities which they afford.

Within modern Western society trees and forests are not devoid of meaning beyond their economic potential. Indeed, far from just being places of natural resources they are potent symbols for nature and the natural (Jones and Cloke 2000, 38). Discourses of global environmental damage have placed the destruction of the rainforest at the forefront of such discussions and trees and woodland have become casualties of industry. Such environmental losses have demanded a response often involving tree planting, constituting both the symbolic and material response to such issues (*Ibid.*, 38-9). Indeed, Zelter has argued that the tree is our most potent symbol, with different aspects of the tree as metaphors for various qualities:

> sheltering and protecting us within its branches; ... giving us strength and resilience in its sturdy trunk; feeding and nurturing us with its fruits; giving us everlasting hope in the constant regeneration and rebirth of its seeds (Zelter 2001, 222).

This symbolic nature is also highly evident in the wide range of tree images used to promote identities of nature, growth, peace, health and organic or environmentally friendly products.

Our perception of different species is also greatly varied and culturally constructed. Different species have differing qualities which affect the land in different ways. Different trees capture and reflect light differently, as particular types of leaves move in various ways in different wind speeds (Jones and Cloke 2000, 91). Likewise, the sounds made by trees also vary between species; the ash hisses, the beech rustles, the holly whistles and the fir tree moans (*Ibid.*, 91). Tree bark differs remarkably both in colour and texture, from the smoothness of the beech to the roughness of the oak (Figure 8.1) and smells, such as the lemon-musk of the sassafras or the turpentine smell of the longleaf pine, also vary greatly. The wildlife they attract also differs, offering different things to different creatures such as the attraction of bees to the lime tree. Thus, far from being merely static, passive agents their presence physically alters a place, showing trees to have their own form of agency and bringing many different qualities to a place, qualities which have been ignored in favour of mechanical properties. As these qualities differ by species they lend themselves to certain social conceptions of those species and the places where they are found. Within modern British society for example, conifers are generally disliked, seen in a negative light despite their usefulness as a resource (Condry 1974, 132) whereas oak trees are symbols of freedom and the longevity and resilience of the English state (Jones and Cloke 2002, 35). Individual species have diverse qualities which not only afford different uses as raw materials, but also differing experiences of place. However, whilst one species has particular characteristics, this is not to say that they are all experienced in the same way. The individuality of trees and their interaction with the surrounding world (not only other plants, but animals, people and activities occurring around them) along with how they are socially perceived allows them to be involved in the creation of place in a dynamic way and actively forms the context for social action. It is aspects such as these which are ignored when wooded landscapes are considered.

What is 'a Tree'?

The division between what is and what is not a tree is generally taken to be an obvious distinction. However, the actual classification of a plant as a tree is not clear-cut and is further complicated as the term 'tree' has no standing in scientific taxonomy. The distinction between shrubs and trees is generally agreed that a tree is a plant with a single trunk rising to over 4.5m high, whereas a shrub is smaller with several stems rising from the base and no obvious trunk (Hillier 1972, 10 and 18). However, some trees and shrubs do not fit into these categories. Both hazel and willow trees frequently branch at ground level but can still produce a crown 8-10m high and so fit into both the shrub and tree categories. Plants vary incessantly in terms of size, woodiness and multiplicity of stems and do not neatly fit into the categories devised

Figure 8.1 Differences in tree bark. A: Ash B: Beech C: Birch

by the modern West (Hunn 1987, 149). Ellen (2001) has clearly demonstrated the cultural ambiguity of the status of palms, as in both folk and scientific taxonomies they are sometimes classified as trees and sometimes not. Thus, whilst it may seem obvious that some plants should be classified as trees, others can be more ambiguous. In the earlier examples of the symbolic role of trees it is not trees *per se* that are singled out and treated as a class in their own right, but particular kinds of entities which are seen to offer particular qualities, qualities which are not necessarily based on the visual form of the tree as we think of it. Gell (1996) for example, has demonstrated that among the Kaluli, bird classification is not based on shared visual characteristics, but rather on the kinds of songs that they have. Consequently, we can not assume that all societies order reality based on visual qualities as we do. Among the Kwakiutl of the northwest coast of North America, trees are believed to be animate and so are considered to be human, being placed in a broad category with many animals, rather than with plants (Goldman 1975, 192).

Randall (1976) has argued that our standard taxonomic diagrams are inadequate in that they do not go far enough to look at relationships between things, suggesting instead that models where many categories are cross-cutting are more appropriate (Figure 8.2). Within this view things are classified by perceived characteristics such as their tree-ness or shrub-ness or oak-ness etc. (*Ibid.*, 550). He argues that people do not construct taxonomic 'trees' but classify things within particular situations, selecting characteristics which are both specific enough to achieve a result, yet general enough to efficiently accomplish the purpose (*Ibid.*, 552). These choices however, are already caught up in social history and values and so are both limited to and enabled by social conditions.

Thus, it can be seen that the term for tree is not an obvious or natural one but rather it is culturally specific, emerging through the identification of specific characteristics. Consequently our notion of what makes a tree a 'tree' is particular to our classificatory scheme. For this reason, other aspects must be considered when looking at tree use for the Mesolithic, not simply visual characteristics, but how Mesolithic people may have experienced and engaged with different trees and how such entities were classified. Therefore comments making simple claims such as that an area was forested ignore the recognition of other schemes of classification, as trees as a whole are not necessarily a recognized category. A forest may be seen to be comprised of a variety of different entities, other than simply 'trees'.

Technology and Raw Materials

Many explanations regarding technology and raw material use assume that they were chosen simply to exploit the natural properties of different raw materials and consequently ignore technological choices and social conventions. When the symbolic role of trees has been considered within prehistory it is generally "in their capacity for transformation" (Evans *et.al.* 1999, 251) but

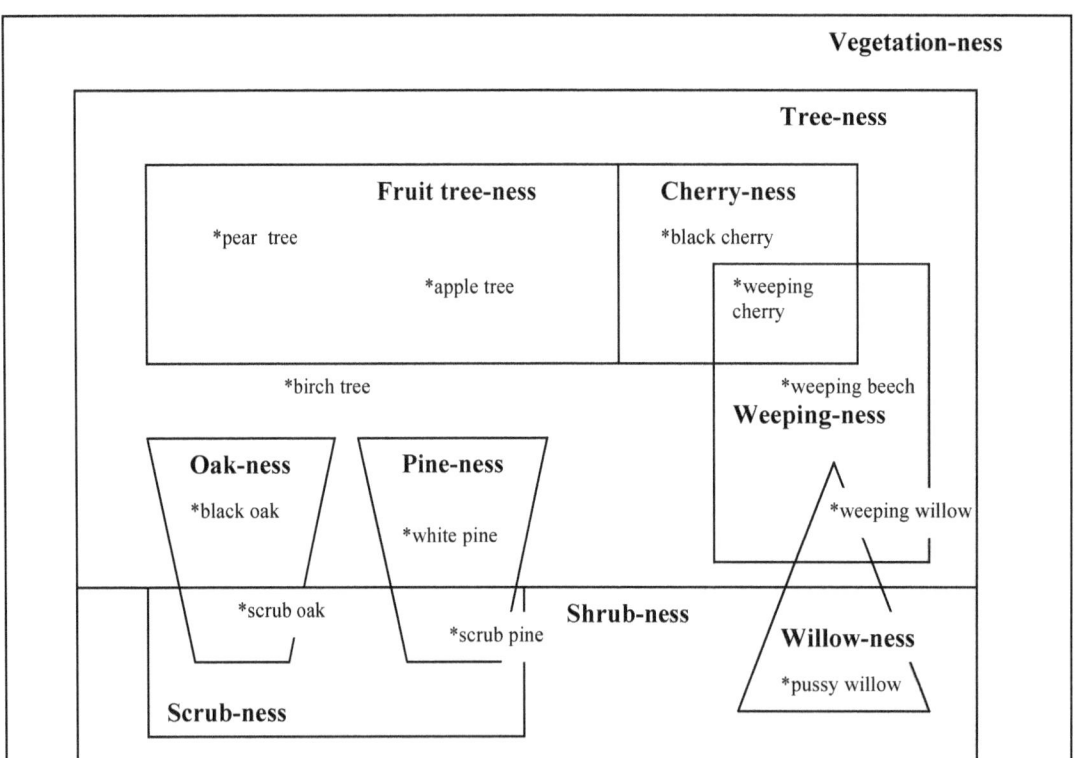

Figure 8.2 An example of a cross-cutting characteristics model of some plant categories. After Randall 1976

these continue to assume that despite their symbolic roles "[t]heir potential as timber is obvious" (*Ibid.*, 251). As such their material properties are brought to the foreground of their role in society, with the social perception of them exerting little influence on technology. These assumptions lead to an ignorance of the social role of wood, with characteristics apparently being designed or chosen to answer technical problems alone and creating explanations in terms of technical properties. A prime example of this is the choice of lime for canoes in the Mesolithic of southern Scandinavia, explained by the fact that lime has a high tolerance to drying, is easy to work when freshly felled and is resistant to splitting (Andersen 1986, 90; Christensen 1990, 131). Likewise, for the Neolithic when alder and oak are preferred, the explanation shifts to the material properties of these woods; that alder lasts longer in water and is easy to work or that oak is very durable (Christensen 1990, 131). Another factor given precedence is the availability of the raw materials. It stands to reason that a material must be available for it to be used, but this does not mean that the most widely available will be the most frequently used, as assumed by many environmental reconstructions. For example, many reconstructions which use charcoal samples (i.e. Andersen 1995; 1996) assume that all available woods are equally burnt. This has been shown to be false, as at Ringkloster where alder was dominant it comprised the least amount of carbonized wood (16%) (Andersen 1994-5, 20).

As discussed earlier raw materials or sources of raw materials must first be recognized as such and the equation of tree and wood is not universal. All human action on the material world is a learned behaviour and therefore varies between human groups. The logic and coherence of technological knowledge is not based exclusively on physical phenomena, but is underwritten by broader symbolic systems, within which the material world is embedded (Lemonnier 1993, 3). If this is the case then it cannot be assumed that Mesolithic people worked with economic efficiency and scientific knowledge. Therefore, through examining how different species of available trees were used in the Mesolithic of Southern Scandinavia, it may offer a suggestion as to how these people classified their world and show that their technological choices were not based exclusively on economic principles. It will also show that their relationship with the environment was not one of it as a passive backdrop of raw materials, but was one which allowed different relationships to be explored and expressed.

The Social life of Trees in the Mesolithic of Southern Scandinavia

Through an examination of the species of tree that various types of wooden objects are made from in the Southern Scandinavian Mesolithic, striking patterns begin to emerge, suggesting a relationship between plants and people which was different from our own. Particular trees and shrubs were singled out for use for certain things, others were interchangeable and some were not used at all. By understanding that humanity and nature are not mutually exclusive categories but are engaged in dynamic relationships, it becomes clear that the environment was not merely a set of resources to be exploited. People and the environment were entwined in a series of complex social relationships and unsurprisingly had different systems of classification, rather than classifying the world as we do, which is commonly portrayed.

For people at this time, ideas about what was (and was not) wood were not based simply on form and the identification of a 'tree', but were enmeshed with other modes of behaviour. Indeed, as Lemonnier (1993, 4) has noted, members of a society have ideas about all aspects of the technical process, including the raw material, the actors and when and where it can occur, which play a role in the wider symbolic system. For the manufacture of wooden objects and the appropriate choice of raw materials then, technical properties alone cannot be considered to be the overriding factor governing such decisions. It can therefore be argued that the choices made during the technical process of wooden object creation can demonstrate a much deeper relationship between people and trees than simply as raw materials to be used to the best economic advantage.

In southern Scandinavia at the time of the Ertebølle, the most dominant trees along with oak and elm were lime on well drained soils, and alder dominating in wetter areas (Berglund 1986). As well as their aforementioned properties, lime is soft and so easily worked by hand and highly resistant to splitting, but it is not as strong as many other woods such as oak (Marshal 1785, 154; Willis 1970). Alder is both water resistant and soft, and so also easily worked by hand (Willis 1970, 7). Of the 21 canoes that have been found and identified by species from the Ertebølle, 20 of these were constructed from whole lime trees, with the sole exception of a canoe of aspen. The only other object to be made from lime was a single heart-shaped paddle, an object which is usually made of ash (Pedersen 1997, 164). So although both woods were widely available and easily worked, lime was chosen almost exclusively for the construction of canoes. Further, although alder was widely available, it was rarely used at all (a single fish weir was found at Tybrind Vig (Andersen 1985, 61)). Thus two of the most abundant species were being used exclusively for one type of object (lime) or hardly used at all (alder).

Other profuse species include oak and elm, of which oak is durable yet hard to work by hand and elm is comparatively elastic, resistant to splitting and wearing, but can also be tough and difficult to work (Willis 1970, 6-8). Oak is rarely used in the Mesolithic and the discovery of 2 oak digging sticks at Ringkloster was noted as extraordinary (Andersen 1994-5, 46). Elm, however, is used consistently in the manufacture of bows, although one example has been found of a bow made from dogwood (Grøn and Skaarup 1991). This was also noted as being different from other bows in its technique of manufacture. Rather than being made from a single split piece of wood as elm bows are, this one had a rounded section which followed the surface of the original branch (*Ibid.*, 44). The use of different woods and manufacturing techniques may imply that it was not considered as a bow in the same way that elm bows were. This suggests that particular social conventions and modes of behaviour were associated with activities surrounding elm and bows. Thus it may have been that both elm and lime are classified pertaining to the objects that they are associated with, namely bows and canoes, rather than as wood in general. Interestingly, both elm and lime have also been associated with mortuary practices, as elm bark has been found covering both inhumations and boat burials (in lime canoes).

Hazel dominated as a shrub, along with hawthorn, holly and willow, thriving under the canopy of the lime-oak-elm-alder forest (Berglund 1986). Hazel is easy to work, resilient and pliant (Kindred 1995, 39-40) and as a shrub is available as rods. Hazel was used for a wide variety of objects in the Mesolithic and appears in a much greater quantity than any other species of wood. Objects including digging sticks, arrows, stakes and withies (for fish fences), fish weirs, boat mooring posts, axe hafts, thwarts for boats and leisters were all made from hazel. Arrows and leisters are the only objects made exclusively from hazel, along with fish fences (although one withy if aspen has been discovered) (Pedersen 1997). Although leisters were made from hazel, the barbs were made from a variety of woods, including hazel, dogwood, rowan and hawthorn. This suggests that whilst the body of the leister was constrained regarding what it could be made from, the barbs were less so. Other shrubs such as holly and willow were rarely used, although hawthorn was used occasionally for several objects.

Other tree species available to a lesser extent include ash and birch. As previously noted, ash was most often used in the construction of heart-shaped paddles, although the majority of these have come from a single site; Tybrind Vig. Spears of ash have also been found at several sites (Andersen 1994-5). Its properties include being both resilient and elastic (Kindred 1995, 31; Willis 1970, 7). There is also evidence to suggest that ash was used in mortuary rites, as at Skateholm I ash charcoal was found above a grave (Larsson 1985, 372). Birch wood is strong

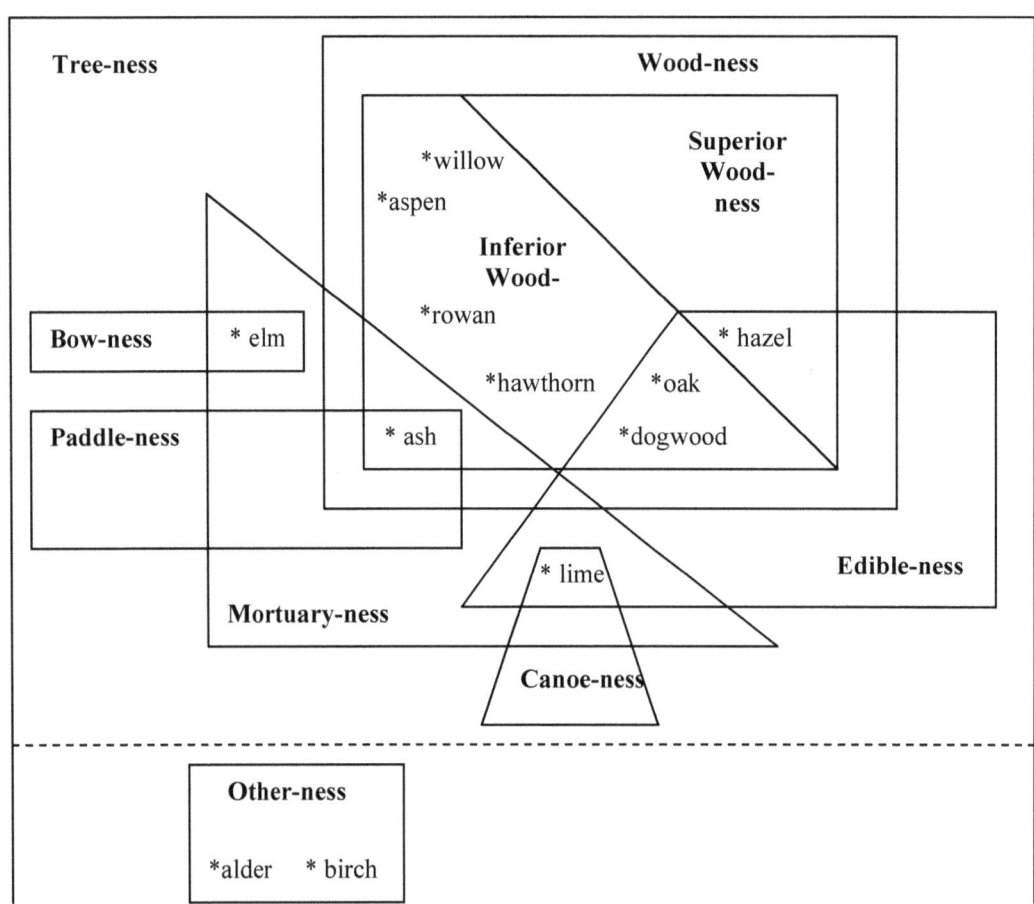

Figure 8.3 Cross-cutting characteristics model for Mesolithic tree use

but also very pliable and easily worked by hand (Kindred 1995, 17-19). It is surprisingly then, that objects made from birch are very rare. Birch bark tar, however, has been found chewed at Segebro in Skåne and parts of Northern Europe (Aveling 1997; Larsson 1982) and is a practice which is also attested in ethnographic accounts (Aveling 1999).

What is apparent from this brief précis is the preferential selection of particular types of wood for particular objects and activities. Drawing on notions discussed at the start of this paper, it is clear than such trends cannot be assumed to be related to mechanical properties alone. There is a clear pattern in the identification of certain species as usable wood, with some species identified with particular objects and particular modes of interaction. The use of lime exclusively for the construction of canoes, for example, may demonstrate the equation of lime and canoe and thus the recognition of a particular mode of interacting with lime, one consequence being that it is not used for other objects (Figure 8.3). The relationship between people and lime was conditioned by socially acceptable modes of behaviour, limiting the possibilities of how it could be interacted with. This could also apply to the use of elm. The choice of specific types of wood for the construction of particular objects is not unusual. Along with the earlier examples, within the Amazonian Ka'apor society, house posts can only be made from a select number of tree species which are "so important as a house post that [they are] tabooed as a firewood source" (Baleé 1994, 54).

Fishing was an important aspect of Mesolithic life, evidenced by the numerous finds of fish and shellfish remains, fishing equipment and stable isotope analysis. It stands to reason that the canoe would have been an essential part of this along with being an indispensable means of transport. The importance of the canoe can also be shown through the finds of decorated paddles, the only wooden objects found to hold such elaboration. Ethnographic examples demonstrate that in many societies the construction of the canoe is embedded in other practices. As shown previously, canoe building among the native groups of the Northwest coast of North America is embedded in specific modes of behaviour regarding how the wood is interacted with. Also among the Achuar of the Jivaro groups of South America, the manufacture of a canoe is performed by a single man who fells the tree and does most of the work at the felling site. During this time he must undergo a self imposed chastity, as without this the boat would be made unstable "like a couple rolling on a bed in each others arms" (Descola 1997, 253). He then issues an invitation to a drinking party, which is held once the participants have helped to drag the canoe overland and to the water. This invitation is open to people from same group as the canoe maker and is extended to those from neighbouring groups. Both men and women help to move the canoe, with the men pushing and the women pulling. Once it reaches the waters edge the women then simulate the launching, struggling to pull an imaginary canoe into the water into which they then fall, splashing one another in order to appease the water spirit. Only after this performance can the canoe be safely launched (*Ibid.*, 252-4). Thus, the construction of the canoe, although performed by a single man who must undergo certain taboos and modes of behaviour, is also a social event, reinforcing beliefs about how things are to be done.

Explanations which hold that mechanical properties are the main reasons for technological choices ignore the social relationships between people and plants. Many trees have properties equally suited to the creation of canoes (alder being the most apparent, with its high water resistance and ease of working), but the choice of a single species has resulted in the properties of the chosen wood being used as an explanation for its choice, with the properties of other woods ignored. The material is believed to have been chosen to accomplish that which its properties are best used for, leading tautologically to the conclusion that it was the best material for the job and consequently removing the social context. The choice of lime assumes that, as it is tolerant to drying out without cracking it was taken out of the water and left to dry, rather than kept in the water. However, that there was little concern about the canoes getting wet whilst not in use can be seen from Horsekær, where 3 boats were discovered to have been moored at the waters edge (Pedersen 1997, 290-294). Indeed, the perishable nature of lime is evidenced on many of the canoes, with holes drilled in them to lash split pieces together (*Ibid.*, 160; 284).

In Ertebølle society, the canoe was a socially important item and as such its use and manufacture were governed by strict modes of behaviour. As previously stated, within society people share sets of ideas regarding how a raw material or object should be made, what it must look like and how it should be used (Lemonnier 1993, 14). Thus the choice to use lime cannot be said to be due to its physical properties alone, but how it is perceived and experienced within that society. So, whilst many trees and shrubs may have been considered to be wood, the lime was not seen in these terms. Rather than having the property of 'wood', it was the 'canoes-ness' of the lime which singled it out from other trees and it is this 'canoe-ness', rather than a 'wood-ness' which governed how it was used, preventing its use for other objects. Consequently, lime and canoe were inseparable and it was not the case that one was a tree and the other a finished object, but rather they were one and the same thing. Elm may have been considered in a similar way in relation to bows. The Elm was not a 'wood' plant, but rather a 'bow' plant. From this, a canoe made from another wood in a different fashion may not have been considered a canoe at all. Likewise, the bow made from dogwood may not have been considered a bow in the same way that elm bows were.

As Dobres (1995, 42) has argued, technical acts involve the defining and expressing of social identities, and therefore produce gendered subjects. As such, the involvement in various relationships with different materials and the construction of particular objects within acceptable modes of behaviour would have created gendered identities. These would have been bound up in particular relationships regarding how different materials and objects were classified and the engagement with these issues in the act of manufacture and use would have served to express social identities. It must be noted, however, that these gendered identities did not necessarily follow modern stereotypes where men would be associated with elm bows and hunting or lime and canoe construction. Rather these gendered identities would have come about through the interplay between people and social conditions, rather than based on modern ideas about sex and identity.

The use of lime for canoes was bound up with particular actions and behaviours, but it can be argued that these were not open to everyone, only certain kinds of people. The use of lime wood demonstrated a particular kind of person, one who was engaged in a dynamic relationship with not only lime but with the whole of society in a different way to others. As all people within the society would have shared ideas and understandings of lime trees and canoes, the active involvement with the lime in canoe production (and use) would have embodied this relationship and reinforced traditions surrounding it. The differing relationships with lime allowed particular people to act within society in ways different to others and to facilitate change through meaningful action. Whilst the modes of interaction with lime were specific and traditional, constraining its use, it consequently also enabled contestation by others. The production of a single canoe of aspen could be seen to be a demonstration of this. While it may have been intended to subvert the social order and create change in social roles, the fact that canoes continued to be made from lime may be due to the unintended consequence that it instead served to bring the legitimate mode of behaviour to the foreground of social concerns. As this action was not socially acceptable behaviour, it may have strengthened traditional behaviours, rather than overcoming them.

The use of hazel for the construction of many objects suggests that this was the main source of 'wood'. There are a few objects which seem to be favoured for construction only with hazel, but due to its abundant use for other objects, it would appear that hazel was associated with wood rather than any particular kind of object in the same way as lime or elm were. Rather, it was preferred, perhaps seen as the best or the most appropriate. So, whilst many trees were recognised for their wood, hazel was the most noteworthy, given a place of precedence above the others. The dominance of hazel as wood enabled the reiteration and contestation of these traditions on a daily level, as it was frequently open to more people. It allowed many people within society to manipulate the social order and display modes of behaviour to help create their own identities and place within society, along with maintaining social traditions or to try to incite change. Given the flexibility of these rules the scope for personal interpretation of them was greater, which also made it much harder to invoke large scale changes in society as such a relationship allowed such personal opinions.

Ash also seems to have been considered as wood but appropriate only for specific things, mainly heart-shaped paddles. The creation of these paddles was understood to involve the use of ash as a part of the social conventions surrounding how paddle making technology was undertaken. Whilst hazel was the preferred wood type for the creation of many different things, ash was technologically linked with heart-shaped paddles. This, however, did not exclude it from use in other areas of technology, and whilst it was seen as 'what paddles should be made from', this does not mean that it was necessarily a good wood for the creation of other things. This also allowed it to be involved in the construction of social identities in much the same way as lime or elm, but it also enabled other modes of action; that of decoration. Given the constraints and the fact that these are the only wooden objects that have been found decorated, paddles could have been a potent medium for the manipulation and expression of social concerns in a highly personal way. However, ash was also used for the production of other objects. So, whilst the creation of paddles from ash was heavily constrained by tradition, the creation of other objects from ash was less so. With the manufacture of other objects, the constraints were less marked, making it no longer a viable means of reproducing or subverting social concerns and ideas.

That alder and birch were rarely, if ever, used can perhaps be explained by highly apparent anomalous features regarding their wood, which may have marked them out as different. Alder is unique in that its wood is white, but when cut turns from white to red (Kindred 1995, 28). Birch is also unique in that its heartwood and sapwood are indistinguishable (*Ibid.*, 17-19) and it also sheds its bark from time to time. These features may have been factors ruling them out as being 'wood'. Bark can be an important resource and the fact that alder bark can be used as a dye and birch bark was occasionally shed may have been considered significant. Care must be taken when stripping bark from a tree to make sure that it is not ringed, and so a tree which sheds its bark may be considered to be offering itself. Also, in many societies the heartwood is an important part of the tree and the absence of it may have played a large part in the classification of the birch as not being a tree at all. So whilst birch was not classified as a tree in the same way as hazel, the bark *was* used. A similarity between the alder and birch is that they also have smooth bark, unlike most other trees at that time which have a much rougher bark. This may also have marked them out as different.

Conclusion

The classification of trees in the Mesolithic cannot therefore be assumed to be the same as our own with the equation of trees and wood. Indeed, specific trees in our society are seen in different ways, a fact ignored in studies of prehistory which seek to recreate the environment. Far from simply seeing trees as raw materials to be exploited, specific trees were recognised as different, not only in terms of their use, but in terms of their *being*. Lime trees *were* canoes, just as elms *were* bows, and as such they were not 'wood'. Their use as a raw material for the creation of other objects was not considered, not because of their mechanical properties, but because of their status within the classification system. This was also the same for other objects not considered to be wood, such as the birch and alder, although not being technologically linked with any objects they were not used. In contrast, hazel was viewed as the preferred, perhaps the best wood but could in most instances be substituted by other plants considered to be wood, including rowan, hawthorn, aspen and willow.

Through dynamic relationships with various kinds of trees, different modes of action were available to different people and with varying degrees of social impact. The heavy constraints surrounding the use of particular types of tree allowed certain people to reiterate and reinterpret traditions from their personal histories and experiences and to manipulate social conventions in socially acceptable ways. As such actions and behaviours were strongly limited, the degree with which they could be altered was also limited, but their effect would have been amplified. This is in contrast to hazel, which was used more often, and was open to many people and many different strategies of expression, reiteration and manipulation of social ideas. Through an active engagement with these principles, different identities could be expressed, changed and re-created.

By viewing trees in this manner this paper has shown that approaches which take it for granted that wood was an obvious resource and that Mesolithic people were efficient economic units ignore the choices and beliefs of the people at that time and how they lived in and experienced the world. Through an examination of how different tree species were utilised and interacted with, we can build up an idea of how people classified their world, in terms of what different trees meant and how they could be used. This paper has also illustrated how people used these to negotiate relationships in order to express and manipulate social identities and values, and it has demonstrated that what constituted a raw material and indeed a tree, may have been much different from our own conceptions.

Acknowledgements

I would like to thank Julian Thomas and Hannah Cobb for comments on earlier drafts. I would also like to thank Chris Fowler, Helena Knutsson and Kjel Knutsson for discussions relating to this research.

References Cited

Andersen, S. H. (1985) "Tybrind Vig - A Preliminary Report on a Submerged Ertebølle Settlement on the West Coast of Fyn." *Journal of Danish Archaeology* **4**, 52-69.

Andersen, S. H. (1986) "Ertebølle revisited." *Journal of Danish Archaeology* **5**, 31-61.

Andersen, S. H. (1986) "Mesolithic Dug-Outs and Paddles from Tybrind Vig, Denmark." *Acta Archaeologica* **57**, 87-106.

Andersen, S. H. (1994-5) "Ringkloster: Ertebølle Trappers and Wild Boar Hunters in Eastern Jutland. A Survey." *Journal of Danish Archaeology* **12**, 13-59.

Austin, P. (2000) "The Emperor's New Garden: Woodland, Trees, and People in the Neolithic of Southern Britain". In A. S. Fairbairn (ed.) *Plants in Neolithic Britain and Beyond: Neolithic Studies Group Seminar Papers 5* Oxford: Oxbow 63-78.

Aveling, E. (1997) "Chew, Chew, that Ancient Chewing Gum." *British Archaeology* **21**, 6

Aveling, E. and C. Heron (1999) "Chewing Tar in the Early Holocene: An Archaeological and Ethnographic Evaluation." *Antiquity* **73**(281), 1-5.

Baleé, W. (1994) *Footprints of the Forest: Ka'apor Ethnobotany - the Historical Ecology of Plant Utilization by Amazonian People.* New York: Columbia University Press.

Ballantyne, C. K. (2004) "After the Ice: Paraglacial and Postglacial Evolution of the Physical Environment of Scotland, 20,000 to 5000 BP". In A. Saville (ed.) *Mesolithic Scotland and its Neighbours: The Early Holocene Prehistory of Scotland, its British and Irish Context, and some Northern European Perspectives* Edinburgh: Society of Antiquaries of Scotland 27-44.

Berglund, B. E. (1986) *Handbook of Holocene Palaeoecology and Palaeohydrology*. Chichester: John Wiley & Sons.

Chritensen, C. (1990) "Stone Age Dug-out Boats in Denmark: Occurrence, Age, Form and

Reconstruction". In D. E. Robinson (ed.) *Experimentation and Reconstruction in Environmental Archaeology: Symposia of the Association for Environmental Archaeology No. 9, Roskilde, Denmark, 1988* Oxford: Oxbow Books 119-141.

Condry, W. (1974) *Woodlands*. Newton Abbot: Readers Union.

De Boeck, F. (1994) "Of Trees and Kings: Politics and Metaphor Among the Aluund of Southwestern Zaire." *American Ethnologist* 21(3), 451-473.

Descola, P. (1997) *The Spears of Twilight: Life and Death in the Amazon Jungle*. London: Flamingo.

Dobres, M.-A. (1995) "Gender and Prehistoric Technology: On the Social Agency of Technical Strategies." *World Archaeology* 27(1), 25-49.

Ellen, R. F. (2001) "Palms and the Prototypicallity of trees: Some Questions Concerning Assumptions in the Comparative Study of Categories and Labels". In L. Rival (ed.) *The Social Life of Trees: Anthropological Perspectives on Tree Symbolism* Oxford: Berg 57-80.

Evans, C., J. Pollard and M. Knight (1999) "Life in Woods: Tree-Throws, 'Settlement' and Forest Cognition." *Oxford Journal of Archaeology* 18(3), 241-254.

Feeley-Harnik, G. (1991) *A Green Estate: Restoring Independence in Madagascar*. London: Smithsonian Institution Press.

Gell, A. (1996) "The Language of the Forest: Language and Phological Iconism in Umeda". In E. Hirsch and M. O'Hanlon (eds.) *The Anthropology of Landscape: Perspectives on Place and Space* Oxford: Clarendon Press 232-254.

Goldman, I. (1975) *The Mouth of Heaven: An Introduction to Kwakiutl Religious Thought*. London: John Wiley & Sons, Inc.

Grøn, O. and J. Skaarup (1991) "Møllegabet II - A Submerged Mesolithic Settlement Site and a "Boat Burial" from Ærø." *Journal of Danish Archaeology* 10, 38-50.

Hastorf, C. A. and S. Johannessen (1994) "Becoming Corn-Eaters in Prehistoric America". In S. Johannessen and C. A. Hastorf (eds.) *Corn and Culture in the Prehistoric New World* Boulder: Westview Press 427-443.

Hillier, H. G. (1972) *Hilliers' Manual of Trees and Shrubs*. Newton Abbot: David and Charles.

Hunn, E. S. (1987) "Science and Common Sense: A Reply to Atran." *American Anthropologist* 89(1), 146-149.

Ingold, T. (2000) *The Perception of the Environment: Essays in Livelihood, Dwelling and Skill*. London: Routledge.

Jochim, M. (2000) "The Origins of Agriculture in South-Central Europe". In T. D. Price (ed.) *Europe's First Farmers* Cambridge: Cambridge University Press 183-196.

Jones, O. and P. Cloke (2002) *Tree Cultures: The Place of Trees and Trees in their Place*. Oxford: Berg.

Jordan, P. (2001) "Ideology, Material Culture and Khanty Ritual Landscapes in Western Siberia". In K. J. Fewster and M. Zvelebil (eds.) *Ethnoarchaeology and Hunter-Gatherers: Pictures at an Exhibition* Oxford: BAR International Series 955 25-42.

Kindred, G. (1995) *The Sacred Tree*: Author.

Larsson, L. (1982) *Segebro: En Tidigatlantisk Boplats vid Sege ås Mynning*. Malmö Museum: Malmö.

Larsson, L. (1985) "Late Mesolithic Settlements and Cemeteries at Skateholm, Southern Sweden". In C. Bonsall (ed.) *The Mesolithic in Europe: Papers Presented at the Third International Symposium* Edinburgh: John Donald Publishers LTD.

Lemonnier, P. (1993) "Introduction". In P. Lemonnier (ed.) *Technological Choices: Transformation in Material Cultures since the Neolithic* London: Routledge 1-35.

Marshall, H. (1785) *Arbustrum Americanum: The American Grove, or, An Alphabetical Catalogue of Forest Trees and Shrubs, Natives of the American United States, Arranged According to the Linnaean System*. Philadelphia: Joseph Crukshank.

Mauzé, M. (2001) "Northwest Coat Trees: From Metaphors in Culture to Symbols for Culture". In L. Rival (ed.) *The Social Life of Trees: Anthropological Perspectives on Tree Symbolism* Oxford, Berg 233-251.

Moore, J. (2003) "Enculturation through Fire: Beyond hazelnuts and into the forest". In L. Larsson, H. Kindgren, K. Knutsson, D. Loeffler and A. Åkerlund (eds.) *Mesolithic on the Move: Papers presented at the Sixth international Conference on the Mesolithic in Europe, Stockholm 2000* Oxford: Oxbow Books 139-144.

Nelson, R. K. (1983) *Make Prayers to the Raven: A Koyukon View of the Northern Forest*. London: The University of Chicago Press.

Pedersen, L., A. Fischer and B. Aaby (eds.) (1997) *The Danish Storbælt Since the Ice Age*. Copenhagen: A/S Storbælt Fixed Link.

Price, T. D. (1985) "The Reconstruction of Mesolithic Diets". In C. Bonsall (ed.) *The Mesolithic in Europe: Papers Presented at the Third International Symposium* Edinburgh: John Donald Publishers Ltd. 48-59.

Randall, R. A. (1976) "How Tall is a Taxonomic Tree? Some Evidence for Dwarfism." *American Ethnologist* **3**(3), 543-553.

Robinson, M. A. (2000) "Coleopteran Evidence for the Elm Decline, Neolithic Activity in Woodland, Clearance and the use of Landscape". In A. S. Fairbairn (ed.) *Plants in Neolithic Britain and Beyond: Neolithic Studies Group Seminar Papers 5* Oxford: Oxbow 27-36.

Willis, W. E. (1970) *Timber: From Forest to Consumer*. London: Ernest Benn Ltd.

Zelter, A. (2001) "Grassroots Campaigning for the Worlds Forests". In L. Rival (ed.) *The Social Life of Trees: Anthropological Perspectives on Tree Symbolism* Oxford: Berg 221-232.

www.ingramcontent.com/pod-product-compliance
Lightning Source LLC
Chambersburg PA
CBHW041707290426
44108CB00027B/2884